DATE DUE

APR 1 1 1989			
APR 25 '90			
APR 2 8 1997			
MAY 5 1997			
JUL 1998			
GAYLORD			PRINTED IN U.S.A.

The Examined Self:

Benjamin Franklin

Henry Adams

Henry James

WISCONSIN STUDIES IN
AMERICAN AUTOBIOGRAPHY

William L. Andrews, General Editor

THE
EXAMINED SELF

Benjamin Franklin
Henry Adams
Henry James

ROBERT F. SAYRE

THE UNIVERSITY OF WISCONSIN PRESS

Published 1988

The University of Wisconsin Press
114 North Murray Street
Madison, Wisconsin 53715

The University of Wisconsin Press, Ltd.
1 Gower Street
London wc1e 6ha, England

First Wisconsin printing
Originally published in 1964 by Princeton University Press

Printed in the United States of America

Quotations from the works of Henry James copyright
1913, 1941; 1914, 1942; 1920, 1948

Library of Congress Cataloging-in-Publication Data
Sayre, Robert F.
The examined self.
(Wisconsin studies in American autobiography)
Reprint. Originally published: Princeton, N.J.:
Princeton University Press, 1964. With new introd.
Includes bibliographical references and index.
1. American prose literature—History and criticism.
2. Autobiography. 3. Franklin, Benjamin, 1706–1790.
Autobiography. 4. Adams, Henry, 1843–1916—Biography.
6. Authors, American—Biography—History and criticism.
I. Title. II. Series.
PS336.A88S29   1988   810'.9'492   87-40372
ISBN 0-299-11640-9
ISBN 0-299-11644-1 (pbk.)

To C. M. S.

CONTENTS

THE EXAMINED SELF REEXAMINED:
A REINTRODUCTION, 1987

SINCE 1964, when *The Examined Self* was first published, American autobiography has gone through a phenomenal renaissance—both in the creative diversity of the writing itself and in the subtle and serious attention it has received from scholars. There is no other period in America's very autobiographical literary history that quite compares with it.

Therefore, it is fascinating to reexamine *The Examined Self*, which was, to many people's amazement, including my own, the first published critical study of this vital subject, and so I am glad to accept the invitation of the editors of the University of Wisconsin Press to write this new introduction. It's a chance to review what has happened in the last two decades and more and also go back, like a man to his small hometown, and comment on what has changed. This is, in other words, an autobiographical situation too—and I think I like it.

Had I not been interested in autobiography, both as reader and someone interested in my own life and times, I never would have chosen this topic for my dissertation. I might have written a study of wit and authorial masks in eighteenth-century satire. But, closet autobiographer that I was, preserver (if not perseverer) of diaries, compiler of photograph albums, and keeper of letters, I thought this was more important.

After all, in our rootless, mobile modern life, what other evidence of our existence, our growth, our change and permanence, do we have? We don't, like aristocrats, own estates that support and express us; nor do we, like peasants or tribal people, know portions of a place so well

that it retains our ancestral spirits and ultimately ourselves. We change dwellings and move between jobs like
interchangeable parts. Perhaps we live and live on in our
friends and families. But they are as mobile as we. Scott
Momaday says in *The Names* that every one should at
some time in his life get to know a *place*. But he wrote his
first autobiography, *The Way to Rainy Mountain*, in part
because he had left Rainy Mountain the place and had
never known the places where the Kiowa people had
come to know themselves. He needed to discover a tribal
sense of place—and "placed it," thereby, in *Rainy Mountain*, the book. It was a very modern act.

Autobiography also matters in America because it can
have a profound social and cultural impact. The influence of Franklin, Puritan autobiography, and Adams'
Education I describe in *The Examined Self*. But what I
could not anticipate in 1964 was the subsequent impact of
new first-person (and third-person) autobiographical
writing. Works like James Baldwin's essays, Eldridge
Cleaver's *Soul on Ice*, and *The Autobiography of
Malcolm X* did not start the Black Civil Rights movement, but they did interpret it, express its urgency, and
carry it on. Norman Mailer's *Armies of the Night* and
Michael Herr's *Dispatches* shaped our judgments of the
Vietnam War. The Women's Movement found its expression in a host of books by Adrienne Rich, Tillie Olsen,
Maxine Hong Kingston, Lillian Hellman, Margaret
Mead, and others. Whatever the movement or group, it
somehow did not become real until it had the deeper,
thoughtful voices of at least one or two autobiographers.

One reason for this, I increasingly believe, is that we
are such indomitable sentimentalists. The cliché is "in-
curable sentimentalists," but I reject that because I don't
think sentimentalism is a disease. It is simply a fact of national character. We don't really understand ideas until

they are embodied in persons and the stories of their suffering, hope, strength, sacrifice, courage. Then we feel sympathy and respect for the individual person and want to join him or her in some way. Therefore it is no surprise that during the last twenty or twenty-five years the more conventional kinds of autobiography—business success stories, celebrities' confessions, politicians' memoirs, the apologetics of officials involved in Watergate and other scandals—have continued to pour from publishers and attract wide attention. They feed the national appetite for inside news, even if out of date or trivial, and reassure readers that American individualism is still rugged and rewarded or repentant and resilient. TV, with its morning and evening talkshows, interviews hundreds of these authors and, rather than reducing booksales, as once predicted, vastly increases them. Which leads me to believe that there is an underlying kinship between television and popular autobiography. Both give audiences a sentimental illusion of intimacy, as both also inflame curiosity about other people's lives. They may be related agents of what Tom Wolfe calls our really serious vice of the 1980s, plutography, celebratory writing about the rich, "the lifestyles of the rich and famous." Autobiographical plutography—*autoplutography*—is a big part of it.

The autoplutography gets consumed and consumes itself. The great new autobiographies, meanwhile, have become college textbooks. They not only have redeeming and rejuvenating social value, they are structurally, thematically, and verbally original. Here at the University of Iowa, for instance, we set up a new undergraduate course in 1972 called "American Lives." The reading material was American autobiography, from classics like those of Franklin and Thoreau to moderns like *Malcolm X* and *Armies of the Night*. Similar courses using mainly black autobiographies and women's autobiographies soon followed. Some faculty curmudgeons did grumble from time to time that this was not true literature: autobiographies should not replace poetry, fiction, and drama. But we had good precedent.

Predecessors of modern biography and autobiography, like *Plutarch's Lives, Caesar's Gallic Wars,* and the *Lives of the Saints,* were once schoolroom standards. It was American departments of English, with their somewhat colonial obsequiousness toward pure "literature," that drove them out. "American Lives," however vague and rather naive the title, turned out to be not only a popular course, with up to nine hundred students a year, but a surprisingly traditional one. The differences were that its material was more contemporary—as happens in American colleges—and that it did not have the direct moral didacticism of those long-ago classes in which schoolboys compared the lives of the Greeks and the Romans. A great many early American autobiographers, it is true, wrote as exemplary men—lives that were to be studied and imitated. But the majority of American autobiographers were interesting to modern students precisely because their experiences were so different. Writers like Malcolm X and Black Elk, Maxine Hong Kingston and Frank Conroy introduced the students to other lives and other cultures, here in America, their own country, that they had never known.

This in turn suggests another more recent reason why Americans need to write and read autobiography: it is a way of getting to know people outside our own class, race, or society. A writer's "account of his own life," Thoreau wrote in *Walden,* is like "some such account as he would send to his kindred from a distant land." And Americans have always had this need. But in the social revolutions of the last quarter-century, in which we have tried to maintain both our unity and our separateness, to affirm our different ethnic and personal identities and also our sense of still having a common national culture, autobiographical writing has become more essential than ever.

In 1960, when I started work on *The Examined Self* as my Yale dissertation, I could not have predicted this phenomenal American autobiographical renaissance. The only preliminary rumblings of it were in James Baldwin's powerful essays in *Notes of a Native Son* (1955) and *Nobody Knows My Name* (1961), Robert Lowell's *Life Studies* (1959), and Norman Mailer's *Advertisements for Myself* (1959), and each was highly controversial. Critics on the left urged Baldwin to stop attacking Richard Wright, clench his fists, and write a real "protest novel." Lowell's early readers lamented the disappearance of "the old Lowell." And reviewers told Mailer to stop making a public spectacle of himself and write another book as good as *The Naked and the Dead*. It seemed unlikely that other writers would take similar risks.

Besides, it was not clear that these books were really autobiography. The definition of autobiography was uncertain, beyond the simplest dictionary one, "a person's book about his own life," and the word itself carried such pejorative connotations that when I asked James Baldwin during a panel discussion at Yale whether he considered himself an autobiographical writer, he protested. He clearly did not want that stigma.

The orthodoxy at Yale was the New Criticism, taught with great vigor and dignity by Cleanth Brooks and William K. Wimsatt, and autobiography was the antithesis of high literary art, just as any kind of biographical criticism was avoided. So when I needed a dissertation advisor, I went to R. W. B. Lewis, who had just come from the Newark campus of Rutgers and was rumored to be more a man of letters, students said, than a scholar or critic (the main terms we knew). And he took me on gladly. Autobiography? Why not? *All* American authors are autobiographical. Do you know Auden's introduction to James's *American Scene?* He warns young American writers never to write their autobiographies, because "it's your whole stock in trade." Do you know Dick Blackmur's essays on Adams? Dick's been working on a book about Adams for years. He's coming up to lecture in this fall in my undergraduate course. Talk to him.

But aside from this enthusiasm and dazzling use of first names, Dick Lewis gave me little advice. I felt intimidated by other graduate students with their long bibliographies and all-night arguments over critical vocabulary. And when I did find Louis Kaplan's *Bibliography of American Autobiography,* with its 6,000-plus entries, I did not know how I would ever read a hundredth of them. Nevertheless, Lewis' optimism was actually the best support. "You don't have to write a history . . . just do an essay. Pull things together. And keep a commonplace book. You know, like old students and authors, with your notes, quotations, gossip, all the ideas that come to you."

So that summer I sat by an open window in my hot New Haven apartment and read and took notes. I felt I had to define autobiography, then define *American* autobiography, which took me into the great issue of a lot of post–World War II American criticism, the uniqueness of the American experience. Finally, I wanted to select three or four principal books to write about, since the major method of the critical writing I'd done was explication of texts.

My commonplace book records my meanderings . . . and my dutiful seriousness and naiveté. Pages and pages of notes on Franklin, Dana's *Two Years Before the Mast,*

Jefferson's *Autobiography*, Howells' *Italian Journeys*, Hawthorne's *English Notebooks*, American Puritans like Thomas Shepard, Increase Mather, Samuel Sewall, and John Williams, Orestes Brownson's *The Convert*, Adams and the Adams family, William and Henry James, plus essays and biographies.

Besides the quantity of material, what also kept distressing me were the slighting references to autobiography by the critics and writers I'd learned to respect. Here are some samples from my notes.

Inner & Outer Life. F.O. Matthiessen, in *Amer. Ren.*, 390–5, claims that fall from yard-arm chapter at end of *White Jacket* was Melville's first successful fusion of inward and outward experience. A similar experience never happened to H.M., but by adapting the account of Nathaniel Ames in *A Mariner's Sketches* (1830), he could exert all his energy on imagining and so improve composition.

Robert E. Spiller on H.A. in *Lit. Hist. of the U.S.*— Adams meant *Educ.* and *Chartres* to be taken together. They are "a planned work of the imagination rather than an historical, autobiographical, or scientific record."

Ezra Pound on James: High approval of *Middle Years*—& respect for *Small Boy & Others.* Says not autobiography.

James: "that accurst autobiographical form which puts a premium on the loose, the improvised, the cheap and easy." Said of Wells, *The New Machiavelli.*

Imagination was supposedly present only in fiction; the easy way of praising an autobiography was to say it wasn't one; and James himself had more bad than good to

say about it! Today I am able to understand these remarks, placing them in the context of a period in which
autobiography had become simply the loose self-history
of some notable person and was therefore scorned; but in
1960 they made me wonder. Would anyone take autobiography seriously?

What finally brought some clarity and encouragement
was the discovery of Roy Pascal's *Design and Truth in
Autobiography*, which had just been published in
England. A friend had seen it advertised in *TLS*, I
ordered a copy, and then wrote an admiring review of it
for the *Yale Review* (Summer 1961). By distinguishing between autobiography and all the other kinds of autobiographical writing like letters, diaries, and memoirs,
Pascal enabled me to cut the subject down. Second, he
provided the standards of autobiography that I adopted
—unity, reasonable comprehensiveness, a balance between inner and outer life, a tension between "design"
and "truth." And, as a final bonus, the review (my first
professional publication) was read by Bernard Perry,
managing editor of the Indiana University Press, who
wrote to ask to see the "study of American autobiography"
which the contributors' notes advertised that I was "en-
gaged in'." As I think any graduate student can still
appreciate, with that news my shyness and timidity
about writing on a noncanonical subject almost changed
to cockiness. Even though Indiana later rejected the
manuscript, complaining about its "dissertationese," I'd
had its encouragement. And when Dick Lewis learned
that James M. Cox, "Jim Cox," had been a favorable
reader, he had Cox send his report to Princeton University Press, and the book was accepted.

As I reexamine *The Examined Self*, I wish that I'd become less cocky and more bold, for the book might have

been stronger than it was. But boldness would have required really having confidence in the subject, whereas cockiness was just the manic side of my insecurity, and I was in this situation because I continued to like and admire the New Critics—and their close and distant followers. They were an "old-boy network," as people would say today, that was also being extremely generous and helpful to me. It would, of course, be more dramatic to cast my young graduate student self as a solitary, self-reliant rebel who struggled against neoformalism. But that would oversimplify, would impose the very kind of reductive pattern a true self-historian should avoid. I really did not know, at that time, how thorough the differences between later autobiographical criticism and the orthodoxies of American literary criticism circa 1960 would turn out to be. The truly dramatic revolt did not come until the late 1960s, in movements like the New University Conference, culminating in the MLA meeting of 1968—though that is a public story I won't try to tell here. Instead, let me run a different autobiographical risk. Let me speak with a retrospective, confessional harshness and list the book's weaknesses.

First, all the writers studied are white males who were already well accepted in the American academy. There is only one reference to Emily Dickinson, and it is of no consequence. I cut Gertrude Stein's complex words "autobiography is easy like it or not it is easy anyone can write it" down to "autobiography is easy," just to make a point, and thereby eliminated her irony and the way she was mocking conventional opinions. I mention Louisa Catherine Adams' "Record of a Life . . ." and "The Adventures of a Nobody" and Alice James's *Journal*, but never go into how both these women's works expressed their difficulties in nineteenth-century male culture. In the back of my commonplace book is a note to buy one other book which

—today—no study of American autobiography could possibly neglect: "Benjamin Quarles (ed.), *Narrative of the Life of Frederick Douglass, An American Slave* (Belknap Press of Harvard U. Press, 1960). $3.50." But I didn't. I was not consciously prejudiced against the writing of women, blacks, Indians, immigrants, and all the other thousands of people who have written autobiography as a way of justifying their lives, protesting, or gaining recognition; I just knew little or nothing about it. And what kept me ignorant and negligent was mainly the definition, in the early 1960s, not of autobiography alone but of literature in general. We were not fully enough aware of how absorbed we were in *belles-lettres*. We had little idea how crude simplicity, engagement, or anger could result in equally interesting, urgent literature—that all autobiographies could be revealing personal and cultural signs and artifacts.

An even more prominent example of this bias, some people will say, is my devotion to Henry James. James and Adams both, they might add, were also notable autoplutographers, though I do not agree. Anyway, *A Small Boy and Others* and *Notes of a Son and Brother* are still not widely read, and my respect and affection for them may appear dated, shadows of the great James revival of the 1950s and 1960s. Indeed, in 1958 I had spent a whole semester in Charles Feidelson's American literature seminar reading only James, and I drew heavily on that class. But James still is the American autobiographer with the most insight into his processes of perception and memory and composition. His only rival, or successor, is Vladimir Nabokov in *Speak, Memory*. Reexamined twenty-five years later, the James chapter of *The Examined Self* may be long; but it still belongs in the book. And fortunately a few readers of autobiography in the 1980s, like Paul John Eakin, share my admiration for *A Small Boy* and the *Son and Brother*.

Finally I wish I had not so fully accepted Roy Pascal's definition of autobiography. As Francis Hart argued six years later in "Notes for an Anatomy of Modern Autobiography" (*New Literary History*, 1970), the most interesting modern autobiographers did not abide by such a narrow and restrictive definition. They had refreshed and revived autobiography partially because they had broken the old forms, and had I included a chapter on Lowell, Baldwin, and Mailer, the writers I already liked so well, I would have had to face this. In my commonplace book was also a leading insight: "*Autobiography needs categories:* Renaissance, metaphysical, Augustan, Romantic, Gothic, historical, picaresque, etc. Possibilities: Puritan, literary, confessional, professional, poetic, fictional, polemic." My proposals came just off the top of my head, and too much such categorization would have been deadly, but I must have felt a desire to break down the monolithic single category that was so baffling.

Because of these defects, it's possible that, today, *The Examined Self* may fall into a kind of critical vacuum between two schools of readers of autobiography. On the one side of the contemporary university curriculum, as I've already suggested, autobiography has become essential reading for recovering or discovering the experience of Americans who were not part of our literary and cultural establishments, while on the other side it provides some of the key texts for deconstructionists and literary theorists. The split came in the 1970s, with the setting up of women's studies programs and minority studies programs whose initial interest was in cultural history, quite rightly, and the simultaneous discovery of the new French structuralism and its rapidly expanding derivatives. From where I stood it appeared that the intellectual new left, which had in fact been interested in both expanding the curriculum and questioning the objectivity of the old kinds of historical and literary study, broke in two. One flank turned to specializing in new subjects and recovering lost books, the other cut off and established new hierarchies of epistemological theorists.

Autobiography had great meaning to both. Indeed, James Olney wrote *Tell Me Africa* (1973), which was a very original use of African autobiographies as cultural introductions, and *Metaphors of Self* (1972), which established him as the American expert in the theory of autobiography. At about the same time I published "Vision and Experience in *Black Elk Speaks*" (*College English,* February 1971) using *Black Elk* as an introduction to American Indian life and cosmology, and "Autobiography and Images of Utopia" (*Salmagundi,* 1972) which, while hardly an example of literary theory, continued my implicit thesis that autobiographies are not simply historical and retrospective.

But as time passed most of the study of American autobiography was re-discovery of the many works in this genre that had been lost or nearly forgotten and fresh interpretation of them in the light of urgent new social priorities. Because the genre was so rich, the study was incredibly rewarding. It took up canonical writers like Whitman, Thoreau, Melville, Howells, and Mark Twain, and it also turned up or turned to such "new" classics as *Black Elk,* Douglass' *Narrative,* Charlotte Perkins Gilman's *Yellow Wallpaper* and *The Living of Charlotte Perkins Gilman,* Emma Goldman's *Living My Life,* Alexander Berkman's *Prison Memoirs of an Anarchist,* Zora Neale Hurston's *Dust Tracks on a Road,* Alfred Kazin's *A Walker in the City,* Mary Antin's *Promised Land,* Jane Addams' *Twenty Years at Hull House,* Richard Wright's *Black Boy,* and, more recently—but certainly not last— Aldo Leopold's *Sand County Almanac.*

The best comprehensive study of such newly recovered classics and their significance to American culture is

Albert Stone's *Autobiographical Occasions and Original Acts: Versions of American Identity from Henry Adams to Nate Shaw* (1982). Stone, who is now my colleague at Iowa and had earlier been among the first readers of *The Examined Self,* in its dissertation form, also takes up the problems of dictated autobiography, violence in autobiography, and what he calls "factual fictions"—the modern autobiographies that have novelistic structures.

Not all study of autobiography has been so topical and so oriented toward American Studies, however. In 1963 the psychiatrist Robert Butler put forward his theory of "the Life Review," arguing that autobiography and other forms of reminiscence are essential acts of people approaching old age and death. (See "The Life Review: An Interpretation of Reminiscence in the Aged," *Psychiatry,* [February, 1963]). In 1966 John Morris published *Versions of the Self: Studies in English Autobiography from John Bunyan to John Stuart Mill* with an investigation of how seventeenth-century religious autobiography, by confronting the problem of the individual anomie, anticipated the psychological crisis of nineteenth-century English intellectuals. Stephen Shapiro, in "The Dark Continent of Literature: Autobiography" (*Comparative Literature Studies,* 1968), questioned why autobiography was so unknown and uncharted on our literary maps, and anticipated the contemporary issues of how we make up our literary canon. Then, in the mid-1970s American critics like Jeffrey Mehlman and Michael Ryan discovered modern French autobiography and French and continental literary theory. The marriage of autobiography and literary theory was made, and Americans began discussing Jean Starobinski, Georges Gusdorf, Philippe Lejeune, and the autobiographies of Michel Leiris and Claude Lévi-Strauss and Roland Barthes.

An extreme example is Paul de Man's article "Autobiography as De-facement" (*MLN*, 1979) in which he argued that the whole referential foundation of autobiography was based upon an illusion, that autobiography was not a life but a text. Such an argument, tendentious as it may be, is quite unsettling to most Americanists and all readers who would like to believe, with Whitman, that when they touch a book they are touching a living person—or coming as close to one as they can. And yet there is sobering sense in such a deconstructionist point. Indeed, Henry Adams anticipated de Man's "de-facement" pun when he used the metaphors of murder to describe biography and suicide to describe autobiography. Adams was talking about de-struction, not decon-struction, but we need to remember that in reading autobiography we only metaphorically read "a life." We read a book.

To my mind, therefore, the best theoretical writing is Elizabeth Bruss's *Autobiographical Acts: The Changing Situation of a Literary Genre* (1976). As the title suggests, Bruss was interested in autobiography as an act, like the act of speech, and she argued that the changes in its definition follow the changes in the commitments and cultural situation of its authors. John Bunyan was committed to trying to represent an exemplary Christian life, Boswell to representing his individuality and subjectivity, De Quincey his higher quest for poetry, and Nabokov the process of memory that makes his life-and-book. Such a summary does not do justice to Bruss's originality; nor is it quite fair to call her just a theorist, because her book is also a literary history, in outline, and an excellent explication of each of her texts. In fact, her use of modern speech-act theory invigorates the arts of explication, making her readers more aware of the wider implications in the writers' choices of their particular rhetorical stances, their choices of words.

Janet Varner Gunn, in *Autobiography: Toward a Poetics of Experience,* also analyzes closely the rhetoric of autobiography and how the writers of it shape their audiences, beginning with themselves, in the diction, syntax, and points of view from which they write. Like Bruss, she takes us back from excessive attention to the "self" and "life" in autobiography and toward greater attention to the act of writing—and its implications in creating the other two.

In the end, the vast range of different interests between the topical-cultural approaches to autobiography and the structural-theoretical ones are but confirmation of how fundamental and still lively the subject is. A subject that attracts both the professor of Comparative Literature who feels himself to be working on the cutting edge of contemporary literary theory and the professor of American Studies who is seeking new methods for interpreting American culture—two disciplines which, otherwise, have lamentably little contact—is indeed many-sided. And since my own continuing interests in autobiography are both rhetorical and cultural—in the ways Revolutionary War and Civil War prison narratives contributed to American national identity, in the rhetorical defenses of World War I and II Conscientious Objectors, and in American sentimentalism—I believe the theoretical and cultural approaches are equally important.

Hence my belief that this book still has some things to say to both the Americanists and the literary theorists. The portion at the end of the Franklin chapter, on autobiography and American culture, is in embryo the line of argument taken by a great many of the investigators of this subject. The chapter on James does not just insist that James turned to his past as a way of reviving his creative power. It attempts, difficult as any attempt at this is, to show how art, experience, and memory were all for James

[xxiii]

an intricate tapestry. That is the book's best contribution to what is now called literary theory. The chapter on James and Adams and their literary friendship also lays out some of the differences in approaches to autobiography. Further, it supplies necessary biographical information about them, for I still believe that to read autobiographies critically one has to know a lot more about the authors than they choose to say in their books. One has to know history as well as the author's "fictions." One constantly has to do what Albert Stone calls, borrowing a term from Freud, "reality testing." Then one is ready to engage in the close rhetorical analysis or explication that Elizabeth Bruss has exemplified. For autobiography is indeed, to use another insight from Paul de Man, a kind of revolving door, constantly revolving between fiction and reality, art and life. To de Man this is an ultimate defect, the reason it can never be a great genre . . . or even *a* genre at all. But to some of us that is actually its great interest. It takes us in and out, between them, and increases our pleasure in both.

PREFACE AND
ACKNOWLEDGMENTS

THIS book is a study of the autobiographies of Benjamin Franklin, Henry Adams, and Henry James. They are studied in relation to each other and against the background of some of the conditions of American experience, conditions which they also help to expose.

Such a project may need certain explanation and justification. This is not a history of American autobiography, though I hope eventually to write something akin to that. The field is vast, and I have chosen to begin on what now seems to me best and most revealing in it. For the time being the huge thicket of the writings of officials, celebrities, and entrepreneurs, for instance, is entirely avoided. "We have the reputation of always boasting and bragging and waving the American flag," James' Mrs. Westgate says in *An International Episode*; "but I must say that what strikes me is that we are perpetually making excuses and trying to smooth things over." She was right, essentially, and the "excusers" are the more interesting because they are the true examiners of themselves, whose lives seem to us, on reflection, to have been most worth living. Adams, James, and Franklin were such men and became the writers of three of the most absorbing American autobiographies. One reason they are so absorbing is that these increasingly intense examinations somehow account for other men's lives as well; they comment profoundly on the American experience.

It still may seem inexplicable to study Franklin in the same volume with James and Adams. All the assaults of the 1920's on Poor Richard and that "snuff-colored Doctor Franklin" (as D. H. Lawrence called him) cannot lower the stature of his *Autobiography*, however. In that work American autobiography came of age, and it remains one of the best pictures of American life we have. Greater insight, of course, can correct our provincial blindness to the artfulness and clever naïveté of the man. Both Adams and James were discriminating admirers of Franklin, and the *Autobiography* was one of Adams' several models in the writing of the *Education*. The contrast developed in the Introduction between Franklin and St. Augustine helps us to see the difficulties of writing autobiography without the ordering beliefs of religion. Franklin reveals how autobiography can be organized around other achievements and purposes and partially indicates how autobiography can itself serve to bring life form and meaning. He therefore prepares us for Adams and James. Yet four generations later, the certainties even Franklin enjoyed were no longer available. Franklin illustrates that the stable "eighteenth-century" world Adams knew had vanished forever, the same one, ironically, which as scientist, middle-class businessman, and diplomat he had played a part in destroying. Thus Franklin showed how much might be done in autobiography and also left behind him some of the barriers blocking the way of later serious autobiographers. He is essential to any discussion of American autobiography.

The advantages of working on Adams and James together are numerous. As an historian and a novelist, they approached autobiography from different directions; while as friends and comrades they had a great many other values in common. Consequently they offer suggestive contrasts and comparisons at every turn and almost always to the improvement of our knowledge of autobiography. Their correspondence contains many perceptive remarks about it, not to mention the comments on each other, on each other's writing, and their mutual problems as survivors of a vanishing world. Later in life, each wrote with the other in mind. Moreover, Adams learned from the methods of his friend's fiction, and James possessed a memory and sense of detail any historian would envy. He could also, as a sensitive and contemplative observer, give meaning to his vivid memories in a way Adams sometimes refused to do and sometimes refused to recognize. This is my answer to readers who may believe that James' autobiographies are inferior work and not worthy of such extended treatment. They are an entirely different kind of autobiography from the *Education*, but just as good, in their way, and therefore just as important to the subject. It is only by pursuing such contrasts that we can realize the scope and variety of this genre. Adams stretches it out to become something approaching an epic, while James uses it to recreate all that he can of his own unfolding sense of life. James cultivated his imagination—"gaping" at other people, examining his own responses—to the point where art and memory gave life form. Therefore his books have an inner continuity of a very vital kind, one just as necessary as the intellectual and political order Adams sought. We can use Adams' search to help us recognize James' achievement, just as James makes us freshly aware of the greatness and tragedy of Adams, while always remaining safely detached from it.

For all the attention to James and Adams, I still hope most for this book's service to our appreciation of autobiography. James and Adams, manifestly nineteenth-century men, are two beginners of the twentieth-century concern with autobiography. The key difference in them and later men may be that they do not write so much out of egotism and romantic excitement at the powers of the individual as out of a need to defend the individual and to establish the beliefs he lives by. A better understanding of their works should thus be useful to our understanding of contemporary autobiography and autobiographical fiction and poetry. Autobiography is not "easy," as Gertrude Stein joked, nor can anyone write it, although many modern Americans have tried. Our distinctions between it and the novel, indeed between "truth" and "fiction," strike me as shamefully unanalyzed.

In certain quarters, as always, fiction is treated as frivolous falsification, and in others autobiography is regarded as pedestrian truth and therefore not art. A novelist who writes an "autobiographical novel" has relinquished the right to be treated as an "artist"; he is a mere solipsist. These errors of the tribe have had a wider-than-ever circulation, I feel, because of a number of modern academic errors: excessive reaction against the nineteenth-century emphasis on personality, overemphasis on internal structure in art (removed from its reasons and wider consequences), a decline of biographical criticism, and a scorn for biographical elements. American writing has always been autobiographical to a large degree and seems destined to remain so. This in itself is neither good nor bad; it is a description of the art. To improve that description and to improve the art as well, we need a fuller notion of the aims and achievements and implications of American autobiography.

The possibilities for a kind of "autobiographical criticism," would seem to be very great. Such an approach would not tie itself to the reduction of art to moments of a man's biography, and would not simply chase every fictional episode back to some precedent in "real life." The more moderate, but also very difficult and ambitious, purpose would be to relate each part of a man's writing to his own changing needs for form and to describe and contemplate the image created. Autobiographies are much more than the personal almanac of dates and doings many critics accept, or reject, them as. If he is to tell a real *story* of his life, or even a phase of his life, an autobiographer is committed to making as many selections and judgments of his material as is the historian or the novelist. As a result, his work is as undeniably an image as both the other kinds of work, and they as much an image as it. We have a lot to learn about how these images are made, what their components are, how they are different, and how they are related, in general and within kind. I know that a great amount of what I have to say about autobiography does not apply to it alone. Much of it was first learned or practiced in the reading of works of other genres. At various points, therefore, particularly in the last chapter, I try to suggest how qualities of these autobiographies may be found in other books and in other authors. These references are sometimes just for clarification and illustration, but I hope they will sometimes have a wider interest and that the reader will also see further correspondences and connections of his own.

A last word of explanation may be needed about texts and footnotes. Wherever good library editions existed and were available, they have been the basis of the quotations and references. In other cases, however, various paperback editions have been much more available, and some of them are very carefully edited or have been printed from the plates of hardbound editions. To distinguish the paperback texts and because the same titles have sometimes been brought out in the same city and same year but in different editions, I have always given the name of their publisher; with hardbound texts this has not seemed necessary. I have also tried to avoid unnecessary footnotes. This means that page references to Franklin's, Adams', and James' autobiographies, in the separate chapters on them, have been given first in a footnote but in parentheses from then on. By the same token, where a letter by James or Adams is well known or can be located in the standard volumes of their *Letters* by its date, a footnote is not given.

Here, too, I want to thank the people who have assisted me in the many stages of the growth of this book. To Charles Feidelson, Jr., I owe my real introduction to Henry James, and without his fresh insights and sophisticated view of *A Small Boy and Others* and *Notes of a Son and Brother*, and also of Franklin, I never would have pursued my own interests in them. In a somewhat similar connection, I am in debt to Norman H. Pearson for my introduction to Henry Adams. For a variety of other things, I want to thank both Martin Price and Davis Harding, also of Yale University; Sherman Paul and Miss Cornelia Kelly, of the University of Illinois; and Alistar Sutherland, of University College, London. Dean F. T. Wall and the University of Illinois Graduate College Research Board have been of great assistance in typing expenses, research costs, and a Faculty Summer Fellowship. The Massachusetts Historical Society and the Houghton Library, Harvard University, have been very obliging in letting me study unpublished letters by Henry Adams and Henry James. Herbert Bailey and Miss Miriam Brokaw of Princeton University Press have given me good advice about the manuscript, as have the Press' readers. The manuscript was first written under Richard W. B. Lewis, whose criticism was always friendly, discerning, and comprehensive. He has not seen its changes, but his constant interest has been indispensable.

The following holders of copyrights and owners of manuscripts have kindly granted permission to use their materials: The Adams Manuscript Trust and The Massachusetts Historical Society (the Adams Papers Microfilms, unpublished letters of Henry Adams, and letters of Henry James to Henry Adams); The Houghton Library, Harvard University (items from the correspondence of Adams and James); Paul R. Reynolds & Son (*A Small Boy and Others*, copyrighted 1913 by Charles Scribner's Sons and 1941 by Henry James; *Notes of a Son and Brother*, copyrighted 1914 by Charles Scribner's Sons and 1942 by Henry James; and *The Letters of Henry James*, ed. Percy Lubbock, copyrighted 1920 by Charles Scribner's Sons and 1948 by Henry James; and items of unpublished correspondence of Henry James); Mrs. Ward Thoron (*The Letters of Mrs. Henry Adams*, ed. Ward Thoron); Mr. Leon Edel (*The Selected Letters of*

Henry James, Henry James: The Conquest of London, and *Henry James: The Middle Years*); The University of California Press (*Benjamin Franklin's Memoirs: Parallel Text Edition,* ed. Max Farrand); Houghton Mifflin Company *(The Education of Henry Adams, The Letters of Henry Adams (1858-1891),* and *The Letters of Henry Adams (1892-1918))*; and *Texas Studies in Literature and Language,* in which a portion of this study first appeared.

Permission to print the two letters from Henry James to Henry Adams, dated July 15, 1912, and May 26, 1913, is gratefully acknowledged to James' literary executors, Paul R. Reynolds, Inc.

The Examined Self:

Benjamin Franklin
Henry Adams
Henry James

But if I go further and seek among these characteristics the principal one, which includes almost all the rest, I discover that in most of the operations of the mind each American appeals only to the individual effort of his own understanding.

Alexis de Tocqueville,
Democracy in America

CHAPTER ONE

Benjamin Franklin
and American Autobiography

Lord, when shall we be done growing? As long as we have anything more to do, we have done nothing.

Melville to Hawthorne, November 1851

Dante's praise is, that he dared to write his autobiography in colossal cipher, or into universality.

Emerson, "The Poet"

HENRY ADAMS always chose good models. His taste was not infallible, for he frequently showed the prejudices of his caste. But this is no more culpable than modern failures of taste, which are prejudices of time. Taste, however, is the need of a dilettante; good models are the mark of an artist, and Adams was an artist as well as a dilettante. Teacher, biographer, historian, and dilettante novelist, he was most completely an artist in *The Education of Henry Adams*. With that in mind, in this introductory chapter, I want to talk about two of his models for that work: *The Confessions of St. Augustine* and the *Autobiography of Benjamin Franklin*. Adams said that "St. Augustine alone has an idea of literary form,"[1] but that Franklin was "a model . . . of self-teaching."[2] The choices were acute, for together these are the most important models for autobiography in America. In needing to use both

---

[1] *Letters of Henry Adams (1892-1918)*, ed. Worthington Chauncey Ford (Boston and New York, 1938), p. 490.

[2] Henry Adams, *The Education of Henry Adams* (Boston and New York, 1918), p. ix. Adams' private edition was published in 1907.

and in trying to achieve the form of self-teaching, Adams perceived the fundamental challenge to American autobiography.

Defining autobiography can be as difficult as defining the novel. Everyone knows what it is until he is asked to explain it. The coinage was put in circulation by Robert Southey in *The Quarterly Review* only in 1809, and yet there is a large number of works written before then to which we apply it. The term has now become so corrupted that it takes in things ranging from a college freshman's first theme to an elder stateman's several volumes. Furthermore, there is a quantity of writing which is autobiographical without being autobiography. But the critic has no choice but to try to rescue the word, and the best way to begin is by describing what is not autobiography.[3]

Diaries, journals, and collections of letters may present a self-written story of a life, but they are not autobiography. They are different, as one scholar has put it, because "an autobiography is one work, a series of entries in a diary several; in an autobiography the whole life, or at least a considerable segment, is seen in long perspective; in a diary the temporal depth is shallow."[4] The autobiographer, like the biographer and the novelist, ideally composes a complete and unified work. I say "ideally" because he very often does not. We speak of Franklin's *Autobiography*, bestowing that title, although Franklin generally referred to his unfinished manuscript as his "memoirs." Augustine's *Confessions* ends with his thirty-third year. Henry James' *A Small Boy and Others*

---

[3] Discussion and definition of autobiography may be found in Leslie Stephen, *Hours in a Library* (London, 1909), III, pp. 220-251; Anna Robeson Burr, *The Autobiography, A Critical and Comparative Study* (Boston and New York, 1909); André Maurois, *Aspects of Biography*, trans. Sydney Castle Roberts (New York, 1929); Arthur Melville Clark, *Autobiography, Its Genesis and Phases* (Edinburgh and London, 1935); Wayne Shumaker, *English Autobiography, Its Emergence, Materials, and Form* (Berkeley and Los Angeles, 1954); Richard G. Lillard, *American Life in Autobiography, A Descriptive Guide* (Stanford, 1956); Roy Pascal, *Design and Truth in Autobiography* (London, 1960).

[4] Shumaker, *English Autobiography*, p. 103.

ends with his boyhood. *Notes of a Son and Brother* ends with his youth in 1870. His third volume was unfinished at his death. Adams' *Education* leaves out the twenty years from 1872-1891. The subtitle "An Autobiography" was not in fact Adams' own; it was added by Henry Cabot Lodge. Nevertheless, these writers all have a perspective on their lives which is missing in journals and diaries. The incidental is either forgotten or ignored. Momentary excitements or outrages are as dead as old banner headlines in a dusty morgue, and what was once insignificant may have been given great attention. Also, however many years are not treated, those which are represent substantial portions of the life. In these and other autobiographies, childhood is crucial. Indeed, the inclusion of fifteen years of childhood is more important than twenty years of middle life or thirty of old age.

The second distinction to make is between autobiography and memoirs. In *Everybody's Autobiography* Gertrude Stein made the popular point (one that has been stupidly allowed to become virtual dogma) that "autobiography is easy" and that anyone can write it.[5] Roy Pascal's reply is that "she is wrong like it or not—though everybody might be able to write memoirs."[6] The two statements imply much more. Miss Stein's little ingenuity has helped foster the strange fallacy that fiction is harder to write than the truth. She assumes that the one great book that is supposed to lie in us all is the book about ourselves, a sort of doubled egotism. Mr. Pascal is correct in emphasizing the dedication of autobiography to internal and mental history as well as exterior events. "True autobiography can be written only by men and women pledged to their innermost selves." Memoirs, in their most usual and marketable form, are lives of generals in which the focus is on their battles, lives of public officials in which the focus is on their quarrels and achievements, or lives of

[5] New York, 1937, p. 6.
[6] *Design and Truth in Autobiography*, p. 195.

[5]

secretaries with open doors to their employers' privacies. Thomas Jefferson's "memoranda" written in 1821, though published as his *Autobiography*, is properly a memoir, for the bulk of it is about the writing of *The Declaration of Independence*, reforms in the government of Virginia, and the activities of the Paris Ministry. Franklin, on the other hand, while vigorously chronicling his deeds and projects, always relates them to his inward life. Autobiography is an examination of the self as both a sovereign integrity and a member of society. In fact, the self is at all times both these things, and autobiography is an endless stream of demonstrations of their inseparability.

In being a man's story of his own life, both as an individual and as a member of society, autobiography is most closely connected to the apology and the confession. Augustine's *Confessions*, after all, is the great colossus of Western autobiography, and the Medieval works like Abelard's *History of my Calamities* and *The Book of Margery Kemp* are dependent upon it. The difference is modern. Augustine's *Confessions*, as I shall shortly show, may concentrate on the story of his conversion, but the importance of that conversion made it the great and all-embracing fact of his life. That was the only story to tell, and other events are brought in to lead up to it. Such inclusiveness is usually missing from modern confessions and apologies. Bunyan's *Grace Abounding* impresses us by its monomania, Rousseau's *Confessions* by its exclusion of everything but the ego. In common practice the confession and the apology have become a kind of autobiography in which the subject is one particular concern or sequence of experiences. Examples range from the *Apology for the Life of Mr. Colley Cibber, Comedian* to De Quincey's *Confessions of an English Opium-Eater* to Newman's *Apologia pro Vita Sua*. For this very reason, both of these kinds of writing are apt to be more unified than true autobiography. The task of representing the whole of one's inner and outer experience over a significant

period of years is an exceedingly difficult one, and the task
of unifying those years even more difficult. But if an autobiography is really to be a man's own *story* of his *life*, these
are the essential requirements which it must meet.

In *Design and Truth in Autobiography* Roy Pascal has
admirably isolated these qualities of unity and completeness
as the indispensable conditions of true autobiography. After
all, to go back over the kinds of personal history which it is
not, letters and diaries may have completeness but they lack
perspective and unity; apologies may have unity but they
lack a sense of the writer's whole life and experience. Memoirs are also different because they concentrate on public
events to the exclusion of private and psychic material or
because they describe affairs to which the author is only an
observer or bystander. It goes without saying that the autobiographer is also not writing fiction, that he is not passing
off the imaginary as actual or willfully falsifying important
facts. Against this background the foolery and folly of Gertrude Stein's quip that "autobiography is easy like it or not
autobiography is easy for any one" is clearly apparent. Good
autobiography requires both "an idea of literary form" and
a capacity to record the progress and process of "self-teaching." These are the standards Adams set for himself, and by
the very success of the *Education* they are the ones which he
has left for others to try to meet. Proper appreciation of the
autobiographies of Henry Adams and Henry James must
begin with brief study of Adams' opposing models, Augustine
and Franklin.

I

The context of Adams' remark, in a letter written to his
friend William James shortly after William had read the
Education, proves how much value Adams placed on Augustine. He asked the author of *Varieties of Religious Experience*: "Did you ever read the Confessions of St. Augustine,

or of Cardinal de Retz, or of Rousseau, or of Benvenuto Cellini, or even of my dear Gibbon? Of them all, I think St. Augustine alone has an idea of literary form,—a notion of writing a story with an end and object, not for the sake of the object, but for the form, like a romance."

Adams credited Augustine with having perceived what almost all critics of biography and autobiography today agree upon, namely that the writing of a life is a work of art. Its materials are the events and realizations of life, but the selection, emphasis, and joining of them is a work of art. Something must make them cohere. It is interesting that six days before, in an earlier message to William James, Adams placed the *Education* not in connection with other autobiographies but as "a literary experiment." To picture the American man, it was necessary by some means or other to work in greater "contrasts and backgrounds" than the landscape naturally provided. This took a *tour-de-force*. He told James, "Your brother Harry tries such experiments in literary art daily, and would know instantly what I mean; . . ."[7] Autobiography is different from a work of fiction, however, in that the contrasts and backgrounds cannot be written to order. In his prefaces the brother Harry insisted that they were not supplied that way in his fiction either. To do so would break the illusion. They had to be organic. Adams' vision of St. Augustine's *Confessions* was of a work as harmonious, as carefully constructed, and as formally eloquent as we today consider a James novel.

St. Augustine gave his autobiography literary form by making the story of his youthful paganism, his errors, and his wanderings in search of truth all find their meaning in his conversion to Christianity. Submission of himself to God in confession was, in turn, the act which gave meaning to past and present and to future as well. It is futile to debate whether he first *gave* his life this form or whether the form

---

[7] *Letters (1892-1918)*, p. 490.

was actually *given* to his life by his knowledge of God. He was a careful rhetorician, and he was also a devout Christian. The two characters conflict in some ways, but they also support one another. As a Christian he felt that his previous training in rhetoric had been given to him in order to aid him in his holy undertakings, one of which was the telling of how he became a Christian. As a rhetorician he must have realized that his Christian experience was a perfect climax to the story of his early life. It dictated the incidents he should include. The only ones of any significance at all were those that marked his painful road to conversion, yet from that point everything had some new significance. To dwell on them at length would be to detract from his high purpose. But on the other hand, that purpose could make even the dullest detail shine with value. Of all the experiences of his boyhood, for example, the one he selects to elaborate is the memorable one of stealing pears. It might not have been mentioned at all; something else might have been equally instructive. He uses it, however, as the central episode of the whole Second Book of the *Confessions*. The otherwise not unusual prank becomes a universal figure of childish perversity, pleasure in wrong-doing, theft, and the brotherhood of thieves. Concomitantly, it becomes a universal example of God's abiding forgiveness. ". . . Unto thy grace and mercy do I ascribe, that thou hast dissolved my sins as it were ice: yea unto thy grace do I ascribe whatsoever evils I have not done."[8]

St. Augustine's emphasis on the importance of his mother in his life and his comparative exclusion of his father from the book is another case of his choice of material according to its function in the story of his holy pilgrimage. His father did all he could to supply Augustine with sophistication and

---

[8] *St. Augustine's Confessions, With an English Translation by William Watts*, ed. W. H. D. Rouse, The Loeb Classical Library (London and New York, 1912), I, 89 (Bk. II, Ch. vii).

with training in rhetoric. "But yet this father of mine never troubled himself with any thought of how I might improve myself towards thee, or how chaste I were; so that I proved cultivated, . . ."⁹ His father was a pagan. Monica was a Christian, and Augustine makes her the immortal prototype of the suffering, deceived, ever-patient, ever-hopeful Christian mother. She follows her son to Milan, precedes him in her devotion to his mentor St. Ambrose, and does not die—appropriately—until after his conversion and baptism. Book IX ends with an impassioned prayer to God that He forgive her sins and an entreaty to the readers to remember her with reverence. Such friends as Ambrose, Evodius, and Alypius are included in order that the stories of their experience and conversions can be used as parallels to his own. The long philosophical passages on Manicheanism and the other mistakes and heresies of Augustine's youth help to describe the disorder and frustration out of which he emerged and contrast with the order and purpose of Christian life. The book is quite intentionally instructive, and another purpose of the discussion of false doctrines is that they may at the same time be refuted.

Instruction, indeed, is a vital goal. Confession, the author believed, was both confession of human sins and confession of divine greatness and mercy. Augustine offers up both and speaks not only to God but also to men, saved men and sinning men. Too much is cynically said about Augustine the ex-sinner, who is thought of as reveling in the enormity of his former error and is, in a way, proud of how much he has to confess. The argument goes on to assert this feature as an explanation of the subtlety of his psychological insights. On the contrary, he appears too subtle not to have been aware of this, and therefore forced himself to speak not as the ex-sinner but as the living Christian.

⁹ *Confessions*, I, 71 (Bk. II, Ch. iii).

This is the fruit of my Confessions, not of what I have been, but of what I am: namely, to confess this not before thee only, in a secret rejoicing mixed with trembling, and in a secret sorrowfulness allayed with hope: but in the ears also of the believing sons of men, sharers of my joy, and partners in mortality with me; my fellow citizens, and fellow pilgrims: both those that are gone before, and those that are to follow after me, and those too that accompany me along in this life.[10]

He is not parading himself but making an illustration of himself, addressing himself to God and at the same time speaking "in the ears also of the believing sons of men." He did not display himself naked for mere nakedness' sake, like Rousseau, but for the sake of honesty to his God, who he believed always knew his naked soul, and for the sake of the relief it brought him. And all this was instruction for his fellow men. What he was had passed. That was over, done with, barren, fruitless. The identity that he is presenting is his new Catholic Christian identity which has brought meaning to his life and form to his story. The form, the pattern of disorder and doubt exchanged for order and faith, is not only an end in itself but also an object, a part of the Christian message. The life of a pagan and disbeliever is chaotic; the life of a believer is ordered.

What must be stressed, then, is that the magnificent and original form of St. Augustine's *Confessions* depends upon his identity as a Christian. In the ruin of the decaying Roman Empire he found beliefs which enabled him to put his life in order and show its meaning. It was a compelling discovery. It was a very new one. Augustine might be said to have addressed himself to God because until then there had been no other audience for such a remarkable story. But by speaking also to "my fellow citizens, and fellow pilgrims: both those

[10] *Confessions*, II, 83 (Bk. X, Ch. iv).

that are gone before, and those that are to follow after me, and those too that accompany me along in this life," he helped others to receive the special organizing Christian identity and thus make the form a convention and perpetuate it.

II

St. Augustine's achievement was not only literary but philosophical. Part of the beauty of the *Confessions*, as Adams saw it, lay in the correspondence between the philosophy and the form. Franklin's deism, therefore, demanded an entirely different form. Furthermore, neither Adams nor James could review their lives from the standpoint of one all-encompassing revelation. They had, like Franklin, to recollect the past as a succession of moments of "self-teaching." They both admired Franklin. James was impressed by his friend Thomas Sergeant Perry's "so clean and comfortable affiliation to the great Benjamin Franklin."[11] (Franklin was Perry's great-great-grandfather.) Adams was impressed by Franklin's "masterly diplomacy"[12] and by his sensitivity to the "new forces" of the eighteenth century.[13] "Benjamin Franklin of Boston and Albert Gallatin of Geneva" were "the two great historical Pennsylvanians," an understandable paradox to Adams, because "The true Pennsylvanian was a narrower type; as narrow as the kirk; as shy of other people's narrowness as a Yankee; as self-limited as a Puritan farmer."[14] As self-teacher and as the first cosmopolitan American, then, Franklin was a worthy predecessor. But his *Autobiography* was no model of literary form. On the contrary, it was a lesson in the pitfalls to be avoided and the difficulties to be solved. Franklin's *Autobiography* does not give form to his deism; instead it

[11] *Henry James, Autobiography*, ed. Frederick W. Dupee (New York, 1956), p. 318.
[12] *Henry Adams and His Friends*, ed. Harold Dean Cater (Boston, 1947), p. 129.
[13] *Education*, p. 485.   [14] *Education*, p. 333.

mirrors his pluralism and his unending versatility. It is as shapeless as he was protean. For him self-teaching did not mean conclusions but repeated new beginnings. In Adams' terms, Augustine was a Unity, Franklin the first example of Twentieth-Century Multiplicity.

Now it might be argued that Franklin's *Autobiography* lacks literary form simply because it is in four parts. It is also unfinished, and scholars cannot be sure to what extent the surviving versions represent even the corrected second draft.[15] Franklin wrote the first part in August 1771, while staying at the home of his friend Bishop Shipley near Twyford in Hampshire. He did not write the second part until 1784 at his home in Passy, outside Paris, after the conclusion of the Revolution and the signing of the treaty with England. He returned to America in the summer of 1785, but with the excitement of his homecoming, his duties as President of the Executive Council of Pennsylvania, and his work at the Federal Convention, he did not sit down to the third part until August 1788. The brief fourth installment was apparently written only shortly before his death, April 17, 1790. The first section treats the years in Boston, the early work in Philadelphia, his adventures in London, and his marriage to Debbie Read in 1730. Franklin did not have this part with him when he wrote the second part at Passy. He did have his outline, however, and he picks up almost exactly where he left off and proceeds to describe his advancement of the subscription library project and the famous effort to arrive at moral perfection. In the third part he resumes the record of his life in the early 1730's and carries on with an account of his activity and reflection down to his arrival in

---

[15] For more complete discussion of the problems with the MS. of the *Autobiography*, see Max Farrand's introduction to *Benjamin Franklin's Memoirs: Parallel Text Edition* (Berkeley and Los Angeles, 1949). An earlier edition of this essay was published in the *Huntington Library Bulletin* (October 1936), X, pp. 49-78.

England as agent for the Pennsylvania Assembly in July 1757. Part four is a memoir of his dealings with the Proprietaries in London.

The odyssey of Franklin's manuscripts of the *Autobiography* and the resulting minor imperfections of all editions of it are too complicated and confused to be treated here. The original manuscript, containing all four parts, is extant and in possession of the Huntington Library. Franklin had his grandson Benjamin Franklin Bache make two revised, fair copies of parts one through three, and these he sent to England and France to his friends Benjamin Vaughan and Louis le Guillaume le Veillard for comment and criticism (somewhat as Henry Adams was to send the private printing of the *Education* to a larger number of friends). Although these two copies were apparently the basis for all editions of the *Autobiography* until 1868, they themselves are not extant. The early editions were not completely faithful renderings of them; consequently there is much anxiety among textual scholars as to exactly what these fair copies were. It is an exceedingly involved problem.

Nonetheless, it is preposterous to believe that a recovery of one of the fair copies would give the world a more unified, more formally perfect *Autobiography of Benjamin Franklin*. The version published in 1818 by William Temple Franklin is as faithful an English text of them as is known. The differences between the Temple Franklin text and the manuscript are not structural. They are small orthographic and stylistic differences. There is no change in the plan of the narrative, the order of incidents, or in the overall meaning and value of the life. Chronologically the parts fit together like beads on a string, and in both versions the incidents within the parts succeed one another in the same clear, chronological order. It is almost as wrong to believe, uncritically, that it lacks form because it was written at four separate times. Franklin endeavored to keep the story perfectly coherent. He drew up an outline before starting to write in 1771, and he followed it carefully. His American friend Abel James enclosed a copy of it in the letter to Franklin which, along with Benjamin Vaughan's letter, is inserted between parts one and two of the Temple Franklin text. He used this outline, then, in 1784 and again in Philadelphia in 1788.

The interesting feature of this outline, which is frequently pointed out to young readers as evidence of the exemplary Franklin's good preparation and orderly memory, is that it is absolutely shapeless. It is not an *outline* at all; it is a mere list. Everything, big and little, comes up in an order only chronological:

> . . . Affection of my Brother. His Death, and leaving me his Son. Art of Virtue. Occasion. City Watch. amended. Post Office. Spotswood. Bradfords Behaviour. Clerk of Assembly. Lose one of my Sons. Project of subordinate Junto's. Write occasionally in the papers. Success in Business. Fire Companys. Engines. Go again to Boston in 1743.[16]

It indicates no intention to weight the events, to frame and compare them, or to design chapters. The writer of the outline had no certain picture of himself; he was but secretary to his own history, putting it all down in a sequence as near to the way it actually occurred as he could remember. So it is incorrect to attribute the formlessness of Franklin's *Autobiography* to the absence of a finished manuscript or to the hiatuses in the writing of it. There are no conspicuous hiatuses in the narrative. Had Franklin held a more fixed and permanent notion of the story he wished to tell and of the character he wished to present, he could presumably have written a more modeled outline. This too he could have worked on at widely spaced intervals. But when he started and when he

---

[16] *Parallel Text Edition*, p. 420. All quotations from the *Autobiography* are from the version of the original MS. in this volume. Succeeding references will be in parentheses.

started again and recommenced, he had only a sense of order, no sense of form.

But the exception to this rule is that each of the three major parts does have a form. The fragmentary fourth part is too short to consider, but the first three are outstanding in American literature as three separate explorations in self-discovery and self-advertisement. Franklin never, like Augustine, found one form and identity which could be made to stand for the whole life; he never even gives the appearance of having discovered one form and then written in it. He composed like the scientist rather than the saint. He assembled the materials and then worked with them and arrived at their intelligence. The life, as so starkly represented in the outline, was the raw material. The three bouts of writing were the investigations of it which produced three forms and identities. The image of himself, so variable that it grew as he wrote, altered materially between writings. Such is the hazard and the advantage of self-teaching. Had he written the whole work at one time, in 1788, for example, the picture might have been steadier, but it would not be the fascinating multiple exposure it is.

The problem Franklin unconsciously illustrated was the problem of the man whose life and character was one of change and discontinuity. He was, as he delighted in telling, the Philadelphia printer who had dined with kings. There are certain fundamentals of his character which were always the same, but they are by no means as prominent as the fundamental facts about Augustine's character, though his life had witnessed many revolutions and turnings about, too. With his paramount knowledge of himself as a new Christian, Augustine had a unifying and organizing identity. The chaos out of which he described himself as having emerged was a planned one; it was developed for the purpose of representing the disorder which he had already overcome. The Saint's pilgrimage had concluded in conversion, and the writer had undertaken the task not of completing the quest but of telling and explaining it. The scientist's life is in disorder right up to the time at which it is written. The pilgrimage is not complete. The writing of it becomes a kind of tentative completion, and the informing identity is discovered on the way. But Franklin's three parts of his *Autobiography* (in a sense three autobiographies in one) not only show that a man may write differently at ages 65, 78, and 82, but also that reproducing at any age one's portrait at another is extremely difficult. Between the first and second parts of the *Autobiography*, for example, is a parallel change in the picture of the youthful Franklin. Augustine's religious conviction made revisions in his idea of his youth inevitable but also justifiable. No other idea mattered. A modern writer, however, is committed to displaying his youth as it was. But what it was, as James said, was so "other," or, as Adams looked back on it, so "troglodytic." The finding of a form to span such a gulf is a challenge to autobiography.

Each of the three parts of Franklin's *Autobiography* reflects the time and circumstances of its composition. When Franklin wrote the first portion while visiting the Shipleys in Hampshire, he liked England. He was enjoying a welcome period of relief from his official duties, and he assumed the role of a retired country gentleman giving a private account of his unusual and adventurous history. This is certainly the character taken in the opening.

> Dear Son,
> I have ever had a Pleasure in obtaining any little Anecdotes of my Ancestors. You may remember the Enquiries I made among the Remains of my Relations when you were with me in England; and the Journey I took for that purpose. Now imagining it may be equally agreeable to you to know the Circumstances of

my Life, many of which you are yet unacquainted with;
and expecting a Weeks uninterrupted Leisure in my
present Country Retirement, I sit down to write them
for you. (p. 2)

As Franklin wrote, this piece began to take the shape of a
short picaresque novel. It has the young Benjamin Franklin
as a hero; and the themes are his ambition to be in business
for himself, his education in writing, his inner struggle over
religious questions, and his uneven progress toward marriage.
He is a bright youth, but a proud one, and his pride and
impatience to succeed make him incompatible with his older
brother and vulnerable to the praise and promises of other
men. Men like Governor Keith of Pennsylvania, the printers
Samuel Keimer and Andrew Bradford, Franklin's friend
James Ralph, and the merchant Mr. Denham appear in
several spots, and Franklin the writer manipulates their
entrances in order to give the story suspense and continuity.
They also represent various types of villains and friends.
Governor Keith is deceitful; Keimer is a braggadocio; Ralph
and other young tradesmen and apprentices are indigent, dissipated, incompetent, or slow witted. Mr. Denham, Andrew
Hamilton, and Sir William Wyndham are important older
men who take notice of the young Franklin and help him
along. It is interesting that Franklin describes one such man,
Sir Hans Sloane, as having heard of an asbestos purse he
had brought from America, come to see him, and "invited
me to his House in Bloomsbury Square" (p. 110). In actual
fact Franklin had heard that Sloane was "a Lover of Curiosi-
ties" and had written offering to sell the purse to him.[17] Either
by design or by failure of memory, Sloane is forced into the
category of influential men attracted to the young Franklin.

In such ways does the older Franklin publicize his youth
and also demonstrate to himself a continuity between the re-

[17] *The Papers of Benjamin Franklin*, ed. Leonard W. Labaree and Whitfield J. Bell, Jr. (New Haven, 1959), I, p. 54.

tired gentleman who is writing and the boy and young man who was already receiving attention from men like the indulgent writer. There is a distinct juxtaposition of youth and age in this part of the *Autobiography*, symbolized by the device of writing it as a letter to his son William Franklin. One is led to believe that William was about the age of the young Benjamin, somewhere in his teens or twenties; yet in 1771 he was about forty years old and Governor of New Jersey! The piece was certainly intended for publication, although probably not until after death, and the signs of a letter are literary devices by which the author established his particular relationship to his material.[18] In a sense Franklin was writing to himself as well as about himself, developing correspondences between the past and the present. It is the changes, the lack of coherence which another sensibility might have found alarming, which Franklin works upon to find dramatic and striking. The famous arrival in Philadelphia, "eating my Roll," is recognized to have enormous emblematic value, and the elder Franklin does all he can to bring out the contrast, "that you may in your Mind compare such unlikely Beginnings with the Figure I have since made there" (p. 60). The writer gives the exact itinerary of the boy's walk through the town, the people he met, the things he did, the places he stopped, and the "Meeting House of the Quakers near the Market . . . the first House I was in or slept in, in Philadelphia" (p. 64). Franklin was not quite the penniless waif he made himself out to be. He had arrived tired from the boat journey down the Delaware River, he had spent his last pocket money, and he had no change of clothes. But his luggage was coming around from New York by ship. He exaggerated the "unlikely Beginnings" in order to set them off against the adult Franklin. The penniless waif is built up as the opposite yet the origin of the gentleman "expecting

---

[18] Robert E. Spiller, "Franklin on the Art of Being Human," *Proceedings of the American Philosophical Society* (August 1956), C, p. 313.

a Weeks uninterrupted Leisure in my present Country Retirement."

Continuity between these extremes exists because Franklin discovered it. It is customary to assert that the *Autobiography*, especially this first part of it, owes its structure to Bunyan and Defoe and is a sort of "American Pilgrim's Progress" or American *Robinson Crusoe*,[19] but this is to be too ingenious about supplying sources or to overemphasize Franklin's secularization of religious biography and autobiography. Franklin indeed knew Defoe and Bunyan well, and he refers to both of them in this part of the *Autobiography*. There is, however, a touch of amusement in the elder Franklin's attitude towards Bunyan ("Honest John," "my old favourite Author"), and his interest in Defoe was primarily in the *Essay on Projects*, an interest that shows up chiefly in the second and third parts of the *Autobiography*. The suggestive feature about the supposed debt to these writers lies in the assumption behind it that Franklin's life was a plastic and unformed substance that could be pushed and prodded into whatever mold he chose to put it. This is a rough but valid assumption. It tallies with Franklin's emphasis on the individual's large range of freedom in his own destiny and also with his method of writing about that life—to gather up the materials and see what forms appear. The distant structural approximations of *Crusoe* and *Pilgrim's Progress*, though, are discovered rather than imposed.

The question next arises, how were they discovered? The explanation lies in Franklin's talent for posing and for imagining roles for himself, an aspect of his character that has already been touched upon in his description of his arrival in Philadelphia. It is obvious that the waif was seized and care-

[19] John Bach MacMaster, *Benjamin Franklin as a Man of Letters* (Boston, 1887), p. 269. Charles L. Sanford, "An American Pilgrim's Progress," *American Quarterly* (Winter, 1954), VI, pp. 297-310; reprinted in *Benjamin Franklin and the American Character*, ed. Charles L. Sanford (Boston, 1955), pp. 64-73.

fully developed after it had once shown itself as a striking illustration of "unlikely Beginnings." It and the other role of the retired gentleman are held together by the professed purpose of writing an imitable tale for the instruction of posterity. The intention is stated in a sentence in the opening paragraph: "Having emerg'd from the Poverty & Obscurity in which I was born & bred, to a State of Affluence & some Degree of Reputation in the World, and having gone so far thro' Life with a considerable Share of Felicity, the conducing Means I made use of, which, with the Blessing of God, so well succeeded, my Posterity may like to know, as they may find some of them suitable to their Situations, & therefore fit to be imitated" (p. 2).

The trouble with this pretense, however, is that not all the deeds are so exemplary; therefore there is another theme of the indulgent older man who "should have no Objection to a Repetition of the same Life from its Beginning, only asking the Advantages Authors have in a second Edition to correct some Faults of the first" (p. 2). This gives him license to remark "errata" such as running from his brother's printing shop, trying to seduce James Ralph's mistress, and not having married Debbie Read earlier. Whimsically building upon his days as both author and printer, he thus gives himself considerable liberty in what he chooses to include. The narrative becomes an adventure in living over the various provisional identities he found for himself until he unwinds, in the natural course of history, with the modest and ever so flexible one he used from 1728 until the end of his life, "B. Franklin, Printer."[20]

[20] This is, of course, the way he describes himself in the famous epitaph, generally believed to have been composed in 1728. See the discussion of the matter in *Papers*, ed. Labaree and Bell, I, p. 110. The epitaph is a beautiful illustration of Franklin's play in assigning identities to himself: "The Body of B. Franklin, Printer; Like the Cover of an old Book, Its Contents torn out, And stript of its Lettering and Gilding, Lies here, Food for Worms. But the Work shall not be wholly lost: For it will, as he believ'd,

It is one demonstration of the number of his provisional identities just to list the various occupations he at some time or another entertained for himself: clergyman, seaman, tallow chandler and soap boiler, printer, poet, swimming instructor, and merchant. It is sententious to call the first part of the *Autobiography* a bourgeois adaptation of spiritual autobiography, with Franklin's progress in trade taking the place of knowledge of God, conversion and baptism.[21] Poor Richard's pithy sayings were never so magisterial as that! It is better to think of Franklin merely trying on hats until he found that the printer's fit. And even when work as a printer expressed some of his talents very well (his playfulness, his love of attention, his spirit of adventure and eagerness for public good), he by no means thought of it as an end of his endeavor but as a base around which to build further images of himself: scientist, politician, diplomat.

A nice picture of the freedom Franklin had in the choice of his occupation appears in his recollection of his father's taking "me to walk with him, and see Joiners, Bricklayers, Turners, Braziers, &c. at their Work, that he might observe my Inclination, & endeavour to fix it on some Trade or other on Land" (p. 28). (Franklin's father did not approve of his going to sea.) The similar freedom he felt he had in the development of his habits and personality is demonstrated in his readiness to take up any idea he met in a book and give it a try. Happening "to meet with a Book, written by one Tryon, recommending a Vegetable Diet" (p. 38), he gave up meat and became a vegetarian. After reading some poems and ballads, he composed two broadside ballads for his brother's press. And what is most revealing, when he discovered the Socratic method in Greenwood's *English Grammar* and Xenophon's *Memorable Things of Socrates*, he "was charm'd with

---

appear once more, In a new & more perfect Edition, Corrected and amended By the Author. He was born Jan. 6. 1706. Died   17   ."
[21] *B.F. and the Amer. Char.*, pp. 72-73.

it, adopted it, dropt my abrupt Contradiction, and positive Argumentation, and *put on* the humble Enquirer & Doubter" (p. 40, italics mine). The poses and masks which Franklin came across in his reading—not only in Bysshe's eighteenth-century translation of Xenophon,[22] but in Addison, Swift, Defoe, Arbuthnot, Gay, Dryden, Pope, and other Augustan satirists[23]—were more than literary ones to be assumed in his scores of hoaxes and pieces of satiric journalism; they were "real" ones to be tried out in life as well. This is evident in Franklin's tireless affection for pranks, for practical jokes, and disguises. Franklin readily slipped into poses in the *Autobiography* because he had lived in a fluid world. His day-to-day identities approached poses.

If no strict and dogmatic religion exactly defined man's role in respect to Heaven and no rigid social structure exactly defined his role on earth, then man's role could be whatever he chose to make it. Franklin was scrupulous in his religious convictions and he was not selfish or single-mindedly accumulative in his worldly activity. The point is that he arrived at both his religious and social philosophies by his own experimentation and intelligence. He recognized his freedom and realized that whatever actions he took were in a dramatic sense, "acts," roles to some degree thrust upon him but also consciously selected and therefore open to whatever interpretations he wished to make of them. The fact that he conducted such a large amount of his business by writing—letters, reports, scientific papers, pamphlets, proposals, propaganda pieces—is interesting in this respect because the printed page was obviously the medium through which he learned many of the gestures and postures of his multiple lives. Still,

[22] Personal letter from Edwin Wolf, 2nd, Librarian, the Library Company of Philadelphia, December 14, 1960. Mr. Wolf says that "the Library Company in its first order of 1732 asked for a copy of Bysshe's translation and since Franklin helped draw up the list, I had assumed that he was speaking of that version."

[23] Francis Davy, *Benjamin Franklin, Satirist* (University Microfilms, 1958), p. 160.

several lessons from "real life" (as handed on in the *Auto-biography*) are to be noticed.

On his way through New Jersey after having broken his apprenticeship to his brother, Franklin says that he "cut so miserable a Figure" that he was suspected of being "some runaway Servant." As a runaway apprentice he nearly was, but a night later he was not so tired and wretched looking. The innkeeper, his eventual friend, Dr. Brown, "entred into Conversation with me while I took some Refreshment, and finding I had read a little, became very sociable and friendly" (p. 58). Neither the notion of Franklin as the fugitive nor the notion of him as the young travelling scholar expressed the whole truth. If people were to make such hasty judgments, however, it made sense to encourage the more favorable one.

A chase, the iron frame surrounding type, happened to break one evening as Franklin the printer was closing shop. Understandably, he stayed up late to reset the pied pages. From outside his window, nonetheless, he appeared to be working like a man extraordinarily devoted to his trade. Word spread that he was a hard worker and that his house would survive despite the competition of two other printers. The elder Franklin cites this as an instance of the usefulness of the virtue of industry, but from another anecdote it is evident that in actual fact he was not so pedestrian.

> In order to secure my Credit and Character as a Tradesman, I took care not only to be in *Reality* Industrious & frugal, but to avoid all *Appearances* of the Contrary. I drest plainly; I was seen at no Places of idle Diversion; I never went out a-fishing or Shooting; a Book, indeed, sometimes debauch'd me from my Work; but that was seldom, snug, & gave no Scandal: and to show that I was not above my Business, I sometimes brought home the Paper I purchas'd at the Stores, thro' the Streets on a Wheelbarrow. (p. 172)

Note the props: the plain dress, the debauching book, the wheelbarrow! Being industrious and frugal was for Franklin a game, a cheerfully entered role. Having noticed that the burghers of Philadelphia (Adams' "true Pennsylvanians . . . as narrow as a kirk; as shy of other people's narrowness as a Yankee; as self-limited as a Puritan farmer") paid attention to industry and frugality, Franklin quietly went about attracting their attention.

Carl Becker observed that Franklin was never thoroughly submerged in anything he undertook. Everything he did he gave his best to, and most everything he did he did well, but behind the gestures and routines of his participation was always a reserve, a certain ironic sense which took amusement as well as satisfaction from the experience.[24] This was the actor in him; one might almost say the dead-pan comedian in him, and it owed much to the fact that each participation was easily and freely chosen. The man behind the actor was always bigger than the single part. This is a most important fact about Franklin's personality, and it operated in all his achievements on all his many stages. The first section of the *Autobiography* is the story of Franklin's building of his roles—sampling sundry occupations, hoaxes, disguises, and literary masks— and of fitting himself out in the "plain dress" of his first and most lasting public character, flexible and adaptable as it was always to be for him, "Benjamin Franklin of Philadelphia, Printer."

He found it again as he wrote the Twyford part of the *Autobiography*. A step towards the vacationing gentleman who is correcting his "errata," it is also the string that draws everything else into place. Having returned from London and gone into the partnership with Hugh Meredith, he soon organizes his Junto. He and Meredith start a newspaper, the *Pennsylvania Gazette*. Meredith realizes that he was not meant to be a printer, so Franklin gets a loan and takes on the whole

---

[24] "Benjamin Franklin," *Dict. Amer. Biog.* (New York, 1943).

business by himself. He writes a pamphlet on *The Nature and Necessity of a Paper Currency* and later receives the contract to print the new money. He adds sidelines of stationery and begins to pay off his loan. His tenants leave after a failure in negotiations for Franklin to marry one of their relations. The whole house left to himself, Franklin marries Debbie Read, who, he says, had first seen him (and laughed at him) when he arrived in Philadelphia eating his roll.

Franklin finds his identity in the first part of the *Autobiography* by reassessing all the provisional roles he played as a young man. The final character of Benjamin Franklin, Printer, is a satisfactory conclusion because it holds within itself both the retired gentleman of Twyford and the penniless waif of "unlikely Beginnings." The work is an amalgam of the man writing and the man written about. The same generalization applies to the two later parts composed at Passy in 1784 and in Philadelphia in 1788. What Franklin wrote in France is a most delicate manipulation of his youthful experience to the purposes of the public character he played at Versailles, in the salons of Mmes. Helvetius and Brillon, and in the French press. What he wrote back in Pennsylvania emphasizes his achievements as civic leader and American patriot.

We can begin by noting, however, that the two later parts have one important thing in common: both are accounts of projects. The Passy piece begins where Franklin had left off thirteen years before with the scheme of the Philadelphia Library Company; then, after a few pages on his domestic affairs and church attendance, it launches into the famous "bold and arduous Project of arriving at moral Perfection." The longer Philadelphia memoir is for the most part a chronology of Franklin's many local and colonial projects for a school, hospital, cleaner streets, a better city watch, fire department, militia, and supplies for General Braddock's army. Franklin was fond of conceiving of himself as a projector, and this fondness is one of the most markedly eighteenth-century aspects of his personality. He wrote both satiric projects after the manner of Swift's *Modest Proposal* and Defoe's *Shortest Way with Dissenters* and non-satiric projects like Defoe's *Essay on Projects*. Simply speaking, the non-satiric are supposed to be taken up and acted upon while the satiric are supposed to rally opposition to the actions the writer urges or assumes will be extended. The important point to realize is that the projector is always wearing a mask, be he the man so anxious for the welfare of Ireland that he cannot understand the inhumanity of raising children for food, or be he the conscientious tradesman who would like to make arrangements for female education or for life insurance.

The mask Franklin wears in describing the "Project of arriving at moral Perfection" is his French one of the *naïf* "Philosophical Quaker," a role both thrust upon him by the acclaim given him on his arrival in France and also cultivated by him in his diplomatic mission, his bagatelles, and even in the modest and ingenuous ways in which he showed his amusement with the role and attempted to deny it.[25] John Adams, who was a severe critic of many of Franklin's diplomatic maneuvers and, like Abigail Adams, was scandalized by his personal behavior, spoke the truth when he observed that Franklin "was master of that infantine simplicity which the French call *naïveté*, which never fails to charm, in Phaedrus and La Fontaine, from the cradle to the grave."[26]

The disarming quality of the attempt to reach moral perfection was the logic of it. Of the pretentiousness and vanity of such an aim, the young Franklin was sublimely unaware.

I wish'd to live without committing any Fault at any

---

[25] Alfred Owen Aldridge, *Franklin and His French Contemporaries* (New York, 1957), pp. 59ff.

[26] *The Works of John Adams*, ed. Charles Francis Adams (Boston, 1856), I, p. 663. Reprinted in *B.F. and the Amer. Char.*, p. 25.

time; I would conquer all that either Natural Inclination, Custom, or Company might lead me into.

In the next breath the elder Franklin means to disarm the reader as well.

As I knew, or thought I knew, what was right and wrong, I did not see why I might not *always* do the one and avoid the other.   (p. 210)

The young man was innocently reasonable, so reasonable that reason deceived him. "But I soon found," it is announced with inimitable understatement, "I had undertaken a Task of more Difficulty than I had imagined." Always doing the right and avoiding the wrong was really rather hard. "While my *Attention was taken up* in guarding against one Fault, I was often surpriz'd by another." Yet reality became a challenge to his diligence instead of a reminder to his modesty; so, adding diligence to his reasonableness, he devised his "Method" for concentrating his attention on one virtue at a time. By maintaining constant watch and subjecting his behavior to minute study, he would still persevere in this most charming madness.

The method was the famous list of thirteen virtues, the little maxims subjoined to each, and the book in which he kept the record of his moral progress. To accept the program didactically as an exemplary exercise in self-improvement or to look upon it cynically as a bumbling tradesman's petty commandments is to miss Franklin's *naïveté*, his cultivated "infantine simplicity." Only Franklin could have conceived it. By comparison, Robinson Crusoe's balance sheet of the "Evil" and "Good" in being castaway on his island is primitive, mere arithmetic. Franklin's "moral algebra" is complete with lines in red ink, columns, mottos, dots, abbreviations, headlines. Yet with all these contrivances (or possibly because of them), the method retains its reasonableness and innocence. The intricacy of "arriving at moral Perfection" makes it the most artful of games. Children are absorbed by it.

> I made a little Book in which I allotted a Page for each of the Virtues. I rul'd each Page with red Ink, so as to have seven Columns, one for each Day of the Week, marking each Column with a Letter for the Day. I cross'd these Columns with thirteen red Lines, marking the Beginning of each Line with the first Letter of one of the Virtues, on which Line & in its proper Column I might mark by a little black Spot every Fault I found upon Examination to have been committed respecting that Virtue upon that Day. (p. 216)

A sample page is included in the text. Franklin's procedure was "to give a Week's strict Attention to each of the Virtues successively," at the same time keeping account of his performance regarding the others as well. "Thus if in the first Week I could keep my first Line marked T [Temperance] clear of Spots, I suppos'd the Habit of that Virtue so much strengthen'd and its opposite weaken'd, that I might venture extending my Attention to include the next [Silence], and for the following Week keep both Lines clear of Spots" (pp. 218, 220). Proceeding in this way, the young Franklin could go through a complete course in thirteen weeks, or four courses in a year. The beginning of the book was given over to bolstering mottos and prayers; the end contained the "Scheme of Employment for the Twenty-four Hours of a natural Day," which was necessitated by the "Precept of Order." It is a further instance of his *naïveté* that as time went by he "was surpriz'd to find myself so much fuller of Faults than I had imagined." He found, in fact, that the wear and tear of erasing the spots of "old Faults to make room for new Ones in a new Course" was puncturing the pages of his book with holes, so he transferred his tables "to the Ivory Leaves of a Memorandum Book," from which the marks could be wiped away with a wet sponge (p. 226).

Franklin the writer never breaks character in his story of this project or lifts his mask to expose the man beneath. Instead he even accentuates his innocent reasonableness from time to time. "Something that pretended to be Reason was every now and then suggesting to me, that such extream Nicety as I exacted of my self might be a kind of Foppery in Morals, which if it were known would make me ridiculous" (p. 228). He is so reasonable, as well as so diligent, that he does not let this "pretended" voice stop him. He dwells on the great difficulty he confronted with the virtue of "Order," leaving one to wonder that he should have reached "Justice" or "Moderation" more easily. He goes on and attributes to the effect of the "Project" his wealth and well-being and says it had once been his intention to write a great book to be called the *Art of Virtue*. He even shifts briefly into the third person, stating that "my Posterity should be informed, that to this little Artifice, with the Blessing of God, their Ancestor ow'd the constant Felicity of his Life down to his 79th Year in which this is written" (p. 230). Beginning in the rhetoric of understatement, he thus works up to the full-blown language of the *naïf* who has mastered his task and then been mastered by it. He becomes exhortative, rotundly pedagogic. The only way out is by coming back to the subject of "Humility," the last of the thirteen virtues. He says he never succeeded in "acquiring the *Reality* of this Virtue; but I had a good deal with regard to the *Appearance* of it" (p. 234). The concluding paragraph is on pride and humility.

> In reality there is perhaps no one of our natural Passions so hard to subdue as *Pride*. Disguise it, struggle with it, beat it down, stifle it, mortify it as much as one pleases, it is still alive, and will every now and then peep out and show itself. You will see it perhaps often in

this History. For even if I could conceive that I had compleatly overcome it, I should probably be proud of my Humility.   (p. 236)

Thus Franklin collapses his philosopher's hubris in his "Quaker" simplicity. The two tendencies are beautifully reconciled, the frankly *naïf* young Franklin commencing the project with his scheme to become perfect, the famous elder Franklin carrying the idea along as a worthy endeavor that all men should be interested in, and the sophisticated, consciously *naïf* "Philosophical Quaker" finishing it in a discourse on pride and humility. The experience of fifty years before is thereby examined and recast in the mold of the present. The character of the young man is brought into line with the pose of the older man. His role as rustic philosopher demanded that he should at an early stage in life have entered upon a "bold and arduous Project of arriving at moral Perfection." Naturally, it failed, but the story of that failure was an opportunity to create a plain, reasonable, somewhat comical origin for the sage whose worldliness expressed itself in simplicity.

Franklin's identity in the third part of the *Autobiography* as patriot and civic projector gives it the form of a series of lessons in "doing good." As a series rather than a single story it does not have the interlocking structure of the first section or the roundness of the main part of the second. Perhaps this more literary order was not so available within the material itself. Perhaps the eighty-two-year-old Franklin did not have the artistic control he once had. Yet it is also true that this continued series of experiences does express the multiplicity of his interests and reflect the variety of lives he was leading at the time he wrote it. It bursts with things: fire ladders, dirty streets, smoky lamps, stoves, bags and buckets, wagons, munitions, whiskey, schools, pigs and chickens, bonds and subscriptions, forts. It is also more moralistic than the other parts, and each modern instance is preceded or followed by its wise saw: *"It is hard for an empty sack to stand upright."* *"He that has once done you a Kindness will be more ready to do you another, than he whom you yourself have obliged."* *"After getting the first hundred Pound, it is more easy to get the second."* "The best public Measures are therefore seldom *adopted from previous Wisdom*, but *forc'd by the Occasion."*

In context these aphorisms are not banal. On the contrary, they reflect Franklin's uncanny insight as politician and lay psychologist. Back in the midst of Philadelphia, back in the whirl of civic and national contentions, Franklin reinterpreted his earlier undertakings in terms of their present applications. Of all parts of the *Autobiography*, this one is most like a memoir and of most value to the descendants of early American democracy. Franklin's projects strike the modern reader as entirely in the public interest; personal vanities should not have mattered. He became attentive, however, not only to how people *should* feel and respond but also to how they *do*. He allowed others to save their face instead of worrying always about his own. He helped them to go on living by their convictions. Pennsylvania Quakers, for example, were not opposed to "the Defence of the Country . . . provided they were not requir'd to assist in it" (p. 284). To win support for the public hospital, Franklin devised a system of matching state appropriations and private subscriptions, with the amusing result that members of the Pennsylvania Assembly realized "they might have the Credit of being charitable without the Expence" (p. 310). The trustees of a special meeting house built at the time of Whitefield's revival had to represent each of the many sects in the City. When the same building was taken over by the new Academy, the new governors had to agree to keep open a hall for occasional preachers and "maintain a Free School for the Instruction of poor Children" (p. 298).

When Franklin wrote this part of his *Autobiography* in

1788, the Country was rebuilding from the destruction of the Revolution and in need of new ideas and energies and men with the social and political skill to employ them. Franklin is seeing himself not as the retired gentleman of the first portion of the *Autobiography* or the naïve philosopher of the second, but as the busy Philadelphian. It might be added that this is the only part of the book in which Franklin seems something of an Anglophobe. In the account of General Braddock's campaign, in the offhand remarks about working hours in London, in implications that the Royal Society scorned his scientific experiments, and in criticism of Lord Louden for delaying the ship on which he sailed to England in 1757—in all these places we know that the Revolution has come between the events and the reminiscences. But this section is most strongly American for its emphasis on *doing* and upon self-realization in public life. It does not present the whole Franklin; it does not present the whole American. But it presents the American Franklin as the writer saw himself at that time. The life has once again been made over in a discovery of the present by means of re-discovering the past.

III

It is remarkable that the United States has been the scene of so much autobiographical writing but has produced such a small number of enduring autobiographies. The "founding" of autobiography as a designated and conscious genre fell within the early years of the Republic, and its growth, coinciding with the spread of the romantic movement, has also coincided with the growth of the United States. As evidence of the mere quantity, it is interesting that recently *A Bibliography of American Autobiography* was by necessity restricted to the most exclusive rules of selection, to keep it "from growing so large that no press could afford to publish it."[27] Nevertheless, there are 6,377 entries. All this self-study and

[27] Compiled by Louis Kaplan (Madison, Wisconsin, 1961).

self-representation is a kind of frenzied, inky background to the few achievements. But by the same token, the vital works should be used to define the standards, rather than the rules, by which excellence can be recognized. And works of each kind, good, bad, and those on the periphery of autobiography proper, can help us to understand some of the many problems facing the American autobiographer. Such help is actually essential. Therefore, before going on to James and Adams I want to discuss this background a little more.

In choosing St. Augustine and Benjamin Franklin as two of his models for the *Education*, Henry Adams in effect chose to try to unite the two major traditions of American autobiography. These might be called religious and secular, though the real distinction is that the one tends to be more formal and self-conscious while the other is looser, more inclusive, and somewhat naïve. The American Puritans were all moved by "the Augustinian strain of piety" (to use Perry Miller's phrase[28]) and their so religiously oriented personal writing is also fundamentally Augustinian, allowing for some very pertinent differences. Franklin, on the other hand, is far more certainly an American original, and his *Autobiography* is, at the crudest level, the earliest of American success stories, tales of material progress, and self-congratulatory accounts of self-teaching. The superficial contrast between the two traditions could not be greater, as all who have compared Franklin and Jonathan Edwards, those strange contemporaries, will readily agree. For the Augustinian Christian and the Puritan, personal history had order because God's ways were orderly and life was a period in which God revealed his order to his servants. For Franklin the possibilities of such revelation were exceedingly remote, and everything depended on each man's imposing some rational order on his daily life (even down to eight hours of sleep, eight of work, and eight of eating, study,

[28] *The New England Mind: The Seventeenth Century* (Cambridge, Mass., 1939). Title of Chapter I.

and diversion) or on his discovering order by his own investigations. Furthermore, the writing of autobiography no longer needed to limit itself to those things descriptive of "soul concerns," as Jonathan Edwards called them. It could and should take in all that happened. Possible materials for autobiography became as infinitely broad as to the Puritan they had seemed infinitely deep. All this raised new problems of form, and Adams wanted a new form as suitable to "self-teaching" as the *Confessions* had been to revelation.

In his fine little study, *Literature and Theology in Colonial New England,* Kenneth Murdock has gathered together many of the reasons for the Puritan devotion to the various kinds of " 'Personal Literature.' " Given the conviction that "all religious progress centered on the individual," the most exciting history for the Puritans was the movement of a man or a united band of men from sin to salvation. At bottom, the diary served a daily confessional value for its writer and at the same time kept "fresh in his memory what he learned each day about himself and about his relation to God's law." It was a sort of spiritual account book or log. The same might be said of journals and autobiographies. In addition, published personal histories, including biographies, performed a propagandistic function. They provided to the writers an occasion for didacticism and exhortation, and to the readers, whether pious or faltering, they were "an interpretation of the divine in terms easily grasped by men." Such a function, of course, was in accordance with the Puritan precept that literature be useful, and authentic personal experience thus had a greater prestige than poetry or any variety of fiction. Mr. Murdock goes on to point out that the way in which the covenant theology held the New England Puritans together in a powerful sense of community had the consequence of giving stories of the lives of individual Puritans a strong social significance. This amounts to saying that the autobiographer could become a kind of hero, a spokesman of his culture. All this brought to Puritan personal narrative a great deal of attention and a great deal of skill, and Mr. Murdock is not alone in admiring their growth in self-consciousness, incisiveness, and psychological subtlety.

Still, if we were left with these descriptions of Puritan autobiography, we would have little more than a description of fragments of St. Augustine's *Confessions*. In these qualities and purposes early American autobiography does evince "the Augustinian strain of piety." But in some Puritans, notably Jonathan Edwards, additional features are present which mark their autobiographies as distinctively American and which help to explain further how autobiography in America is both so prominent and so difficult. A brief consideration of Edwards and his *Personal Narrative* is an essential part of the preface to Adams and James.

Edwards preceded Franklin and Adams and to a lesser extent James in seizing his own life as both the starting point and the ultimate test of speculation. In his *Treatise Concerning Religious Affections* and the *Narrative of Surprising Conversions* Edwards tried to distinguish between the signs of false and true religiosity. The *Personal Narrative* is, as Perry Miller puts it, a "case history,"[29] an inquiry into sincerity in religious behavior. But the grim and humble candor of the study is not its only remarkable feature; another is Edwards' terrify-

[29] *Jonathan Edwards* (Meridian Books, Inc.: New York, 1959), p. 206. Professor Miller begins his next paragraph, "The *Personal Narrative* must be read, not as autobiography or as reminiscence of early Connecticut but as a revelation of the point at which Edwards turned from asserting his doctrine of causality against the Arminians to an examination of those who took him at his word, who conceived grace as emotional and then ran riot." The implication that it is not autobiography shows what disorder we face for not having an adequate definition and respect for autobiography. The *Narrative* is very short. As the biographer makes clear, it has its possible factual errors. But it does cover a large period of Edwards' life (approximately twenty-five years), it aims at a coherent record of life, it is intensely personal, and the author's own life is the subject. It is a far cry from conventional autobiographies, but this is just what must be appreciated. It was probably the only kind of autobiography Edwards would have cared to write.

[36]

ing isolation. The passionate interest of his life has been salvation and his awareness of God, and the world around him is left the very blankest and most desolate. Edwards' hours of contemplation came "on the banks of Hudson's river," "in a solitary place in my father's pasture," or "walking alone in the woods." Augustine's conversion, after all, occurred in a garden in Milan—his friend Alypius inside, a young voice chanting in a house nearby—but Edwards is without these marks of civilization and companionship. He travels, he stays with a few friends, but there is the scantest description of places and peoples, and the story continually returns to himself, his solitude, and his moments of religious insight.

Edwards was not a solipsist. He was eager to draw lessons from the histories of his contemporaries, from the "surprising conversions" of enthusiasts like Abigail Hutchinson and Phebe Bartlet, for they too, although they were not so aware of it, were faced with the same problem. It was the need to build an entirely new structure for experience. What are the outlines of life? What are its foundations, its sides and corners, and what are the values? In the search for salvation Edwards was trying to follow the vanishing lines of the old forms, yet in his awareness of the innumerable possible deceptions about salvation he had come to question the validity of the forms themselves. The *Personal Narrative* does not have the rhythm of conventional religious autobiography, of which the great archetype is the *Confessions*. Edwards seems to have witnessed so many stories of sin, conversion, and rapture and to have become so self-conscious that he is examining himself with fresh care and not permitting easy acquiescence to old patterns. "And I am ready to think," he says of the piety of his boyhood, "many are deceived with such affections, and such a kind of delight as I then had in religion, and mistake it for grace." Consequently, the *Personal Narrative* is a scrutiny of each of the author's successive religious moments. The long chain of insights and affections, many of them on record in his diary and other writings, was taken up link by link, and the conclusion was exasperatingly uncertain. He could not be sure where the chain led; he could not be sure of his lasting conversion!

Edwards encountered in his own deeply serious but now abandoned religious context what remains one of the lasting perplexities of American life and thus, inevitably, of American autobiography. As had been the case for William Bradford, Cotton Mather, and many others, his Biblical images supplied him with a fine storehouse of analogies for his search, the Puritan people, their little cities, and the American wilderness.[30] But the wilderness remained the wilderness, solitude remained solitude, and a "vision . . . of being alone in the mountains, or some solitary wilderness, far from all mankind, sweetly conversing with Christ, and wrapt and swallowed up in God" was but temporary relief from the actual barrenness around him. This was by no means a romantic or a Wordsworthian loneliness, one of silhouetted dairy maids or shepherds. The American landscape, as James wrote in his study of Hawthorne, offered no such rural vistas, "no castles, nor manors, nor old country houses, nor parsonages, nor thatched cottages, nor ivied ruins." (When James himself at last looked out on the picturesque European scene of solitude, "a sordid old woman scraping a mean living and an uninhabitable tower abandoned to the owls," the associations thus brought together were so numerous as to leave him stunned.[31]) The American loneliness was more than romantic because it was without the emblems of history and civilization, without the inescapable relics of old manners, classes, and values. Among them, while an individual might be away from human company, he still retained some social and traditional identity. In other words, Edwards could and had to seek self-discovery

[30] Charles Feidelson, *Symbolism and American Literature* (Chicago, 1953), pp. 77-84.
[31] *Henry James, Autobiography*, ed. Dupee, p. 161.

[38]

within himself because there were so few avenues to it outside himself.

The loneliness and the need for new forms really go together. They are consequences of one another and serve jointly as inducements and as difficulties to autobiography. The
Puritan was initially driven to his introspection by the severi-
ties of his faith, but the self-examination of Edwards' kind
became a way, hopefully, of bolstering the faith and eventually of re-making the world, of building a New World. As a
result, the student of autobiography can see that the continued
interest in self displayed by Franklin and with added energy
by Emerson, Thoreau, Hawthorne, Melville, and their contemporaries is not just the lingering of a Puritan tradition
but the perpetuation of an American tradition. Edwards and
his fellow colonials were not yet nationalistic enough to conceive of the problem in the almost chauvinist terms of a century later, but the need and the zeal were just as great. Edwards' predisposition to his inner or personal affairs with
God even while in New York or with friends was no weaker
than Emerson's absorption in self at the beginning of his
European travels in 1833. Emerson wrote in his *Journal*:

> Perhaps it is a pernicious mistake, yet, rightly seen,
> I believe it is sound philosophy, that wherever we go,
> whatever we do, self is the sole subject we study and
> learn. Montaigne said, himself was all he knew. My-
> self is much more than I know, and yet I know nothing
> else. . . . And I bring myself to sea, to Malta, to Italy,
> to find out new affinities between me and my fellow men,
> to observe narrowly the affections, weaknesses, surprises,
> hopes, doubts, which new sides of the panorama shall call
> forth in me.

Throughout the nineteenth century in American writing
there is a kind of debate going on over the advantages and
disadvantages of a new country as a subject of literature.

Cooper, for example, is of the opinion that the "poverty of materials" is a definite obstacle to the American author. Speaking in *Notions of the Americans*, he anticipates James' famous catalogue of the things missing in American life.

> There is scarcely an ore which contributes to the wealth of the author, that is found, here, in veins as rich as in Europe. There are no annals for the historian; no follies (beyond the most vulgar and commonplace) for the satirist; no manners for the dramatist; no obscure fictions for the writer of romance; no gross and hardy offences against decorum for the moralist; nor any of the rich artificial auxiliaries of poetry.

Hawthorne would have agreed, and he made similar statements of his own in his prefaces. In the preface to *The Blithedale Romance* it is the absence of a "Faery Land" that he mentions, and in the preface to *The Marble Faun* he announces that "romance and poetry, ivy, lichens, and wall-flowers, need ruin to make them grow." Emerson and Thoreau, on the other hand, could not be more pleased. They acknowledge the situation but see it only as a great opportunity. As Emerson says in "America, My Country," it is

> Land without history, land lying all
> In the plain daylight of the temperate zone, . . .
> Land where—and 'tis in Europe counted a reproach—
> Where man asks questions for which man was made.

This absence of manners and traditions was not only a dearth of materials, as authors then used the word, but a dearth of forms, in both a social and a literary sense. Hawthorne's lament that America is no country for romance is comment on his surroundings and comment, too, on the lack of precedents to follow in his writing. Autobiography was looked to, in one way, as the thing which would cover the blankness or fill in the void. Even Hawthorne, who felt himself to be the most reticent of autobiographical writers, turned to "romanticizing" his own experience at the Salem customs house in order to prepare the required introduction to *The Scarlet Letter* and then to building a whole novel from his life at Brook Farm. But, from another angle, what was generally received by novelists as a tremendous handicap was apprehended by autobiographers as a tremendous asset, at least by the more naïve ones. Where everyone's life was as good as the next man's, where no one needed to feel constrained by tradition or by traditional forms, in that state every man's life was of potential interest. Any man could become President, the saying went, and any man could be an autobiographer. Behind this, autobiography finds a certain philosophical justification because, as Tocqueville noticed, every democrat is empowered "to seek the reason of things for oneself, and in oneself alone."[32] Franklin is the ideal demonstration. The cultural and philosophic origins of the *Autobiography* are exactly the same as those of his versatile achievements and the legendary phenomenon of his "rise." Yet Franklin was not particularly concerned with form—was content to copy Defoe or Addison in his essays and satires and satisfied to see his memoirs take their own shape and teach him as he wrote. It is in this way, of course, that he has contributed to the merry American folk myth of the untutored genius, of the writer who writes best because he never learned to write, though this is hardly the truth about him.

Both the myth of natural genius and the great prospects for autobiography find their strongest defense in Emerson and Whitman. To them the autobiographer was a potential national bard and epic poet. Such histories as Augustine's, Cellini's, and Rousseau's are among the most influential books in Western history and are also great mirrors of their eras. What work was to do the same for the United States? Indeed,

<hr>

[32] *Democracy in America*, ed. Phillips Bradley (Vintage Books: New York, 1960), II, 3.

who was to be the American Dante? "Dante's praise is that he dared to write his autobiography in colossal cipher, or into universality," Emerson said in "The Poet," and when he went on to put out his call for the poet who would celebrate "our log-rolling, our stumps and their politics, our fisheries, our Negroes and Indians, . . . the southern planting, the western clearing, Oregon and Texas," he implied that such a man would be his own historian and that his "poem" would be such an "autobiography in colossal cipher." Whitman's acceptance of this spirit is one of the things which makes *Leaves of Grass* and particularly "Song of Myself" the ambitious works they are, for the "Walt Whitman" of the poems—as opposed to Walter Whitman, the holder of the first copyright—is the "kosmos" whose life is the "sign of democracy" and whose experience is made the representative experience of his race. Yet Whitman's great problem of form is the American autobiographer's problem again raising itself amid the additional problems of the form of the undefined American epic. For just as he was without valuable precedents for the American epic, so was he without sufficiently mature models for autobiography. The result, as recent critics have tried to show, is that his best poems are not so much a form as a process, a representation of himself in the very act of realizing himself.

"Song of Myself" is not Whitman's autobiography, any more than "The Custom House" is Hawthorne's or *Walden* is Thoreau's. Yet these mid-nineteenth-century classics are all autobiographical and all illustrations of the manifold ways of using personal experience in American literature. They also testify to the necessity that an American author be, somehow, a *character*. This can mean everything from his actually being the hero of his own books ("I, on my side, require of every writer, first or last, a simple and sincere account of his own life," Thoreau says) to his appearing in public in some mask related to his work (e.g. Hawthorne the shy customs inspector or Whitman the "good grey poet"). The more autobiographical writing and the more masks, the more complicated the task of autobiography proper, as Mark Twain's (Samuel Clemens'?) nearly forty years of struggle to write the story of his life clearly proves. Going about it by fits and starts from the early 1870's until just before his death, he never decided either how to write it or how to organize it. He might have produced a book with rich insights and assimilations, and there is no denying that some of the reminiscences chosen by his editors are among his finest pieces. But his numerous varieties of attempts at autobiography are evidence of the difficulty having so many possibilities for the mode naturally presented to him. Was he to be Mark Twain the funny man or was he to expose his pessimistic, misanthropic side? Was he to continue to tell tales, to eulogize his daughters, or was he to indulge his perverse plan for settling old quarrels and damning his enemies? By this time many of the old possibilities for personal history had become some of the most entrenched of the problems.

It is time to stop discussion of the difficulties. James and Adams could see by the end of the nineteenth century that understanding and conveying American experience required an examination that would have to begin by examining the viewer's own consciousness. The story lay not just in the life itself but in the making of the mind that in turn made the life, shaped it and studied it. Such autobiography would have to combine the introspection and desire for form of religious autobiography with all the variety of events and materials of secular "self-teaching." "Self-teaching" would take on a really religious seriousness. Here lay challenges of a new and perhaps greater kind, and James and Adams, almost alone among their contemporaries, were prepared to deal with them.

CHAPTER TWO

Henry Adams and Henry James

We all began together, and our lives have made more or less of a unity, which is, as far as I can see, about the only unity that American society in our time had to show.

Adams to James, January 22, 1911

WITHIN the principality of American autobiography, the two royal houses are the Adamses and the Jameses. In one kind of self-examination or another, the ascendency of the Adamses goes back to 1776, when Henry's great-grandfather John Adams purchased a folio notebook from a Philadelphia stationer and began to keep copies of all his correspondence.[1] John Quincy Adams followed by keeping a diary, and Charles Francis Adams faithfully did so too. The custom went on in Henry Adams until in 1888 and 1889, looking back over this burden of the past, he burned the diary he had kept since his years at Harvard.[2] He thereby committed himself to the less arduous but more complicated medium of autobiography itself. Yet for this too there was a family tradition, going back to John Adams' autobiographical sketches of 1802 and 1809. Henry's grandmother Louisa Catherine Adams had begun autobiographies during periods of depression and gloom in 1825 and 1840,[3] and in 1869 Henry had prepared to publish them.[4] Finally, two years be-

---

[1] Lyman H. Butterfield, "The Papers of the Adams Family: Some Account of Their History," *Proceedings of the Massachusetts Historical Society*, LXXI (1953-57), pp. 328-329.

[2] Butterfield, p. 338.

[3] "Record of a Life, or My Story" and "The Adventures of a Nobody." See Martin B. Duberman, *Charles Francis Adams, 1807-1886* (Boston, 1961), pp. 2, 3, 26, 425.

[4] Butterfield, pp. 346-347n.

fore *The Education of Henry Adams* was offered to the public in 1918, Brooks Adams, the youngest brother, published the autobiography of Charles Francis Adams, Jr., the eldest brother.

The activity of the Jameses made up in concentration what it lacked in age. Of the seven members of the family of Henry James, Senior, the only ones not to respond to the impulse were Mrs. James and Garth Wilkinson James, the third son. Henry Senior's work was "Immortal Life: Illustrated in a Brief Autobiographical Sketch of the late Stephen Dewhurst; Edited, with an Introduction by Henry James," printed by William in *The Literary Remains of the late Henry James*, 1885. William kept diaries and at one time made the very revealing confession to Henry Adams that "autobiographies are my particular line of literature, the only books I let myself buy outside of metaphysical treatises, . . ."[5] The youngest son Robertson left a few pages of autobiography, wishing he could write more—ghostly impressions of a childhood so like his elder brothers' crossed by a maturity so different.[6] The last companion and predecessor to Henry Junior's achievement (a work for a time appropriately and respectfully referred to as the "Family Book")[7] was the journal of his sister Alice James. Starting it in May 1889, she applied herself to it so doggedly that the last entry was dictated to her attendant on March 4, 1892, as she lay on her deathbed.[8]

Such an inheritance of self-examination and self-portraiture is imposing, to say the least. In this chapter, however, I do not want to compare fathers or to compare the diaries of

[5] *Letters of Henry Adams (1892-1918)*, ed. Worthington Chauncey Ford (Boston and New York, 1938), p. 485n. In the letter William asked for a copy of the *Education*.
[6] *The James Family*, ed. F. O. Matthiessen (New York, 1947), pp. 270-271.
[7] *The Letters of Henry James*, ed. Percy Lubbock (New York, 1920), II, p. 346.
[8] *Alice James, Her Brothers, Her Journal*, ed. Anna Robeson Burr (New York, 1934), pp. 87-252.

Charles Francis Adams with the "Immortal Life" of "the late Stephen Dewhurst," suggestive as such an inquiry might be. Instead I want to trace the lives of the bearers of the inheritance from the time they met until the time when, influenced to some degree by each other, they transformed these family traditions of personal narrative into their contrasting autobiographies. The story of the harmonious difference of the *Education* and *A Small Boy* and *Notes* really begins with the long agreements and differences of their authors. The friendship of Henry James and Henry Adams is something of a critic's cliché. It needs documentation—more, unfortunately, than exists, but the chronicle here will show what is available. On the other hand, the story does not need to stop with these things, and we are compensated by being able to consider other works which are introductions and supplements to the autobiographies.

The advantages of trying to see James and Adams together should become apparent. Their acquaintance, strong during the seventies and early eighties, rose up in the later years of their lives as a kind of camaraderie, a mutual respect of veterans. When James died, Adams wrote that he had lost a friend of over forty years and that the news had hit him "harder than any stroke since my brother Charles' death a year ago."[9] Adams also thought of James as being part of that group of his friends who were the distinguished spokesmen for his generation: H. H. Richardson, Augustus St. Gaudens, John La Farge, Alex Agassiz, Clarence King, John Hay, and William James. The list deserves thought. Intent as we are today on locating James in other contexts, it must be remembered that this was, after all, a large part of his own American setting. And Adams had the vision to see how they were "more or less of a unity . . . about the only unity that American society in our time had to show."[10] Whether James would have made such a statement is doubtful; his list, cer-

[9] *Letters (1892-1918)*, p. 638.   [10] *Letters (1892-1918)*, p. 558.

tainly, would not have included all the same names. By such slight human divergences does the conversation between James and Adams begin to take on significance. Underlying it, and spreading out further from it, are some of the greater, almost chaotic disunities of our own so nonorganic age. To put it simply, James and Adams were a novelist and an historian who could still talk to one another. They naturally thought of themselves—at least Adams did—as being in a "unity" with an architect, a sculptor, a painter, a mining engineer, a geologist, a statesman, and a psychologist because their various professions were held together by common professions of belief. By listening in on James and Adams (and by listening for the equally profound things not said), we can get a year-by-year story of how the break-up happened. We can also begin to realize what Adams meant by "Twentieth-Century Multiplicity," what he was trying to do in the *Education*, and what he thought James had failed to do.

I

The two Henrys probably first met in the fall of 1870. Adams was at Harvard for his first year as Assistant Professor of Medieval History and Editor of *The North American Review*. James was living in Cambridge and writing for such periodicals as the *Atlantic*, the *Nation*, and the *North American*. They could have met at the monthly dinners of the Club, a group of young editors, writers, lawyers, and teachers that included other young men of promise like Howells, William James, and T. S. Perry.[11] Already their experiences had been unique enough to separate them markedly from even their own fellows and peers. Neither had served in the Civil War. Adams' seven years abroad as his father's secretary at the London embassy had been anticipated by James' years of familial vagabondage in England

[11] John T. Morse, Jr., *Thomas Sergeant Perry, A Memoir* (Boston and New York, 1929), pp. 63-64.

and Europe in the 1850's. In the fall of 1870 Adams had just returned from a summer in Europe, and James had been back only several months from his first solitary year and a quarter in Europe. Such exposures and opportunities for young men of thirty-two and twenty-seven were mainly open because of the Adams-Brooks and James wealth, which did not need to be large still to be considerably above average. Yet these coincidences were hardly more than superficial, and if the two men did not immediately become close friends there are good reasons why. "We knew each other to the last nervous center, and feared each other's knowledge,"[12] Adams wrote James much later. But he was not speaking of themselves; he was describing the nervousness of his own more intimate circle of Harvard men and Unitarians, and James was not one of them.

In later years, Adams grew more and more critical of Cambridge, Unitarianism, and his Harvard education. This was a kind of comfortable and conformist influence which he had to break free of. James, on the other hand, had never really had such an indoctrination. In 1870, Adams was being drawn back into an environment he thought he had left ten years before. His important assignments at Harvard and to the *Review* could have represented places in which a man of thirty-two might have *settled*, might have sunk foundations in anticipation of a successful career or might have slowly become complacent in and decayed. He instinctively saw both possibilities for himself and saw them in the parallel lives of his intimates. "We looked through each other like microscopes. There was absolutely nothing in us that we did not understand merely by looking in the eye." In retrospect he wondered how he had ever endured such group self-consciousness and suspicion, created by the group's unnatural uniformity and isolation from the mainstream of American life; and he also saw that while James had been tacitly aware

[12] *Letters (1892-1918)*, p. 414.

of the condition, he had never been drawn aside by it. In 1870, being five years younger than Adams, he was not on his way back to Boston but resolutely on his way through. The house at No. 20 Quincy Street, Cambridge, had simply been another of his parents' many more or less temporary quarters. Previously the Jameses were Newporters, New Yorkers, or just "hotel children." Henry's matriculation at Harvard had been quite casual; he had not even graduated. And two years before Adams came as Editor of the *North American Review*, James had been offered an editorship on the same periodical and turned it down.[13]

Yet these differences between Henry Adams and Henry James must still not obscure the fact that the Boston and Cambridge of 1870 had brought together two men of somewhat similar interest and background and given them further common experience to be the basis of closer friendship. James' not being a Bostonian by birth may even be counted a future advantage to the relationship. They therefore need not have looked back and forth as if at mirrors of each other and given one another the distrustful and predatory kind of interior watching exchanged between the local boys. Compared to Adams' impulses to self-examination, which were the consequence of an overconcentration of environment and a piling up of inheritance, James' were the result of too varied an environment and an inheritance still open to definition. In the long run the opposite approaches to self-cultivation would be beneficial. In the meantime James' shrewdness of observation meant that he could begin to understand Adams and yet understand him without embarrassment. And Adams must have been constantly surprised by the range and profundity of the novelist's comprehensions.

A fact of considerable portent to their friendship is that in June 1872 Adams married Marian Hooper, an old admira-

[13] Leon Edel, *Henry James: The Untried Years* (Philadelphia and New York, 1953), p. 246.

tion of James', "He belonged to the circle of my wife's set long before I knew him or her," Adams wrote forty-four years later on getting word of James' death. James had liked "Clover" Hooper not just as the member of a "set" but as one of the three or four girls he and William appreciated as intellectual and conversational sparring partners, a wit, a "genius of my beloved country,"[14] a spirit whom their imaginations foresaw as the focus and interest of whatever America could hope for in the way of real *sets* and salons. Clover— the nickname seems suggestive—drew the men closer together than they might independently have come. In Chanticleer-ish moods a few months before the wedding, Adams described his fiancée as rich, sympathetic, given to learning languages, and a bad dresser. She "laughs at the idea of being thought a blue," he said in one place, and yet her forthrightness and independence seem to have overpowered him occasionally. "She rules me as only American women rule men, and I cower before her. Lord! how she would lash me if she read the above description of her!" Thus, despite Clover's own Brahmin lineage, the devious course of married life may actually have worked towards Clover's improvement of her husband, towards a breaking down of the Boston rigidities which had encumbered his and James' earlier encounters. When they were dinner guests together in Rome in the spring of 1873, James found Adams "improved,"[15] apparently less self-conscious and restrained in his public manner. From now on they were united enough for Adams to supply James with letters of introduction and for James to help the Adamses with hotel reservations and lodgings.[16] They jointly

---

[14] *Selected Letters of Henry James*, ed. Leon Edel (London, 1956), p. 67.

[15] Leon Edel, *Henry James: The Conquest of London* (London, 1962), p. 127.

[16] *The Notebooks of Henry James*, ed. F. O. Matthiessen and Kenneth B. Murdock (New York, 1947), p. 28. And Henry Adams, Letters to Robert A. Cunliffe, April 18, 1879, and Charles Milnes Gaskell, May 21, 1879. Adams Papers Microfilms.

became busy, urbane, and established members of the transatlantic scene, and Clover's turbulent mixture of acuity, sophistication, and enthusiastic Americanism is both a center and a record of the friendship.

Both Adams and James were aiming at a kind of self-realization and self-knowledge which required the thickest possible contexts within which to see themselves and then a consciousness of their own minds' manners of making the observations. The knowledge of consciousness without the complex and suggestive backgrounds would have led only to redundant introspection; the mere agglomerations of backgrounds would have led to bored worldliness. It is revealing that in the 1870's they both left Boston to seek new homes, James preparing almost throughout the decade for his "Conquest of London" and Adams first renting a house in Washington in 1877. Both moves, moreover, were carefully weighed and considered, and the two men to a degree used each other in trying to understand the meaning and consequences of the decisions. This is an underlying theme or "action" to the comedy of the international scene which in the late 1870's and early 1880's becomes both the subject of James' fiction and an issue in many of Henry Adams' letters. All the while Clover comments too, for she was present at the debate, presiding over the tea service, giving her own vigorous views.

The Adamses were in Europe in 1879-80, so that Henry could mine the resources of the various libraries and foreign offices for his *History*. James was with them in London in the summer of 1879, in Paris in the fall of 1879, and again in London in 1880. His first impression on reopening acquaintance was that Adams "could never 'in the nature of things be a very gracious or sympathetic companion,' "[17] but this was soon revised. The Adamses' rooms in Half-Moon Street were but two streets away from his own in Bolton

[17] *The Conquest of London*, p. 377.

Street. Marian's letters to her father are full of references
to James, of his dropping in on the spur of the moment,
and statements that he "came in to dine on his own suggestion,
and sat chatting till late."[18] In Paris they were even more
frequent companions. "Mr. James comes in at about six-thirty
and towards seven we go off to dine, and three times a week
to the theatre afterwards," Marian said in an account of
their usual habits. On his side, James wrote his family, "I
have become very fond of them—they are very excellent
people." Back in London the easy familiarity continued and
one Sunday afternoon Adams described James "standing on
the hearthrug, with his hands under his coat-tails talking with
my wife, exactly as though we were in Marlborough Street."[19]

They were three Europeanized Americans—but ones who
still needed to analyze and clarify their impressions and
choices, and, naturally, they did so with each other's help and
each in relation to the others as examples. The Adamses
were, as James did in fact put it, his *"confidants."* When they
returned to Washington in the autumn of 1880, he wrote
Grace Norton:

> I go in an hour to bid farewell to my friends the
> Henry Adamses, who after a year of London life are
> returning to their beloved Washington. One sees so
> many "cultivated Americans" who prefer living abroad
> that it is a great refreshment to encounter two speci-
> mens of this class who find the charms of their native
> land so much greater than those of Europe. In Eng-
> land they appear to have suffered more than enjoyed,
> and their experience is not unedifying, for they have
> seen and known a good deal of English life. But they
> are rather too critical and invidious. I shall miss them

---

[18] *The Letters of Mrs. Henry Adams*, ed. Ward Thoron (Boston, 1936),
p. 155.
[19] *Letters of Henry Adams (1858-1891)*, ed. Worthington Chauncey
Ford (Boston and New York, 1930), p. 321.

much, though—we have had such inveterate discussions and comparing of notes. They have been much liked here.[20]

He thus used their experience as a way of increasing his own. Their criticisms may originally have given him doubt about his decisions, but such insights as this one enabled him to rise even higher in his good-humored international point of view, becoming neither more European nor more American but more like himself. Clover provided the crackling and witty American viewpoint. "It is high time Harry James was ordered home by his family," she once wrote her father from London. "He is too good a fellow to be spoiled by injudicious old ladies in London. And in the long run they would like him all the better for knowing and loving his own country. He had better go to Cheyenne and run a hog ranch."[21]

James was a sort of ideal example of the Europeanized American, against whom she and Henry placed their own desire to be Americans who could still practice and expand a grand manner in the United States. Whatever joking and irony she might practice on James in his presence or *en famille*, she stood up for him, of course, among strangers and phillistines. Back in Washington in December 1880 she told her father, "I stoutly defended Henry James and *Daisy Miller* to stout Mrs. Smith of Chicago, and protested that the latter was charming and that the author adored her."

II

The perceptive, sometimes satiric comments on themselves and the dialogue about international manners continued through the early 1880's. That James was now a celebrated authority on the subject did not stop the Adamses; they had sufficient experience of their own. When he was in Wash-

---

[20] *The Conquest of London*, pp. 379-380.
[21] Marian Adams to Robert W. Hooper, April 4, 1880, Adams Papers.

ington in 1882, they made light of what they considered his affectations. Clover was amused that he should have "sheltered under an alias" in order to avoid the newspapers. ". . . That young emigrant has much to learn here," she quipped, adding that he was surprised to find he needed no permit to attend debates in a democratic Capitol. "He may in time get into the 'swim' here," she blithely said, "but I doubt it."[22] The Adamses were now in the thick of their social and political skirmishes, and they watched James' reactions with great interest. Clover was happy to have his opinion that Oscar Wilde, also in Washington and sponsored by a rival household, was a "fatuous cad." When James dined with their arch enemy, James G. Blaine, she predicted the worst: " 'And a certain man came down (to? from?) Jerusalem and fell among thieves . . . and they sprang up and choked him.' " Actually Blaine had invited James to meet President Arthur; James liked the evening, and the Adamses, he said, were "eagerly anxious to hear what I have seen and heard at places which they decline to frequent."[23] Yet Adams could sense James' distress at seeing friends so embroiled, and also his desire for cities requiring less strenuous cultivation of impressions. He could tell that James thought his and Marian's life "revolting in respect to the politics and the intrigues that surround it," and described James as "very homesick for London and for all the soft embraces of the old world."[24]

A difference in point of view is plainly evident. This was the period in Adams' life when he was most committed to self-discovery by action. To him James G. Blaine was a vicious and cynical scoundrel; getting Blaine out of power was an important exercise of his own power and a kind of test of the soundness of democratic government. We can sympathize.

[22] *Letters of Mrs. Adams,* pp. 327, 320.
[23] Leon Edel, *Henry James: The Middle Years* (Philadelphia and New York, 1962), p. 30.
[24] *Letters (1858-1891),* p. 333.

On the other hand, we can also sympathize with James' mode of life, which appeared so aloof. His means of action was writing, and fiction was his means of understanding the queer and varied world history had thrown up around him. This necessitated imitation, and imitation required detachment, not in a some Olympian sense but in a strangely personal sense. "Art requires above all things," he had written in his review of Whitman's *Drum-Taps*, "a suppression of one's self, a subordination of one's self to an idea." Thus we have the phenomenon of James using the Adamses and even using himself in the fiction of this period and yet coming up with something quite separate from both "sources" as they initially were. It is almost as if he had written: "Self—or knowledge of one's self—requires a suppression of one's self, a subordination of one's self to art." Under this discipline he might have seemed aloof—and anglicized and nostalgic for some sentimental London—but it would have been only in a superficial way. Deeper down, he had loosed his imagination to his American travels as liberally as he could.

This paradox is illustrated even in the two fairly light short stories which incorporate the Adamses, "The Point of View" (1882) and "Pandora" (1884). In "The Point of View" James assigned Clover's patriotic vernacular to Marcellus Cockerel, a young Californian just freed from the compulsory grand tour: "I've got Europe off my back. You've no idea how it simplifies things and how jolly it makes me feel. . . . Disagreeables for disagreeables I prefer our own. . . ." And James caught a side of Adams in the letter of Miss Sturdy, a fifty-year-old spinster who had spent most of her life in Europe. Writing from her piazza in Newport, she represented his sophisticated estrangement: "It's true I've been for a longer time than usual on the wrong side of the water, and I admit that I feel a little out of training for American life. They're breaking me in very fast, however. I don't mean that they bully me—I absolutely decline to be bullied." Or, in a forecast of one of Adams' later poses: "The privilege of indifference is the dearest we possess." Transforming Clover and Henry Adams into Marcellus Cockerel and Miss Sturdy is in one way James' reply to the kidding and criticism he took from them—the implications in Mrs. Adams' remark that he should "go to Cheyenne and run a hog ranch." These portraits further prove that James had studied his friends closely. There indeed was something masculine and western about Clover, and "Marcellus Cockerel" just brought it to clearer view. The same goes for the spinsterish, haughty qualities of her husband. Adams' humor was simultaneously sprightly and corrosive, and he tended sometimes to be more "Miss Sturdy" than himself. James could not make these discoveries, however, without a certain subordination of himself to his art, or to the latent and underlying features in his material which seem to have suggested the art. And yet the outcome was not only a discovery about the Adamses but finally one about himself and his surroundings. If the imagination appeared aloof, that was really because it was so busy in the life right around it.

In "Pandora" James set out even more consciously to "do Henry Adams and his wife," as he put it in his *Notebooks*. There, seen through the eyes of a reflective German diplomatic officer, they are "Mr. and Mrs. Bonnycastle," two Washington socialites who have resolved the question of where to live, at least to their own satisfaction, and who thus seem both amusing and also rather perplexing. "The couple had taken upon themselves the responsibilities of an active patriotism," the articulate German observes; "they thought it right to live in America, differing therein from many of their acquaintances who only, with some grimness, thought it inevitable." He is puzzled by the care with which these citizens of a democracy make their social distinctions; he has heard that the usual Bonnycastle party "left out, on the whole, more people than it took in." Spring, however, made Mrs. Bonnycastle become "whimsically willful, vernally reckless," and the eccentric Mr. Bonnycastle was in that season briefly allowed a wider choice of guests: "Vogelstein still remembered the puzzled feeling . . . with which, more than a year before, he had heard Mr. Bonnycastle exclaim one evening, after a dinner in his own house, when every guest . . . had departed, 'Hang it, there's only a month left; let us be vulgar and have some fun—let us invite the President.' "

But besides imitating the Adamses' "active patriotism" and highly unpredictable brand of snobbishness, James has also reached a kind of parody of himself. His surprise at American manners, his confusion in a country he thought he knew, his supposed fastidiousness and formality, and his reflectiveness are all registered in the German narrator. Concomitantly, Vogelstein is the least severe and straight-backed of Germans; that tendency is challenged on one side by American ingenuousness and checked on the other by Jamesian curiosity and good humor. Still, what survives of it is left as the parody. James could have realized that he seemed excessively Old-World and frowning in his attitudes in America; the treatment of himself as a critical "Vogelstein" is a confession of these sins and thus a kind of prevention of their overdevelopment. Here, still more explicitly, though more complexly, art has been first a subordination of self, right down to fitting the self into a restricted portrait—and then a discovery of self.

Though the Adamses undoubtedly read and enjoyed these shorter pieces, they continued to regard him only familiarly and irreverently as "that young emigrant." They also found his longer, more ambitious writing unnecessarily drawn out and difficult. Adams admitted that he "broke down on *The Portrait of a Lady*"[25] and Clover was equally at a loss, though at no loss for words.

[25] *Letters (1858-1891)*, p. 333.

It's very nice, and charming things in it, but I'm ageing fast and prefer what Sir Walter called the "big bow-wow style." I shall suggest to Mr. James to name his next novel "Ann Eliza." It's not that he "bites off more than he can chaw," as T. G. Appleton said of Nathan, but he chaws more than he bites off.[26]

Their so similar, if so differently phrased, responses show the disappointment of friends who are bothered by an author's suddenly not writing according to their experience of him. But there is something else, and the obvious way of putting it is that neither Adams nor Clover could share James' manner of looking at life. So long as they all three remained on the comic level of the International Scene, there was a rich profusion of anecdotes and cases which could be debated with great pleasure and interest. The difficult old "question of Europe," as James called it, was a lively dispute between friends. The Adamses could see James as some one of their own set who had made different choices. They did not need to go further, and James did not need to try to enter Adams' intricate kind of vision. But the presence of these differences is announced even by the positions taken in the international question and the choices of London and Washington for residences. The two men were seeking more suggestive settings, but they wanted different kinds.

Adams' most famous announcement of his reasons for going to Washington is in his letter to Charles Milnes Gaskell of November 25, 1877. The immediate reasons were dissatisfaction with Harvard and Boston and the advantages of Washington in writing his *History*, but he had more profound ones, and it is worthwhile to quote portions of this letter at some length.

We have made a great leap in the world; cut loose at once from all that has occupied us since our return

[26] *Letters of Mrs. Adams*, p. 306.

from Europe, and caught new ties and occupations here. The fact is I gravitate to a capital by a primary law of nature. This is the only place in America where society amuses me, or where life offers variety. Here, too, I can fancy that we are of use in the world, for we distinctly occupy niches which ought to be filled.

He continues by hinting at the role he wishes to play as host and unofficial public personage and by mentioning his needs as scholar. The next paragraph begins:

One of these days this will be a very great city if nothing happens to it. Even now it is a beautiful one, and its situation is superb. As I belong to the class of people who have great faith in this country and who believe that in another century it will be saying in its turn the last word of civilization, I enjoy the expectation of the coming day, and try to imagine that I am myself, with my fellow *gelehrte* here, the first faint rays of that great light which is to dazzle and set the world on fire hereafter.

It was a dramatic moment for Adams, and as he wrote his old English friend he seemed to want to send up flares, fire salutes. In saying a law of gravitation drew him to capitals, he summoned up both his family heritage and their ordered Newtonian world, and yet he added to that his dilettantish affection for a society of amusement and variety. However, lest that seem merely frivolous, he also spoke of being useful and of filling important "niches." His grand objective, after all, was not just to bring the capital gentility and society but to give it some link between political manipulations and national history and life, some sense of Society.

As an Adams, he could see this need, and the second paragraph conveys his awareness of national possibilities. Still, the reader should not be distracted by the "active patriotism." "To be an Adams was by definition to make history rather than to record it. The hand of the fathers lay heavily upon the young boy. . . ."[27] So long as that ponderous sentiment overhangs Adams criticism, his decision will be only jingoistically interpreted. Without depreciating the power of the heritage, we should be able to see that Adams had learned to live in it in order to use it. It added emphasis to his concept of history as motion. The eighteenth-century references and metaphors, the assumption of civilization's movement westward, the figure of himself as a beginner, a "*gelehrte,*" all underline his strong sense of time and change. History was motion, and his consciousness was built around such a definition. He already sought to identify himself as a position along the path of the motion ("the first faint rays of that great light"), and upon this identification arose the force of much of his writing. Some years afterwards, at the time of the first printing of the *History*, he wrote Gaskell, "I am writing for a continent of a hundred million people fifty years hence."[28] This infers that the language itself was in a position along the course of history. "I enjoy the expectation of the coming day."

It was this vision that James could not share and work in with Adams. Neither could Adams make his way in James' esthetic orientations. When James wrote in his *Hawthorne* that "the flower of art blooms only where the soil is deep, that it takes a great deal of history to produce a little literature," Adams would have agreed with the desire for backgrounds and social contrasts, but he would not have agreed with the image of history as merely a soil pleasingly sending up the flowers of art. Yet James little needed any more serious or theoretical notion of history. A part of a letter from James to Charles Eliot Norton in 1873 makes a poignant contrast to Adams' letter to Gaskell.

[27] Robert E. Spiller, "Henry Adams," *Literary History of the United States*, ed. Spiller, Thorp, Johnson, and Canby (New York, 1959), p. 1082.
[28] *Letters (1858-1891)*, p. 357.

I don't pretend in the least to understand our national destinies—or those of any portion of the world. My philosophy is no match for them, and I regard the march of history very much as a man placed astride of a locomotive, without knowledge or help, would regard the progress of that vehicle. To stick on, somehow, and even to enjoy the scenery as we pass, is the sum of my aspirations."[29]

Thus the preference for learning by his art, which was a sort of concentrated way of studying and enjoying "the scenery." Thus the only passing interest in Washington and the deep preference for London, which provided more impressions and "notes" and gave them up more freely. Adams took his experience linearly; he looked ahead and behind. James took his roundly; he scanned the immediate horizons on all sides of him. It is a sign of their unity and a tribute to their success in their respective visions, even so, that what they saw was so much the same.

III

By the time James returned to London in 1883, to begin over twenty years of continuous residence abroad, both he and Adams were established in their elected cities, their preferred settings, and their chosen lines of work. James was forty, Adams forty-five. Pictures of them from around these years show them both balding or nearly bald, both with high, prominent foreheads, and with thick beards and mustaches. Both are elegant dressers. James, however, looks more full-cheeked and solidly round-faced; Adams' face has begun to look more narrow and his eyes seem slightly sunken, speculative, and distance-gazing. James' eyes are large and set in fine big lids and brows. Both men also look very serious and intent. Both, after all, were dedicated to their work, disciplined

[29] *Selected Letters*, p. 73.

in their efforts, and hopeful of substantial fame. For the time being neither cared to relax for long, and the two did not see each other again until the winter of 1891-92 when Adams was briefly back in London. By then, though, Adams' life was vastly changed. His wife had died in December 1885. He had finished his *History* in 1890 and had gone on the voyage to the South Seas which dramatically marked the end of the middle period of his life. By the 1890's he and James mutually regarded themselves as elder statesmen or survivors of an earlier age who were preparing for their last projects. But the "middle years," despite the lapse in contacts and the hiatus in correspondence (their letters probably having been destroyed),[30] remain an important part of this essay. The most compelling reason is that Adams here made his two experiments as a novelist, and this provides another insight into his and James' methods of consciousness, as well as their images of women and society.

A great deal has been written and even more imagined regarding the devastating effect on Adams of Marian's suicide. It has already been shown that James' affection for her, although of another kind, naturally, was by no means small. She was, he once told her, "the incarnation of my native land." (With her habitual sense of irony Clover felt that, coming from James, the compliment was "most equivocal.")[31] James' regard for Clover is fixed forever in his figures of the American Girl, to which she, along with the bright, responsive, and responsible of her contemporaries, was a partial contribution. Two years before her marriage, James had seen fit to write his brother that she and Minnie Temple possessed qualities missing from the plain, stiff, and dowdy English women he was then among. "I revolt from their dreary deathly want

[30] Edel, *The Middle Years*, p. 166. Mr. Edel suspects, and I agree, that Adams probably burned all James' letters to him and Clover in his bonfires of 1888 and 1889. It is also conceivable that correspondence from them to James was by some means intentionally destroyed, too.
[31] *Letters of Mrs. Adams*, p. 384.

of—what shall I call it?—Clover Hooper has it—intellectual grace—Minnie Temple has it—moral spontaneity."[32] Marian Adams' death may be counted among the various factors which brought to an end James' early comic stories of the International Scene. She had been a part of it; her death closely coincided with its conclusion.

It is distracting, however, to lay too much stress on the importance of Marian Hooper Adams (or any single, so limited source) to the work of either James or Adams. It is also distracting to try to assess too carefully the psychological impact of her death. From a critical standpoint Clover is really best seen as introductory; she is a sort of emblem of James' and Adams' devotion to women. The women they went on to celebrate have a significance much broader than any shadow she can cast. The importance of the female figure, of the Virgin, in *Mont-Saint-Michel and Chartres* and the *Education*, is something to which Marian Adams was only a bare beginning. Similarly, the Minnie Temple of the last chapter of *Notes of a Son and Brother* represents a great deal more than Minnie herself did to James at the time she died in 1870. The love which the two men actually gave in life was but a starting point for the symbolic value attached to imaginary women in their work.

The further reasons for this idolatry are complex. For one thing, as Leslie Fiedler has insistently pointed out, the readers of novels in the nineteenth century were largely women. But behind this fact (and who is to say the condition has changed?) lay the division of labor which left to women the fields of art and culture and crowded men into the close dens of the market place. On the other hand, when men such as Adams or James had been released from trade by the activity of their grandfathers or fathers-in-law and maternal grandfathers, the shops and offices became to them a world of which they were regrettably ignorant. "Business in a world of busi-

[32] *Letters*, I, p. 26.

ness was the thing we most agreed (differ as we might on minor issues) in knowing nothing about," James said of his family.[33] Adams, in his studies of economics and in his investigations of the Gould and Fisk scandals, had informed himself to some degree, and he was also more knowledgeable in political matters than James. Yet both of them, by the time they had dedicated themselves to their careers of fiction and history, were "feminine" in their social roles and, to a large extent, in their social companions. It is an old generalization that society is feminine, that it is civilized according to how much liberty and opportunity it offers women, but the basis of such a rule is the assumption that men will still be present, that they will remain in the company of the women they have emancipated. That nineteenth-century men, American nineteenth-century men especially, did not was a tragedy that both James and Adams frequently took occasion to notice. James' departure for Europe was in part an effort to find male company and a heterosexual society. Adams' move to Washington, the "City of Conversation,"[34] as James called it, was a similar search. "The business-man in the United States," James said, "may . . . never hope to be anything *but* a businessman."[35] And the remark is good background for a favorite dinner-party gambit of Adams': What is the cause of the failure of the American woman? His smarter partners answered, "Because the American man is a failure."[36] The woman's plight was therefore not just more acute, more melodramatic, or more familiar to readers; it was above all more representative. It denoted mankind's.

The figures of women in James' and Adams' work are revered as spokesmen of life and culture. They stand courageously for themselves, but their battles are those of their

[33] *Henry James, Autobiography*, ed. Dupee, p. 35.
[34] Henry James, *The American Scene*, ed. W. H. Auden (New York, 1946), p. 351.
[35] *The American Scene*, p. 345.
[36] *The Education of Henry Adams*, p. 442.

authors as well. the goals of free men and the society of free men. It is a mistake to think that Adams' characterizations of Madeleine Lee in *Democracy* and Esther Dudley in *Esther* are simply projections of his own wife. As critics such as R. P. Blackmur, Ernest Samuels, and J. C. Levenson have variously noted, Esther and Mrs. Lee are intellectually nearer to Adams himself. "Madeleine Lee, *c'est moi,*" the author might have said, meaning that she faces his dilemma, that the things she wants and the pressures that resist her were the same as his own. And James might have made similar adjustments of Flaubert's remark. The heroines of *Democracy* and *Esther* and of James' many novels with feminine protagonists are all in various subtle ways images of the authors. They anticipate the "protagonists" of the *Education* and *A Small Boy* and *Notes.*

Madeleine Lee is a very gifted young widow, thirty years old and backed with an income of $20,000 to $30,000 a year, but with no purpose in life. She read philosophy, but "the more she read, the more she was disheartened that so much culture should lead to nothing—nothing."[37] She "plunged into philanthropy . . . saturated herself with the statistics of vice, until her mind had nearly lost sight of virtue" (Ch. 1). Her Boston friends suggested she crusade for higher education, while her New York friends suggested she lecture on women's rights or go upon the stage. The one source she had not exhausted was Washington. "She was aware that the President, the Speaker, and the Chief Justice were important personages, and instinctively she wondered whether they might not solve her problem" (Ch. 1). Consequently, with all lesser paths and purposes tried or dull, she gayly throws herself into the center of the maelstrom. She decides to spend a winter in Washington. "She was bent upon getting

[37] Henry Adams, *Democracy and Esther*, intro. Ernest Samuels (Doubleday Anchor Books: New York, 1961), p. 3. Further references will be given in parentheses; because of the number of new editions, they will be to chapter rather than page.

[65]

to the heart of the great American mystery of democracy and government" (Ch. 1).

The fundamental workings of the novel are those of a love story and the familiar triangle. The attractive Mrs. Lee cultivates a salon of office holders, diplomats, and lobbyists, but her two most regular instructors in politics are her two suitors. One is a Virginian and ex-Confederate officer, John Carrington, and the other is crafty Senator from Illinois and possible President, Silas P. Ratcliffe. Carrington is the relic of a distinguished Virginia family. He retains the moral values of an age when politics were the domain of gentlemen, yet he is the one man in the book who is out of office, without ambition, and without a political ax to grind. He simply practices law, practices it simply to support himself and a hungry household of sisters and female relations. In this position he is able to assist Mrs. Lee in meeting politicians and in becoming acquainted with the Washington scene, and, should they marry, her income would assist him in bailing out his family affairs. But marriage to Carrington hardly enters Mrs. Lee's head. " 'Ten years ago, I could have loved him,' she thought to herself . . ." (Ch. 9). The fact is that she wants power, substantial power, and Carrington does not have it.

Ratcliffe, on the other hand, is the most powerful voice in the Senate. Mrs. Lee hooks him ("like a huge, two-hundred-pound salmon") by telling him his speeches have the force of Webster's, and he soon becomes such a steady guest at her salon that the City's gossips begin to whisper impending marriage. Mrs. Lee's rivals send out tales that she is a young scamp bent on being the wife of a President, and Ratcliffe's friends hope her wealth and cultivation will reform his frontier gaucherie and further his chances. Meanwhile Mrs. Lee refrains from moral judgments, listens to her man, and accepts his case for the necessity of compromise and expediency in politics. In this way she is sure to get to understand democracy

and hopes to help him to understand himself. Cleaning up
his manners and morals will come in due season. She even
blinks a voting fraud he managed because he says it was for
the good of the Union and had to be done.

The climax occurs at the end of a great ball at the British
Embassy when Ratcliffe proposes. Mrs. Lee is cornered and
almost accepts on the spot. Fortunately her sister sweeps her
home and gives her a sealed letter from Carrington. Carrington knows of further scandals in Ratcliffe's past. In fact Ratcliffe was so afraid of exposure that he pulled strings to have
the young man appointed to a claims commission in Mexico.
But before leaving, Carrington had foreseen such a crisis. He
left the letter not to blacken Ratcliffe publicly or even to re-
open his own suit. It is only to save Mrs. Lee from Ratcliffe's deceits. Ratcliffe, it reveals, had some years ago with-
held approval of a subsidy for a steamship company until presented with a $100,000 bribe.

The Senator's explanation of the incident is a disgusting
display of amorality, equivocation, and clever self-abasement.
"Not until this moment," Mrs. Lee reflects, "had she really
felt as though she had got to the heart of politics, so that she
could, like a physician with his stethoscope, measure the organic disease. . . . Here she sat face to face with a moral
lunatic, who had not even enough sense of humor to see the
absurdity of his own request . . ." (Ch. 13). For Mrs. Lee to
step in to correct Ratcliffe's behavior would be to "go out to
the shore of this ocean of corruption, and repeat the ancient
rôle of King Canute, or Dame Partington with her mop and
her pail" (Ch. 13). She drives him from the house, and on
going out he receives a humiliating caning from a wiry old
Bulgarian diplomat! Mrs. Lee and her sister pack up for a
long trip to Europe.

"I want to go to Egypt," said Madeleine, still smiling faintly; "democracy has shaken my nerves to pieces.

Oh, what rest it would be to live in the Great Pyramid
and look out for ever at the polar star!"   (Ch. 13)

Democracy is a very amusing and a very revealing novel,
but it is something short of a good novel. James' own comment on it is useful: "It is good enough to make it a pity it
isn't better."[38] The major fault is that the characters are not
complete. They tend to be fleshless and intellectual, as if
they were fastened together to represent types and ideas.
What they enact, instead of being an independent action, is
a sort of ballad tale, "The Legend of Madeleine Lee," about
a lovely woman's discovery of the rottenness of post Civil
War politics. As such, it has most of the standard personages
of a story with whose outlines we are already familiar, but it
does not reach down into the deeper investigation that we
have a right to expect in a novel, even in one so deft and
rather light-handed as this. What does Mrs. Lee really want?
Knowledge of Power is too big a subject for one unoccupied
widow's single winter's study. And if Ratcliffe is the embodi-
ment of both the power and the corruption of democracy,
shouldn't we know more about him? He is hateful but he
is crucial, and a good novel should go further in accounting
for him or in exposing the real moral poverty inside him.
What makes the book so revealing, on the other hand, is the
origin of its defects, as well as a number of its virtues, in
Adams' means of imagining the book, or what might almost
be called his creative process.

To begin with, *Democracy*, like its successor *Esther*, has
aspects of a *roman à clef*, and Ernest Samuels has done a
thorough job of identifying Adams' friends and enemies
among the assorted characters filling out Madeleine Lee's
experience. The President, "Granite" or "Old Granny" is a
composite of Presidents Grant and Hayes; Senator Ratcliffe

---

[38] Virginia Harlow, *Thomas Sergeant Perry: A Biography and Letters
to Perry from William, Henry, and Garth Wilkinson James* (Durham,
N.C., 1950), p. 309.

is mainly based on Senator James G. Blaine; Carrington on James Lowndes, the ex-Confederate officer and gentleman lawyer who was a frequenter of Adams' house. Even the old Bulgarian diplomat, Baron Jacobi, is a portrait of the Turkish diplomat, Aristarchi Bey.[39] Adams' so direct use of his acquaintances tells us of his comparative lack of fictive imagination. When James used the Adamses in "The Point of View" and "Pandora" he was neither so dependent upon them nor so limited to using them as they were. His parodic treatment of himself as Vogelstein was, at its furthest range, a realization of a comic version of himself and a final dissociation from the implications of such manners. But more than this, *Democracy* remains restricted to the issues which worried the people it appropriated and to the issues which worried its author. It is a novel *about* things—about "the great American mystery of democracy and government," or about Washington, politics, and corruption. Although all novels need subjects, better ones make subjects into life and create complete, living worlds of their own. *Democracy* stops at a clever sketch of the world of Adams' Washington.

In Adams' case this need to work with actual people and to confront specific ideas is evidence that he had after all chosen the wrong medium for himself. The idiosyncratic and elaborate circumstances of his two novels' publications indicate that in his own careful way he may have known this perfectly well. With a Walpolean kind of flourish and flutter, he tried his hand at the game twice and then withdrew. The troublesome contradiction was that he was entirely serious about his subjects, but he could not be serious in a medium which influences as various as Puritan tradition, popular taste, and aristocratic *esprit* told him was frivolous. One clear result of this was that his writing tended to decorate very important questions with too much of the ribbon and lace of elegant pat-

---

[39] Ernest Samuels, *Henry Adams, The Middle Years* (Cambridge, Mass., 1958), pp. 89-95, and *Democracy and Esther*, pp. xiii-xv.

ter. The author of *Democracy* had the ability to see the men and women around him and the social questions of his day in all the complexity and depth they naturally had—or which they habitually distorted or disguised. To Adams, James G. Blaine was significant enough. John La Farge, Clarence King, and Phillips Brooks, the models for three of the major characters of *Esther*, were equally suggestive and real. To convert them to Ratcliffes, Whartons, Strongs, and Hazards is only to make them melodramatic or needlessly artificial. They then ceased to have what James might have called sufficient emotional capacity of character. This is even more true of Adams' introduction of himself in the tormented heroines. The person really bent "upon getting to the heart of the great American mystery" is not Mrs. Lightfoot Lee, draped partially as the author's wife and partially in the gowns of a society woman who was a friend of the author's, but the author himself, Henry Adams. Consequently, his better medium was autobiography and the machinery of this certain kind of autobiographical fiction was just encumbrance.

Adams' literary needs were in shocking opposition to James'. Both, as I have said, were strongly attracted to women as their protagonists. They used similar settings and social classes, and in this milieu they readily identified with the woman's plight. Of the two, Adams is the greater idolator of women, and it is interesting to note that the idolatry is somewhat inhibited in his novels by his too immediate kind of identification with them. The apotheosis of these authors' women remained for the autobiographies. Otherwise, James' imagination and creative process is so different from Adams' that they here have nothing in common. In the Preface to *The Spoils of Poynton* James tells the illustrative little story of how the "germ" of that novel happened to have been dropped by the slightest and most casual of anecdotes mentioned by a lady beside him at a dinner. "There had been but ten words," as he would have counted them, and he insists he wanted no more. He even tried to halt the woman's on-flowing words, for they only became another proof of what to him was "the fatal futility of Fact." But had Adams been equally interested, he might have pursued his informant until the very end of the evening. He craved "Fact." The "germ" was all James needed; improvisation, complication, "muddlement," and further characterization supplied themselves. The improvisation did not come so easily to Adams, and "Facts" were both a substitute for it and an insurance that his irresponsible fancy did not go astray. For the writing of fiction, Adams was handicapped by a very stylized eighteenth-century notion of the creative process.

Much more could be said about Adams' two experiments in fiction as compared to James' many achievements. Yet the essential thing to realize is that the novel for Adams was a possibility which nevertheless hampered him. James, on the other hand, intentionally restricted his practice in certain ways in order to work out the novel's ever richer and richer possibilities. The slightest and most impromptu hint, so nurtured (and the genesis of *The Spoils of Poynton* is an excellent example), could become the origin of an entirely new and still believable world. His heroines, such as Fleda Vetch, are not stand-ins or masked substitutes for himself but variously equipped extensions of himself. Each can perform a deeper examination of her consciousness because her emotional capacity exists independently and completely, in fact has been given such existence for the creator's own increased sense of life. Madeleine Lee and Esther, however, are held back by never being able to be more than compounds of the people who contributed to them and never possessing the full dimensions of any of the originals. Clarence King made the acute observation about Esther that suicide would have been the only way out of the impasse the novel had trapped her in.[40] Mrs. Lee's departure for the Great Pyramid is a similar

[40] *Henry Adams, The Middle Years*, p. 256.

eviction from life. But the traps were already set when the characters were made up, since they had been denied the further resources of their models. This is surely one of the factors which gave *Esther* such a haunting quality to Adams after Marian actually had committed suicide. Adams himself always found ways of avoiding such ultimate measures. But having put Marian into Esther alongside himself, it may have looked as if he had forced his wife to the same recourse he had driven the heroine to, then illogically backed her away from.

The contrasts of James' and Adams' fiction is nicely epitomized in Adams' reaction to *The Sacred Fount*, which that close friend and devoted reader of James (though he is little appreciated for it) John Hay had urged upon him in 1901. "I recognized at once," Adams wrote, "that Harry and I had the same disease, the obsession of *idée fixe*. Harry illustrates it by the trivial figure of an English country-house party, which could only drive one mad by boring one into it, but if he had chosen another back-ground, his treatment of it would have been wonderfully keen."[41] "Harry's" concentration on specific illuminating backgrounds, his dedication to consciousness, his envelopment in particularities which are then made wonderfully inclusive—this might well have struck Adams as "obsession of *idée fixe*." But his own obsessions were tellingly different. They lay in selected verifiable facts. They were the confrontations of momentous historical processes and masses. They tended to place individuals in terms of long traditions and to see them as configurations of ideas. And the obsessions clung tenaciously to the real world, at least, as Adams apprehended that puzzle.

IV

James' and Adams' early association as Bostonians and then as ex-Bostonians and Europeanized Americans, pilgrims of cul-

[41] *Letters (1892-1918)*, p. 333n.

ture, bore a bounteous second harvest in the autobiographies and in the pleasant and advantageous contacts of their later years. By then they were both legends, James the Master of Lamb House and Adams the widely travelled resident of 1603 H Street, the fine house on Lafayette Square designed for him by H. H. Richardson. But the fame did not reflect wide public popularity, and one of the further experiences they were to have in common was that of having not received the big successes both deserved and both, to various degrees and in various ways, wanted. Adams' *History of the United States of America During the Administrations of Thomas Jefferson and James Madison*, published between 1889 and 1891, was slow in winning proper esteem from contemporary historians and even slower in winning popular recognition. With his flare for eloquent statistics, he estimated that the work had cost him $80,000 (the figure in the *Education* is $100,000): "twelve years of unbroken labor at (say) $5000 a year, and $20,000 in money spent in traveling, collecting materials, copying, printing, &c."[42] Scribner's wrote him in 1913 that his royalties from 1903 to December 4, 1913, amounted to $1458.27.[43] James' losses can not be so vividly stated in dollars and cents, but it is safe to say that his regret over the lack of attention given his later novels and his humiliation from the theatrical fiasco was even greater.

Adams' solace in this and in graver disappointments was in travel, in new studies and experiments, and in the comfort of his intimate friends. James' solace was in friends, in some travel, and in further work. In both cases the reactions were creative. Part of what makes Henry Adams such a fascinating and baffling figure is the mere fact that he was so contradictory. Much of his writing shows him as melancholy,

[42] "The Making of a History: Letters of Henry Adams to Henry Vignaud and Charles Scribner, 1879-1913," ed. C. Waller Barrett, *Proceedings of the Massachusetts Historical Society* (1953-57), LXXI, pp. 218-220. For the higher figure see *Education*, p. 327.

[43] Barrett, p. 267.

irascible, and pessimistic, yet evidence also exists that he was quick, gentle, and never without new hopes and energies. On the matter of his wife's death he surrounded himself with different defences. "One of these," according to his brother Brooks, who was a man to know the most gloomy side of him, "was that, when his wife died, in 1884 [sic], he insisted that he also died to the world."[44] James was able to see the other side of him as well. Recognizing the amount Adams had continued to grow and ripen and the scores of compensations he had made, James said years afterwards to Margaret Chanler, "We never knew how delightful Henry was till he lost her."[45] Justice Oliver Wendell Holmes offered another viewpoint:

> I knew Adams quite well. He had two sides. He had distinction, great ability, and great kindness. When I happened to fall in with him on the street he could be delightful, but when I called at his house and he was posing to himself as the old cardinal he would turn everything to dust and ashes. After a tiresome day's work one didn't care to have one's powers of resistance taxed by discourse of that sort, so I called rarely.[46]

An amusing sidelight on these contradictions was John Hay's sobriquet for him, "Porcupinus Angelicus." Hay even had Augustus Saint-Gaudens strike a medal of Adams to illustrate the two natures.[47]

Adams was a short slender man; James was of medium height and, as time went on, broad and heavy. His careful precision in speech and his excessive refinement in dress became trademarks. "He was always well-dressed; perhaps even

[44] Brooks Adams, "The Heritage of Henry Adams," *The Degradation of Democratic Dogma* (New York, 1919), p. 2.

[45] Mrs. Winthrop Chanler, *Roman Spring* (Boston, 1934), p. 303.

[46] *Henry Adams and His Friends*, ed. Harold Dean Cater (Boston, 1947), p. lxx; quoted from *Holmes-Pollock Letters*, ed. Mark A. DeWolfe Howe (Cambridge, Mass., 1941), II, p. 18.

[47] Cater, p. 554n.

a little more than that, for he gave the impression—with his rather conspicuous spats and extra shiny boots—of having just come from an ultra-smart wedding ceremony."[48] The appearance of solid respectability housed deeper solidities which the world has been slower to recognize. In the summer of 1891, as he was summoning energies for yet further experiments and new departures, James wrote into his *Notebooks*,

> The upshot of all such reflections is that I have only to let myself *go*! So I have said to myself all my life—so I said to myself in the far-off days of my fermenting and passionate youth. Yet I have never fully done it. . . . All life is—at my age, with all one's artistic soul the record of it—in one's pocket, as it were. Go on, my boy, and strike hard; have a rich and long St. Martin's Summer. Try everything, do everything—be an artist, be distinguished, to the last.

Adams visited James in London in October 1891, as he was returning from nearly a year and a half in the South Pacific with John La Farge, James' mentor of thirty years before in Newport. They talked of Robert Louis Stevenson, whom Adams and La Farge had seen in Samoa, and of Adams' plans for further adventures. "He talks of Central Asia," James told Stevenson, "but can't find anyone to go with him —least of all, alas, me."[49] In January 1892 they were having Sunday lunches together, Adams posing as world-weary and writing that James "is only a figure in the same old wall-paper, and really pretends to belong to a world which is extinct as Queen Elizabeth."[50] James never appears to have been distracted by this side of Adams. Between them they had too much else to talk about, and James was absorbed by Adams' alert mind, his rich memory, and his dazzling per-

---

[48] *The Legend of the Master*, ed. Simon Nowell-Smith (London, 1947), p. 3.
[49] *Selected Letters*, pp. 174-175.
[50] *Letters (1892-1918)*, p 3.

ceptions. "Henry Adams spoke to me the other day of the end of certain histories of which, years ago, in London he had seen the beginning—" and so he recorded a *donnée* Adams had given him to which he was to return for several years.[51]

In December 1897 Adams tried to interest him in a tour of Egypt, but again James declined. Adams' income, Ernest Samuels has estimated, was in the vicinity of $50,000 a year. James, on the other hand, lived modestly and lived within the profits from his writing. As well as being temperamentally unsuited to Adams' globetrotting, he was unable to afford it, either in time or in money.

They were on more common ground in 1903 at the time of the publication of James' *William Wetmore Story and His Friends*. They had both known Story more than thirty-five years before. James, Adams, and Clover had been to his house in Rome in the spring of 1873, and their reactions then were strikingly similar. "So you're acquainted with Story's Muse—that brazen hussy—to put it plainly," James wrote Charles Eliot Norton. "I have rarely seen such a case of *prosperous* pretension as Story. His cleverness is great, the world's good nature to him is greater."[52] Clover's letter to her father was equally frank: "We went to Mr. Story's studio, and oh! how he does spoil nice blocks of white marble. Nothing but Sibyls on all sides, sitting, standing, legs crossed, legs uncrossed, and all with the same expression as if they smelt something wrong. Call him a genius! I don't see it."[53]

Adams had been to a reception at Mrs. Story's in 1865; he was more impressed by one of the other guests, "a pretty blonde in blue," than by his hosts.[54] He was no more taken in by the great hope of the time than James or Clover. His letter to James of November 18, 1903, stays faithful to the old reaction and also shows him in the mood of the author of

[51] *Notebooks*, pp. 113, 119, 135-136, 297.
[52] *Selected Letters*, pp. 72-73.
[53] *Letters of Mrs. Adams*, pp. 94-95.
[54] *Letters (1858-1891)*, p. 117.

the *Education.* I quote it in full, for these reasons, and also for its many other values.

Although you, like most men of toil, hate to be bored, I can hardly pass over your last work without boring you to the extent of a letter. We have reached a time of solar antiquity when nothing matters, but still we feel what used to be called the law of gravitation, mass, or attraction, and obey it.

More than ever, after devouring your William Story, I feel how difficult a job was imposed on you. It is a *tour de force*, of course, but that you knew from the first. Whether you have succeeded or not, I cannot say, because it all spreads itself out as though I had written it, and I feel where you are walking on firm ground, and where you are on thin ice, as though I were in your place. Verily I believe I wrote it. Except your speciality of style, it is me.

The painful truth is that all of my New England generation, counting the half-century, 1820-1870, were in actual fact only one mind and nature; the individual was a facet of Boston. We knew each other to the last nervous center, and feared each other's knowledge. We looked through each other like microscopes. There was absolutely nothing in us that we did not understand merely by looking in the eye. There was hardly a difference even in depth, for Harvard College and Unitarianism kept us all shallow. We knew nothing—no! but really nothing! of the world. One cannot exaggerate the profundity of ignorance of Story in becoming a sculptor, or Sumner in becoming a statesman, or Emerson in becoming a philosopher. Story and Sumner, Emerson and Alcott, Lowell and Longfellow, Hillard, Winthrop, Motley, Prescott, and all the rest, were the same mind, —and so, poor worm!—was I!

Type bourgeois-bostonien! A type quite as good as another, but more uniform. What you say of Story is at bottom exactly what you would say of Lowell, Motley, and Sumner, barring degrees of egotism. You cannot help smiling at them, but you smile at us all equally. God knows that we knew our want of knowledge! the self-distrust became introspection—nervous self-consciousness—irritable dislike of America, and antipathy to Boston. *Auch ich war in Arcadien geboren!*

So you have written not Story's life, but your own and mine,—pure autobiography,—the more keen for what is beneath, implied, intelligible only to me, and half a dozen other people still living; like Frank Boott: who knew our Boston, London and Rome in the fifties and sixties. You make me curl up, like a trodden-on worm. Improvised Europeans, we were, and—Lord God!— how thin! No, but it is too cruel! Long ago,—at least thirty years ago,—I discovered it, and have painfully held my tongue about it. You strip us, gently and kindly, like a surgeon, and I feel your knife in my ribs.

No one else will ever know it. You have been extremely tactful. The essential superficiality of Story and all the rest, you have made painfully clear to us, but not, I think, to the family or the public. After all the greatest men are weak. Morley's Gladstone is hardly thicker than your Story. Let us pray!

Adams' admiration of himself in James, his identification with both the killed and the killer, is remarkable. At this point he should have been conclusively aware of the enormous separation between his historical imagination and James' esthetic one. "Except your speciality of style, it is me." But what greater "speciality" could there be? What Adams did recognize and what continued to unite the two of them was that James had examined Story by examining Story's consciousness. This

Adams knew was what had to be told. This, after all, was what he was at almost that minute doing as the author of the *Education*.

Because of the care and intelligence of James' examination, it is, in truth, difficult not to identify oneself with both James and Story. The book is unlike most biographies in being more the tale of the writer than the subject, the real and more interesting "subject" being James' reflections rather than the deeds of Mr. Story. Never did he give so much to so little. His reply to Adams is evidence of this and evidence of a tactful effort to keep Adams in the company of the imaginative. If one can imagine, then one can know, and if one knows, then he need not feel exposed or trodden on. With his imagination James could make himself at home in Story's world and still preserve his separate identity. The biography of Story had briefly returned Adams to the past without leaving him the sense of the present and future which had become his faith and defence. James had so vividly recaptured the past that it buried the present.

Lamb House, Rye
November 19, 1903

My dear Adams,

I am so happy at hearing from you *at all* that the sense of the particular occasion of my doing so is almost submerged and smothered. You did bravely well to write—make a note of the act, for your future career, as belonging to a class of impulses to be precipitately obeyed, and, if possible, even tenderly nursed. Yet it has been interesting, exceedingly, in the narrower sense, as well as delightful in the larger, to have your letter, with its ingenious expression of the effects on you of poor *W.W.S.*—with whom, and the whole business of whom, there is (yes, I can see!) a kind of *inevitableness* in my having made you squirm—or whatever is the proper name for the sensation engendered in you! Very curious, and even rather terrible, this so far-reaching action of a little biographical vividness—which did indeed, in a manner, begin with me, myself, even as I put the stuff together—though putting me to conclusions less grim, as I may call them, than in your case. The truth is that *any* retraced story of bourgeois lives (lives other than great lives of "action"—*et encore!*) throws a chill upon the scene, the time, the subject, the small mapped-out facts, and if you find "great men thin" it isn't really so much their fault (and least of all yours) as that the art of the biographer—devilish art!—is somehow practically *thinning*. It simplifies even while seeking to enrich—and even the Immortal are so helpless and passive in death. The proof is that I wanted to invest dull old Boston with a mellow, a golden glow—and that for those who know, like yourself, I only make it bleak—and weak! Luckily those who know are indeed but three or four—and they won't, I hope, too promiscuously tell. . . .

Yours, my dear Adams, always and ever,

Henry James

James agreed to the biography of Story shortly after the sculptor's death in 1895. He "succumbed," he said, "to the amiable pressure" of Story's children, who supplied him with the letters and other materials so lavishly distributed across its two volumes of 371 and 338 pages. The contract with the publisher was settled in 1897, but it was not written until after the writing of the three late novels.[55] Thus, though hack work of a sort, it belongs to the "major phase," and its art, as well as having had such a pronounced effect on Adams at a time when he was conceiving the *Education*, also influenced

[55] *Selected Letters*, pp. 224, 129n.

Adams' *The Life of George Cabot Lodge* and anticipated James' own autobiographies, especially *Notes of a Son and Brother*.

The book is suffused with James' consciousness. The later James overcame the cynicism and somewhat nasty revulsion of the young traveler of 1873 by seeing William Wetmore Story as one of the "light skirmishers" in the American advance on Europe. The metaphors of the opening pages are brilliant, each enforcing the others and none as good as all of them. Images of discovery, of conflict, of pioneering, of cultivation, and of pilgrimage are in ordered abundance. The moral, if moral there must be, is that Europe is now easier for Americans because it has been *"made* easy." The relationship between James and Story is thus clear from the beginning as a condescending one, but mutually condescending. Old debts are paid off. If the Master stoops to discussing the "drollery" and awkwardness of Story's "touching experiment," one suspects that the earlier generation had once been patronizing to the younger. Over and above this, however, is the fact that the follower may still owe the predecessor some obeisance, that James sees Story as an important chapter in the destiny his own life has brought to larger fulfillment. Story had a faith, a simple one, yet its strength in part depended upon its simplicity. And if Europe rewarded him richly, he also *"paid,"* paid for his faith, and paid for his lack of faith in the United States. The ultimate cost was in the nature of the achievement: if Story was not an artist, he was an explorer.

Part of the fate of being an explorer, James implies, was being superficial. Story's natural talents were several, and like many such men, "Story, while at college, was inclined to let himself go in almost any direction but that of effort."[56]

---

[56] Henry James, *William Wetmore Story and His Friends* (New York, 1959), I, p. 42. This edition is photo-offset from the 1903 edition, and pagination is the same. All other references will be given in parentheses.

In the United States, on returning in 1855, "he found himself again steeped in a society both fundamentally and superficially *bourgeois*, . . . so that its very virtues irritated him, so that its ability to be strenuous without passion, its cultivation of its serenity, its presentation of a surface on which it would appear to him that the only ruffle was an occasional acuter spasm of the moral sense, must have acted as a tacit reproach" (I, 304). Even though he rejected this society, he was unable to exorcise its influence within him. His provincial idolatry of Robert Browning resulted in Browning's benevolent employment of him as a trusty finder and securer of lodgings, a species of hound. The "generality" of his abilities distracted him from perfecting any single one: he wrote poems and propaganda, sketched and painted, "esthetically speaking, a wonderful all-round sociability" (II, 84). "One might have been inclined to wish him the comparative rest of an exclusive passion" (II, 215-216).

All of these criticisms have a bearing on James' portrait of the New York society of his boyhood and on his response to his father's well-intentioned concern that any commitment to one profession or any specialization, was somehow too "narrowing." At the same time, we can appreciate all the other pitfalls which father Henry James saved his children. "To live over people's lives is nothing unless we live over their perceptions, live over the growth, the change, the varying intensity of the same—since it was *by* these things they themselves lived" (I, 125). This is not the least of the humanities taught by the author of "Immortal Life," and as it is the charm that carried James through *Story*, so had it worked in his fiction and so would it work in his autobiography. Adams arrived at it through self-consciousness, James through an inner life in which consciousness was constantly objectified.

In *William Wetmore Story and His Friends* James uses every device available to try to discover Story's perceptions and to wring value from them. Thus is the man made present. He is a "ghost," but he is there, living in the "golden air" of a "vanished society," and the book is a re-creation, not a dirge. The primary device is the old letters which quicken the pulse of recollection and pass on the beat to the encompassing narrative. James' own perceptions, in turn, frame and dress up Story's letters, and James is writing "pure autobiography" to the extent that in the perceptions he does describe himself. At other times James is imparting observations to Story which he may not have had, skating over thin ice, as Adams said. That James the young pilgrim at some places appears in the history—e.g., in Newport and Rome—is really not to the point. His insights, his revival of the past are everywhere.

Consequently James took Adams' word "thin," which had been applied to the old Boston culture, and, as "*thinning*," gallantly and very acutely turned it onto the art of the biographer. Not that James felt he had failed; he could be sure of the richness of his "little biographical vividness." (An amusing illustration of the book's vividness is a letter of James' to the Duchess of Sutherland. Her reaction had apparently been of an altogether different kind, and he found it necessary to confess his "chronicling small beer with the effect of opening champagne. Story was the dearest of men," he went on, "but he wasn't massive, his artistic and literary baggage were of the slightest and the materials for a biography *nil*." He urged her to keep reading *The Ambassadors!*)[57] James' success as a biographer was exactly what made Adams "squirm." The more the past came to life, the less clearly Adams could see himself as one who had overcome it, the more exposed he felt, and the more James seemed to be turning the knife.

Vividness is what is missing in Adams' *The Life of George Cabot Lodge*. The situations of its composition were quite

[57] *Selected Letters*, pp. 224-225.

similar to the ones behind James' life of Story, and a short comparison is interesting. After Lodge's death in 1909, at age 35, his family asked Adams to write his biography and supplied him with the young poet's letters. The book was published in 1911. The difference in subjects between a poet born in 1873 and a sculptor born in 1819 must be recognized, but the difference this actually made is relatively small. Each, as J. C. Levenson has noted, was "an essay on the social conditions of art."[58] Adams' treatment of these conditions was the reverse of James'. Story failed because he was unable to overcome them; Lodge failed because they overcame him. This would seem to place all the blame with the men and their environments, but their influence in the matter is as nothing to the influence of the biographers who finally prepared such analyses. "A poet, born in Boston, in 1873, saw about him a society which commonly bred refined tastes, and often did refined work, but seldom betrayed strong emotions" (Ch. 1).[59] Adams made no effort, such as James made, to show how the artist might have acknowledged the waste land and scouted for the assumptions on which the conventions were based. "The Bostonian of 1900 differed from his parents and grandparents of 1850, in owning nothing the value of which, in the market, could be affected by the poet" (Ch. 1). This is Adams' conclusion, not Lodge's. "A winter in Berlin is, under the best of circumstances, a grave strain on the least pessimistic temper, but to a young poet of twenty-two . . . Berlin required a conscientious sense of duty amounting to self-sacrifice, in order to make it endurable" (Ch. 3). Again, this is Berlin as Adams remembered it from 1858. Wrapped in this shroud of epigrams and determinism, "a simple vigorous nature like Lodge's" did not

[58] *Mind and Art of Henry Adams* (Boston, 1957), p. 383.
[59] Henry Adams, *The Life of George Cabot Lodge*, in *The Shock of Recognition*, ed. Edmund Wilson (New York, 1943, 1955).

stand a chance. The atmosphere may have been bleak; Adams' presentation of it was bleaker.

Today the usual reasons for reading this document are for background to *Prufrock* or for evidence of Adams' pessimism. I offer it as an image of Adams' sense of himself and, indirectly, as a sign of Adams' failure of imagination, at least by 1910. The curiosity of this *Life*, Edmund Wilson has suggested, is that the author meets in his subject "all the old round of the life-cycle of people from Boston, of people like oneself; and he cannot repress a shiver." Adams, like James in *Story*, is trying to write the record of a class, a small one, but a class of "Improvised Europeans" who represented the cultural aspirations of Boston. But unlike James, he can not separate himself from it. Lodge's Boston, Paris, or Berlin is no different from Adams'. The important thing to do is to breathe meaning into these places, and for once Adams fails to do so. In making the scenes so bleak he robs them of the individuality which would have spelled separate individualities for the author and his subject. In handling Browning, for example, James creates three people: the offhand and worldly poet, the provincial sculptor who is being used, and the amused biographer. When Adams introduces a letter in which Lodge describes a meeting with (coincidentally) Henry James, in Washington in 1905, no effort is made to give the experience the great significance it quite obviously had. Lodge marveled: "in matters of art [James is] incorruptibly honest, and in consequence hugely expensive" (Ch. 7). Adams' laconic preface to the letter takes no advantage of such a perception; the meeting is tossed off as only inevitable: "Naturally, too, in the social and literary sequence, young Lodge fell under the charm of Henry James." In the *Education* he was never so matter of fact about his own new acquaintances, say with Swinburne or Kipling.

James' own epitaph on Lodge further illustrates what Adams failed to do. "I recall him as so intelligent and open and delightful,—a great and abundant social luxury." Thus did Adams quote James, with great approval, in a letter to Elizabeth Cameron. Adams was a good maker of phrases, but his effort was always to generalize and universalize rather than to particularize. His imagination was syllogistic and dialectic; he had no sooner repeated James' comment, in fact, than he began to test its wider applications. "Bay was indeed a social luxury *s'il en fut,* but, for that matter, so is Harry James too, and so are we all,—only not great or abundant."[60] Like many of Adams' remarks, this sentence could start a whole conversation or debate. In the *Lodge* Adams blew up the general without fixing the boundaries that held the parts in place. He did not set up his usual network of opposites (eighteenth century and twentieth century, Boston and Quincy, New England and Washington, morality and ambition, etc.), but surrendered to a single category. The security of James' image of himself depended upon the power of the inexhaustible coffers of his consciousness to bestow particularity. He needed no formal dogmas or dualisms; on the contrary, he persistently destroyed them. Adams' sense of himself lay at the junction of a hundred crossed wires, each one connecting an ingeniously defined pair of opposites. In the biography of Lodge he for once failed to stretch them out, and he and his subject both collapsed into the dull lap of Boston.

V

"We all began together, and our lives have made more or less of a unity . . . about the only unity that American society in our time had to show." This observation, which was Adams' conclusion after the death of William James, might also be taken as a kind of epitaph to the lives of both Henrys and to the brilliant group to which they had belonged. As Adams read the roll—"Richardson and St.

[60] *Letters (1892-1918),* p. 522 and fn.

Gaudens, La Farge, Alex Agassiz, Clarence King, John Hay"
—he mentioned only the dead. Other men like Howells,
Brooks Adams, Charles Peirce, and Holmes were also partners, and together they composed "about the only unity" of
American artists and intellectuals of that generation. It was
a group (perhaps we should say a *school*) whose work, as
Adams says in the *Education*, began in the 1870's and who
faced the responsibility of giving order and expression to a
rapidly expanding and industrialized nation of from sixty to
eighty million people. How uncertainly the school succeeded
could be stated any number of ways. We might note, for
example, the number of members who are now less regarded
and whose fame has been surpassed by men and women
who worked alone—Ryder, Eakins, Mark Twain, Emily
Dickinson, Henry George. Still, this was and remains an
imposing group, and James and Adams were two of its
greatest luminaries. As Adams was also one of the principal
agents in bringing and holding it together (a consequence
of his own needs), so did he become its principal historian
and tragedian.

The needs of the school were large and various, but the
most inclusive way of stating them was as forms. This, after
all, is the heart of their discussion about European and
American culture, about tradition and innovation, about
science and religion, or about private wealth and the public
order. No matter what the individual member's special line of
investigation, and together they covered all the major
ones, this search for viable new American forms remained
a common search. Furthermore, James and Adams were
among the members who pursued the need for new forms
most intently.

As was shown in the first chapter of this essay, autobiography
is not only one of the human enterprises or esthetic genres in
which the need for form is felt but, more particularly, a genre
which holds out peculiar opportunities for giving form to

[87]

other enterprises as well—to life, private and general. But such autobiography can be written only by people endowed with the necessary kind of consciousness of themselves and with the ability to universalize their lives in such a way that the form has more than limited interest and application. In this chapter, therefore, the effort has been made to study James and Adams not only as friends but also as contrasting explorers of consciousness. This, one might say, was their joint distinction within their school, for as self-explorers they even excelled the psychologist himself, William James. The two of them "were concerned with experience as education," as R. P. Blackmur has so nicely put it,[61] and to neither was the experience or education complete until it had been put to concentrated analysis and to their own marked expression of it. In each case, moreover, the manners of analysis and the styles of expression were so different that while the lives made "more or less of a unity," the "Lives" or the treatments of the lives make excellent contrasts in autobiography. In fact a better pair of harmonious opposites can be found nowhere else in American literature.

A good deal more could surely be said about the men's friendship, especially during the later years of their lives, since that was the period in which the autobiographies were written and also the period when their letters and their occasional meetings seem to have been most deeply affecting. Still, not all this biographical material is pertinent to this "autobiographical" study, and that which is will be found in the concluding chapter. It does seem fitting, however, to end this introduction to the creators of the *Education* and *A Small Boy and Others* and *Notes of a Son and Brother* by glancing at the men's reactions to each other's books. The letter James must have written Adams on reading the *Education* and *Mont-Saint-Michel* has been lost or

[61] "Henry Adams: Three Late Moments," *Kenyon Review* (Winter, 1940), II, p. 16.

destroyed, and a similar fate seems to have met Adams'
letters to James after reading his books. What we have is a
letter from Adams to Elizabeth Cameron after reading *Notes
of a Son and Brother*:

> I've read Henry James' last bundle of memories which
> have reduced me to a pulp. Why did we live? Was that
> all? Why was I not born in Central Africa and died
> young. Poor Henry James thinks it all real, I believe,
> and actually still lives in that dreamy, stuffy Newport
> and Cambridge, with papa James and Charles Norton—
> and me! Yet why!
>
> It is a terrible dream, but not so weird as this here
> which is quite loony.[62]

James had, he felt, exhumed the unity of their past, but he
had not expressed the unity of their dream or revitalized it
to retain unity for their present and future. Adams did not
understand James' purpose, and it may be doubted whether
James' famous defence of his book helped him. In autobiography the two men had such different ideas of form that
there appears to be no reconciling them.

[62] *Letters (1892-1918)*, p. 622.

CHAPTER THREE

The Education of Young Men

※€ ※€ ※€

Shall I at least set my lands in order?

The Waste Land

IN the "Editor's Preface" to the *Education*, which Adams wrote for Henry Cabot Lodge's initials,[1] Adams admitted to having said frequently, "half in jest, that his great ambition was to complete St. Augustine's *Confessions*." The difference is, he goes on, "that St. Augustine, like a great artist, had worked from multiplicity to unity, while he, like a small one, had to reverse the method and work back from unity to multiplicity." This is only one of the many references and comparisons to Augustine which crop up in the *Education* and dot Adams' correspondence. St. Augustine, to Adams, was a person of power. The power of a devout Christian, naturally, which he drew from God; but the power, also, of a man with an organizing idea. Of all autobiographers, Adams told William James, Augustine was alone in having literary form. Augustine wrote "a story with an end and object, not for the sake of the object, but for the form, like a romance." And it might be added that the power Augustine brought over his own life in the *Confessions* could also be applied to society at large in *De Civitate Dei*.

Adams knew the power of order. This, I think, is a fundamental thing to remember about "Porcupinus Angelicus"—and Hay's clever nickname describes the peculiarly saintly and prickly elements in the paradox of his nature. But whether we take him as the ultimate pessimist, the way the intellectu-

---

[1] *Henry Adams and His Friends*, ed. Harold Dean Cater (Boston, 1947), pp. xc, 769-770.

als of the 1920's and 1930's did, or whether we take him as the paragon of sympathy, kindliness, and hope that he was for his intimates and closest correspondents, he is still a student of power. This also applies to both the Henry Adams of 1874-76 who tried to engineer a reform movement in American politics and the Henry Adams of later years who lived "as a stable-companion to statesmen" while pursuing his private quest of Nirvana. The *Education* bursts with power, the power of bombs, of coal, of the Virgin, of wealth, and of statesmen, Presidents, and the Senate, but the greatest power is the one all the others are powerless without, order.

How could he bring order to his own life? Adams' *History of the United States* begins with six chapters describing the Nation as it was in 1800, a line of states strung out along the Atlantic seaboard, with little communication between each other and only wagon-roads and trails into the interior. The *History* ends with several chapters in Volume IX descriptive of the Country in 1815 and its prospects for the coming century. The lines of wealth, religion, and character were more clearly defined, and the American who saw these lines could read the history of the United States for the next one hundred years. Such a reading was difficult; it took vision, but a man who had a notion of what had been and what was to come had an idea with which to give his efforts order and therefore power.

The function of a student is to seek order, and the function of a teacher is to seek it and convey it to his students. Adams is both teacher and student. As a boy, as a student, he had been given an idea of what the United States was and what its destiny was. The idea was totally wrong, he said later, and he had not yet learned his responsibility to seek such ideas himself. As the writer of the *Education* he hoped, avuncularly, to spare other young men the same mistakes, but that meant first of all discovering the order of the new century, the twentieth century, in himself. If, like the Augustine of the *Con-*

fessions, he could discover the meaning of his own life, then, like the Augustine of *De Civitate Dei,* he could also give order to the world.

His fancied ambition, however, was not to repeat Augustine, but "to complete" him, to begin where he had left off and where history had ceased to run in his shadow. He had also to think of Rousseau, of "self-teaching," of Franklin, and of the altering influences of which Franklin might be regarded as symbolic. Adams says early in the *Education:* "Of all the conditions of his youth which afterwards puzzled the grownup man, this disappearance of religion puzzled him most."[2] "The Church was gone" (p. 232), he says later. "The stupendous failure of Christianity tortured history" (p. 472). The decline of Christianity (not to mention the remoteness of his own Christian faith) forced upon the autobiographer a new form. What was the new order? The heritage of St. Augustine required some things, but the new time required others. In so far as Adams wanted to write an autobiography that followed a concept of literary form and gave order to public action and private conviction, he was endeavoring to imitate St. Augustine. He also wanted to represent his age. But reapplication of faith in God as the all-embracing theme which should unify experience was impossible. The story of the twentieth century was an education, not a confession.

Education is both power and order. As the theorists of the Renaissance from Castiglione to John Milton divined, it is the cornerstone to the building of a new era. The word is also dear to American hearts in its many possible meanings, and Adams recognizes them all. He makes it refer to basic talents and techniques. It is a facility with French, German, Spanish, and mathematics, the only four tools he really needed, he says, and four he never mastered. A second definition is that knowledge of history, art, and science which the Philistine calls

[2] *The Education of Henry Adams* (Boston and New York, 1918), p. 34. Hereafter references will be given in parentheses.

"culture." His friend Clarence King, Adams said, had all those things, especially science, and Clarence King failed. Thirdly, education means experience—an acquaintance with the ignorance of Congressmen or the self-interest of Boston's State Street. But in all these cases it is useless unless it also means a kind of superior mental and muscular coordination, knowing how "to react with vigor and economy" (p. 314). In the grandest sense, Adams tells us early in the book, education has the common aim of all endeavors.

> From cradle to grave this problem of running order through chaos, direction through space, discipline through freedom, unity through multiplicity, has always been, and must always be, the task of education, as it is the moral of religion, philosophy, science, art, politics, and economy; but a boy's will is his life, and he dies when it is broken, as the colt dies in harness, taking a new nature in becoming tame.   (p. 12)

The Education of Henry Adams, therefore, is the story of the taming of his chaos and the attempt to liberate his energies.

Ideally this should be a coherent process, a story, as St. Augustine's was, with the pieces and digressions all fitting into place eventually, even if they did not seem to at the time. A complete and filled out nineteenth-century education, however, was discontinuous. This is the criticism of his age and this is the challenge confronting the autobiographer. How to tell a story of what was not a story? How to give that "dreamy, stuffy Newport and Cambridge" of youth significance to the present and how to reconnect a life that was broken in two in 1885? It is worth noting that each chapter of the *Education* is a lesson in itself, and that many of them contradict each other: "Quincy" vs. "Boston"; "Political Morality" vs. "The Battle of the Rams"; "The Height of Knowledge" vs. "The Abyss of Ignorance." Chronologically, we can bring some of them together. It is possible to look at Adams' life in four stages: boy, journalist and secretary, teacher of history, and twentieth-century man. One should remember, however, that the divisions are rather arbitrary and that the anarchist in Adams would insist they have nothing to do with one another.

Franklin, that "model . . . of self-teaching," wrote his autobiography in four parts, and the dress of the "hero" of each was chosen to correspond with its author. Adams wrote more continuously, but he poses too. Projecting backwards to what one was at given times years ago means dressing one's self in strange garments. He is not trying to show himself in all the truth of Nature; Rousseau tried that. The terse and necessarily somewhat enigmatic explanation of Adams' "Preface" is that "the Ego has . . . become a manikin on which the toilet of education is to be draped in order to show the fit or misfit of the clothes." The various toilets can be made to represent the various Henry Adamses, the old incomplete and unrelated educations. As "tailor" (we can note the reference to *Sartor Resartus* and beyond Carlyle to Swift's *A Tale of a Tub*), Adams will try to fit his patrons, i.e., "young men, in universities or elsewhere," with the clothes they will need in years to come, but doing this entails showing "the faults of the patchwork fitted on their fathers."

The value of this little device to reading the *Education* is great. Although education is order, the only course of the education of Henry Adams was disorder. Chaos is created by dressing the boy, the journalist, the teacher, and the man in all the old illusions and deceptions he ever wore. Beneath the misfitting toilets—all meant to be instructive to later young men—is the manikin, the effaced Ego, who was inevitably growing into the tailor, the author. Adams the author poses as student of many kinds of power, but the power he never gave up was the power of the man of letters to create order. Bringing it out of the wild and furious power of the twentieth century was the aim and the integrity of Henry Adams.

[94]

I

To the author of the *Education*, the faraway education of the eighteenth-century boy seemed terribly remote. It is no exaggeration to say that no preceding sixty-year period in history had included as much change as the change in the United States between 1840 and 1900. Born February 16, 1838, Adams' way of underscoring such a revolution was to treat his boyhood as "eighteenth-century." He might as well have been born in 1738, a hundred years earlier. It is indicative of their difference that James characterized the remoteness of his youth by calling it "queer" and by recording the effort of memory required to summon back the ancient days. James thought in terms of the distance his mind had traveled; Adams, with equal force, stressed the distance society had traveled. 1838 was "colonial," "troglodytic," and Adams carefully dwells upon all that was so seemingly permanent and eternal about his grandfather and grandmother. John Quincy Adams' house was finished with Queen Anne mahogany panels, furnished with Louis Seize chairs and sofas and Sevres china. "The President," as he was always called, is imagined absorbed in his Quincy library, surrounded by his classics and by experiments in natural history preserved under "the Madam's" tumblers and cut-glass bowls. She, in turn, is remembered at breakfast in her bedroom, "with her heavy silver teapot and sugar-bowl and cream-jug."

Driven in among these roots are pointed signs toward the century that lay ahead. The boy did not know it, but "he and his eighteenth-century, troglodytic Boston were suddenly cut apart—separated forever—in act if not in sentiment, by the opening of the Boston and Albany Railroad; the appearance of the first Cunard steamers in the bay; and the telegraphic messages which carried from Baltimore to Washington the news that Henry Clay and James K. Polk were nominated for the Presidency" (p. 5). The dizzying road ahead led down State Street, through banks, stock-lists, railways, tele-graphs, coal, and steel. While Boston looked backwards to the Revolution and the War of 1812, Adams the author cleverly anticipates "Secession and Civil War."

All promises of change, however, are introduced not as things the boy saw but as things he overlooked. This is an advantage of writing in the third person. Had "I" not been impressed by the opening of the railroads, "I" would have been incredibly peculiar as a child or consciously sentimental as an author. It is tricky to speculate about what a book might have been, but it is safe to say that Adams' presentation of his past as a series of discarded garments rather than as the coherent growth of an individual is definitely aided by the separation of "Adams" the author and "Adams" the early forms of the author. In the first person, the following sentence is more sentimental than Rousseau. "This was in May, 1844; I was six years old; my new world was ready for use, and only the fragments of the old met my eyes" (p. 5). Later in the first chapter, Adams tells the story of an Irish gardener who said to him: "You'll be thinkin' you'll be President too!" Said, "to the child," the remark is amusing and reflects the differ-ence between the child's eighteenth-century outlook and the humorous perspective of the twentieth-century author. Again, to write "I could not remember ever to have thought on the subject; to me, that there should be doubt of my being Presi-dent was a new idea"—to say that would have confessed an ingrained and unreformed egotism. Whether the egotism was in fact still there is another question. The third-person auto-biography was a way of standing off from it, like Gertrude Stein's assignment of her autobiography to Alice B. Toklas. In *A Small Boy and Others* James frequently posed himself as "him," the Small Boy.

This objectivity in point of view assists the author in setting up his antitheses between past and future. The first chapter anchors the eighteenth-century boy in Quincy, and certain lessons, like the old grandfather's impassive and authoritative hand leading him to school, never broke loose. Other lessons were illusory. Quincy, *old* Quincy, *rural* Quincy, was also a town where residents sat every Sunday in the parish church, giving the best pews to gray-headed leading citizens, just as men had sat "since the time of St. Augustine, if not since the glacial epoch" (p. 15). This seemed right, and in such a steady and moral society "the boy" already thought he had the answers to complex questions others would have given more thought to. It takes the author to break in and restore the questions' full import.

Since the boy would not heed the prophetic signs, even the education in "Boston" (Ch. II) did not prepare him for later needs. He participated in the city's self-assured political and intellectual life, not its commercial one. He was novice to the little band of "statesmen" who were his father's friends. This group, Dr. John G. Palfrey, Richard Henry Dana, Charles Sumner, and Charles Francis Adams, regarded office as a sacred trust; "they guided public opinion, but were little guided by it" (p. 32). Seated at a table in his father's library, Henry worked on his Latin grammar, read proof on his father's edition of John Adams' *Works*, and listened to discussions of politics. "England's middle-class government was the ideal of human progress," the author observes ("improvised Europeans, we were"), and his father's associates strove to imitate it in America. Henry accepted their beliefs and assumed that what had been would always be.

> Politics offered no difficulties, for there the moral law was a sure guide. Social perfection was also sure, because human nature worked for Good, and three instruments were all she asked—Suffrage, Common Schools, and Press. (p. 33)

Adams is too ironic to let such complacency stand unmolested, and he leaves various barbed needles in the cloth. The chapter ends with an idyllic image of summers back at Quincy, the boy lying on "a musty heap of Congressional Documents . . . reading *Quentin Durward, Ivanhoe,* and *The Talisman.*" From this perch, he casually (cf. Augustine) "raid[ed] the garden at intervals for peaches and pears. On the whole he learned most then" (p. 39).

In the chapter "Washington" the author recounts an experience which might have overthrown the New England dogma. When his father took him by railroad to New York and then by boat and train on down to the Capital, he had not been impressed until they entered Maryland. There, for the first time in his life, he was in a slave state. Here was something for the Puritan mind to hate. The landscape was ragged; pigs, cows, and Negro babies ran loose in the village streets. "Slave States were dirty, unkempt, poverty-stricken, ignorant, vicious!" And yet, the author interjects, there was something in this ease and indolence which unconsciously appealed to that small portion of Southerner in him; it "soothed his Johnson blood" (p. 45). (Louisa Johnson Adams, the grandmother whose autobiographies he began to edit in 1868, was the daughter of a Maryland merchant and his English bride.) At the terminus of the trip was an even stronger contradiction, this one squarely recognized. He and his father jolted over more bad roads—"bad roads meant bad morals"—to Mount Vernon, and there was the moral order of George Washington. By pondering on this dilemma, he might have reached early wisdom. But he did not; he "had only to repeat what he was told—that George Washington stood alone" (p. 47). The chapter begins with a story of snowball fights on the Boston Common and ends with a story of Charles Sumner's fight for a seat in the Senate, in which the boy readily accepted the Free Soil party's bargain with the pro-slavery Democrats. The sign of the practical man, Adams emphasizes, is the faculty for ignoring contradictions.

Writing the *Education* demanded a large, detached perspective. It is illuminating that in the chapter on "Harvard College" Adams says that the usual graduate showed "moderation, balance, judgment, restraint, what the French call *mesure* . . . but such a type of character rarely lent itself to autobiography" (p. 55). In another place he speaks of Harvard introspection, the "nervous self-consciousness" of the letter to James on Story. Adams transcended both because he had removed himself from the tight Cambridge orbit and because he finally made the autobiography not a study of himself but of himself and his society. When he returns, as autobiographer, to re-examine his Harvard years, he coldly sets up Harvard and the old Harvard undergraduate, Henry Adams, as reflections of each other. His remarks are those of the man who is ultimately the best student, one who has gone on to learn enough after graduation to realize how little he learned before it. "Any other education would have required a serious effort, but no one took Harvard College seriously" (p. 54). He archly dismisses the College's social prestige by saying what he needed was "some one to show him how to use the acquaintance he cared to make" (p. 64). His prize as Class Orator was a political rather than a literary victory. His classmates chose him because he was "the kind of representative they wanted," and thus they were "the most formidable array of judges he could ever meet, like so many mirrors of himself, an infinite reflection of his own shortcomings" (p. 68).

Europe, "his third or fourth attempt at education," was another misspent opportunity. In some senses of the word, listening to Beethoven in Berlin or comprehending the horrors of German State Schools was indeed "education," but the elder Adams' complaint with his youthful self is that the boy was "passive." He left the external world to act upon him instead of reacting to it. Had he been alert, the initial train journey from Liverpool to London through the Midlands Black District might have evoked a response. Eleven years

later at age twenty-five James was to miss the full impact of
the same landscape because of murky weather part of the way
and because he feigned sleep to avoid a garrulous Englishman.[3] The twenty-year-old Adams simply put the experience
from his mind and thus missed having to wrestle with Karl
Marx, who is imagined "standing there waiting for him" at
the end of the line. Adams makes his Wanderjahren a sort
of epitome of the post-graduation travels of all well-con-
nected young Americans, and by treating himself roughly he
also delivers a few blows to his readers. The technique was
Baudelaire's and was to become Eliot's: " 'You! hypocrite
lecteur!—mon semblable,—mon frère!' " Adams says that
the boy failed to learn German, and the Germany he came
to love was "the eighteenth-century [one] which the Germans were ashamed of, and were destroying as fast as they
could" (p. 83).

To impose order on his travels across the Alps and to Rome,
Adams echoes and quotes Matthew Arnold and Gibbon. "He
was in a fair way to do himself lasting harm, floundering between worlds passed and worlds coming, which had a habit
of crushing men who stayed too long at the points of contact" (p. 83). Louis Napoleon declares war on Austria, and
the future pilgrim of the Virgin could not have witnessed a
more emblematic scene. Henry and his sister are caught trying to cross the Stelvio Pass through the tense, opposing
Italian and Austrian armies. Only the power of the "eternal
woman" in his sister subdues the ignorant armies. The next
year the steps of the Church of Santa Maria di Ara Coeli
(to which he was referred by the famous passage in Gibbon's
autobiography, quoted in his guidebook) presented a mystery sufficient to excite even the "tourist." "Two great experiments of Western civilization had left there the chief
monuments of their failure, and nothing proved that the city

[3] Leon Edel, *Henry James: The Untried Years* (Philadelphia and New
York, 1953), p. 282.

might not still survive to express the failure of a third" (p 91). The steps of the Ara Coeli become a constant symbol in the *Education*. Why man? Why his societies? What orders and destroys them? "The greatest men of the age scarcely bore the test of posing with Rome for a background," the author says; his test is to pose America and the twentieth century there instead.

So far, "education" has had little to do with the challenge of an occupation. The young man went to Berlin to study Civil Law, but he had little idea what it was and did little about studying it. The most constructive move he made was in Italy, where he began writing articles on Garibaldi for the *Boston Courier*. The nationalist leader was about to attack near Palermo, and on the strength of the Adams name Henry managed to be sent there by the American Minister in Naples. This was some sign of self-determination. The end of boyhood had come. But the last months in Europe were a genial regression into tourism in Paris, and this gives the author occasion to conclude by saying he returned home with "no education." He might have developed coherence between his early apprenticeship and his later journalism, but this would have been a pat simplification. None of the youthful identities were complete enough. The autobiographer may establish and define the unity of civilization within the context of his life, but to presume to do so in one career only multiplies chaos.

II

It is in the chapter "Treason (1860-1861)" that Adams first puts on the clothes of his father's "private secretary," a suit he wore for the next eight years of his life. Returning to the United States in 1860, in time "to begin the study of law and to vote for Abraham Lincoln on the same day" (p. 98), Henry had not read very far into his Blackstone before Charles Francis Adams, then serving in Congress, invited him to Washington. The son closed the book and went, intending to open it again with his father as his tutor. However, in the rush and turmoil of the winter of 1860-61 the pursuit of the Common Law was as neglected as the pursuit of the Civil Law had been in Germany. As it happened, Adams the aspiring writer published seventeen unsigned "Letter[s] from Washington" in the Boston *Daily Advertiser* during December, January, and February and one unsigned article in the *New York Times* for April 5, 1861,[4] but these are referred to in the one description of himself as "acting in secret as newspaper correspondent" (p. 106). Attention is diverted from the education of the journalist so as to concentrate on the education of the private secretary. All at once, Adams moved from being a recorder of events distant and foreign to a concerned observer and minor participant. War was about to start in the United States.

As the lessons of Harvard and Europe had been mostly literary and dilettantish, the lessons with his father in Washington and London are political. Throughout his boyhood he had regarded Charles Sumner as one of his father's closest friends and allies. That winter Sumner and Charles Francis Adams parted ways, and Henry learned that Sumner "privately denounced [Adams'] course, regarded Mr. Adams as betraying the principles of his life, and broke off relations with his family" (pp. 107-108). The news came as a staggering shock to the private secretary, a kind of treason against friendship that struck much closer than the defection of the South. Henry himself and Sumner remained on speaking terms, but the experience had taught that "a friend in power is a friend lost." This lament is repeated frequently in the *Education*, and the author has to admit that with it "education —for good or bad—made an enormous stride." But if there is no solidarity to friendship (and this is a value strongly

[4] Ernest Samuels, *The Young Henry Adams* (Cambridge, Mass., 1948), pp. 314-315.

affirmed), what order can there be? If power means loss of friends, what kind of power is that?

The chapters on the London Embassy extend the instruction in the behavior of politicians. The private secretary's "teachers" were the most costly and experienced in the world: Lords Palmerston and Russell, Gladstone, their steady opponent Charles Francis Adams, persuasive Members of Parliament like Roebuck and Bright, Monckton Milnes, and the salty American party organizer, Thurlow Weed. As one of a number of influential men sent by Secretary of State Seward to help galvanize British and European opinion, Weed took charge of the Embassy's press relations, and Henry grew to admire him. He illustrated the kind of broad paradoxes and contradictions so strong in Adams' own personality. Weed "grasped power, but not office. He distributed offices by the handfuls without caring to take them. He had the instinct of empire: he gave, but he did not receive." In seeking to get to the bottom of such a philosophy, the secretary asked, " 'Then, Mr. Weed, do you think that no politician can be trusted?' Mr. Weed hesitated for a moment; then said in his mild manner: 'I never advise a young man to begin by thinking so' " (p. 147).

The fact can not be escaped, unfortunately, that these "teachers" did not exist solely for the edification of the American Minister's son. Consequently, there are long stretches where Adams the private secretary is little seen and where Adams the author presents diluted diplomatic history. The longest such anecdote concerns Charles Francis Adams' dealings with Palmerston and Russell. Prime Minister Palmerston was regarded as the more difficult and dangerous and the more likely to lead the British government into open alliance with the South. Russell, his Secretary of State for Foreign Affairs, was regarded as reasonably honest and very doubtful about intervention. Adams says that his father died holding these theories. The value for "education" to be found in a long review of these men's actions is that forty years later new evidence proved the old estimates wrong. Palmerston turned out to have been a "conciliatory" and "cautious" leader who "tried to check Russell" (p. 164). The worth of this to autobiography is that for once it is not only the youth whose clothes do not fit but also the older man and author who had gone on wearing them. The sense of surprise and confusion, however, is typical and deserves comment.

The *Education* proceeds by shocks, and part of its strategy is to display Henry Adams as the man who has undergone the maximum of them. This is not the creation of confusion, as Yvor Winters has called it;⁴⁴ it is more like a re-creation of confusion, a return to the moments of burst illusion so that out of the disorder order may be built again. Adams gave his first precedent for the process in the recollection of his scarlet fever in chapter one. It was the earliest shock, and out of the pain and darkness grew the "fining-down" in his build and sensations and the intensifications of doubt, distrust of personal judgment and rejection of the world's judgment, "the tendency to regard every question as open; the hesitation to act except as a choice of evils . . ." (p. 6). That was the legacy of the fever, and in a sense the legacy of every shock since. Adams felt doubtful and extra sensitive each time, and he re-creates the feeling as he tells the various incidents of the book. Confusion is necessary at moments of education: there was confusion. It must also be repeated so that *the* education, which is "running order through chaos," can reorganize with greater freedom and larger perspective.

Parts of English society were an opportunity for such shocks to a young American as complacent New England rarely supplied him with. Save for the duplicities of Russell and Palmerston, the instances are relatively inconsequential, but the pages on Monckton Milnes and the chapters "Ec-

---

⁴⁴ "Henry Adams: or the Creation of Confusion," *The Anatomy of Nonsense* (Norfolk, Conn., 1943).

centricity" and "The Perfection of Human Society" subject the private secretary to a succession of charged characters.

> The commonest phrase overheard at an English club or dinner-table was that So-and-So "is quite mad." It was no offence to So-and-So; it hardly distinguished him from his fellows; . . . Eccentricity was so general as to become hereditary distinction. It made the chief charm of English society as well as its chief terror.
>
> (p. 181)

Milnes was powerful in London because the majority of men laughed at him. People treated him as Falstaffian, but behind the mask was "a fine, broad, and high intelligence which no one questioned" (p. 124). A better example was John Bright, whose force in debate Adams compares to the energy of a "big mastiff" shaking a "bad-tempered Yorkshire terrier." He tells how some years later he invited Bright and James Russell Lowell to dinner. Afterwards Lowell said Bright was " 'too violent.' " Adams' feeling was that Bright knew England and Englishmen. "He knew what amount of violence in language was necessary to drive an idea into a Lancashire or Yorkshire head" (p. 191).

These lessons are repeatedly knocked away, however, by anticipation of an even stronger one which is to come. The Englishman could afford to leak energy in eccentricity and hyperbolic speech. The American's energies had to be concentrated and efficient, smoothly directed to earning a living. The private secretary's "English education" is constantly jostled by American realities. Just as the author has already undercut his picture of eighteenth-century Quincy with reminders of the twentieth-century banks and railroads which were to change it, so he now satirizes Adams the dandified London socialite and dilettante by moving in references to the America he must return to. The world of embassies and country houses "might fit a young man in some degree for editing Shakespeare or Swift, but had little relation with the society of 1870, and none with that of 1900" (p. 195). "The perfection of human society" is symbolized by such a place as the Gaskells' restoration of Wenlock Abbey in Stropshire. Lovable as it was, "but a few years of it were likely to complete his education, and fit him to act a fairly useful part in life as an Englishman, an ecclesiastic, and a contemporary of Chaucer" (p. 207).

Across the ocean, Lincoln had been re-elected, the Civil War was over, and Adams' friends and contemporaries were leaving the Army and beginning to seek work. News of Lincoln's assassination reaches the dislocated Henry Adams while he is in Rome performing the rituals of escorting members of the family ordered south for their health. "Again one went to meditate on the steps of the Santa Maria in Ara Coeli, but the lesson seemed as shallow as before" (p. 209).

The challenge of choosing a career now for the first time forces the young Adams to face the problem of order. How to find a thread to tie up the "bundle of disconnected memories" which was the nearest thing to an identity he had, and then how to cast it ahead as a coherent plan for the future? For the moment Adams was beset with "an English tone of mind and processes of thought," and the best he could do was persevere in it. He deepened his already deep but wavering path as a dilettante.

In doing so, however, he finally walked straight into his American affection for certainties, for concrete proofs, and for practical applications. Attending auctions under the tutelage of Francis Turner Palgrave, he was one day encouraged to buy a portfolio which was said to contain a drawing by Rembrandt and which Palgrave thought contained a drawing by Raphael. The incident became a merry exposure of the uncertainty of experts. A dealer bought the portfolio not for the Raphael but for the Rembrandt, which Palgrave thought false. This dealer gladly sold Adams the other sketches, and Adams took his prize to the curator of drawings at the British Museum. At first the curator thought it false, but a week later, on the evidence of a watermark, he admitted that it might be genuine. This, Adams noted, was "a method of studying art . . . which even a poor and ignorant American might use as well as Raphael himself." That the drawing, when removed from its mounting, had a barely decipherable poem on the back only confused matters further. The moral of the story was an introduction to scepticism: even experts disagree. Adams kept the drawing and "for forty years" it stayed on his mantelpiece, not for its marketable value or its merit so much as its value to education—and "his amusement even more" (p. 219).

This was as far as he could go in being a dilettante. He could not rest content among uncertainties. Furthermore, dilettantism and its partner antiquarianism only bred more disorder. "History, like everything else, might be a field of scraps, like the refuse about a Staffordshire iron-furnace" (p. 221). Adams, however, would not have it that way. At the suggestion of John Gorham Palfrey, he wrote an article for *The North American Review* on John Smith and Pocahontas. It was published in January 1867, and marked his beginning as a scholar. Later in 1867 he made two more contributions to the *North American* on "British Finances in 1816" and "The Bank of England Restriction." The most important writing he did at this time was a fourth piece for the periodical he was eventually to edit, an extended review of Sir Charles Lyell's *Principles of Geology*. Lyell was Darwin's champion in geology, and this article, which was done with Lyell's approval as a way of advertising the book in the United States, gave Adams an opportunity to inform himself about Darwinism as well as geology.

The advice of the *Education* is that Adams was a Darwinian by instinct, "a predestined follower of the tide" (p. 224). He was first of all united to the social and intellectual atmosphere out of which the theory of evolution emerged and to which it gave expression. And secondly, he was attracted to the possibilities it offered for a systematic theory of history and civilization.

> Unbroken Evolution under uniform conditions pleased every one—except curates and bishops; it was the very best substitute for religion; a safe, conservative, practical, thoroughly Common-Law deity.   (p. 225)

Darwinism was an education in the usual sense, that is a new body of information, and also an education in the ultimate sense, a new belief, a new method of order. It gave a pseudo-scientific foundation to an American's faith in national growth and destiny, and it could even support the kind of faith in moral evolution held by Charles Francis Adams' little club of statesmen. Henry Adams' Darwinism, on the other hand, was peculiarly his own. He reports to having asked Lyell "to introduce him to the first vertebrate" and Lyell's bewildered reply that it "was a very respectable fish, among the earliest of all fossils . . . whose bones were still reposing, under Adams' own favorite Abbey on Wenlock Edge" (p. 228). Adams accepts this fish, called by Huxley the *Pteraspis*, for as honorable a grandfather as the ape and accepts its age, the Silurian, as another metaphor for his own antiquity. The result is that Darwinism, in Adams' hands, becomes a sort of modern bestiary. "La Fontaine and other fabulists maintained that the wolf, even in morals, stood higher than man; and in view of the late civil war, Adams had doubts of his own on the facts of moral evolution" (p. 229). At this point both Adams the author and Adams the young student have rejected the social and political analogies placed alongside the Theory of Evolution. He could prove change, but not evolution. Aspects of Darwinian thought remained brightly prominent in Adams' intellectual life, but he was as far from being a true believer as the most conservative churchman, though for different reasons. He was thus a Darwinian by instinct, but he also "was a Darwinian for fun" (p. 232).

As if to round out the education of the private secretary and apprentice journalist, the author observes that in February 1868 the young man was back in Rome and sitting once more on the steps of Ara Coeli. The years since his first visit "had changed nothing for him there" (p. 236). Rome was still the same, and his comprehension of the questions it asked was still as weak as before. The only differences were that he had become more aware of their difficulty and that, as a young man in need of a marketable education, he was even more poorly prepared for the America he was returning to. Moving from one education to another, however, was becoming a method of organizing chaos. While the clothes of successive educations were put on and off, the manikin grew beneath them into the artful tailor who was directing the operation. The more clothes he put on, the more he represented his age. The more clothes he put off, the more he rose up above his age. Thus did he become both student and teacher, both multiplicity and unity. The most important Adams was the one who was all these others, the tailor, the author.

III

Before surveying Adams' further presentation of himself as journalist and Assistant Professor of History, I should like to re-emphasize the ambition "to complete St. Augustine's *Confessions*." Writing in an age after the philosophical and scientific revolutions of the eighteenth century and after the discoveries of Darwin, Adams could not order his life around Christian faith. He had, like Franklin, to tell a story of education rather than a confession. For the story to have value to others, the education had to be thorough and almost epic in scope. The "consciously assenting member in full partnership with the society of his age" (p. 4) had to have witnessed and examined all the ideas and values of that age. "Running order through chaos" was then a problem of introducing all the chaos of those other ideas as well as of finding the order that held them together. Furthermore, in the nineteenth century, notions like social Darwinism repeatedly became faiths in their own right, ersatz religions which many men accepted as the guiding principles of their lives. Thus the author of the *Education* not only had to touch upon them; he also had to push them over.

Henry Adams and Henry James lived in what R. P. Blackmur has called "the interregnum between the effective dominance of the old Christian-classical ideal through old European institutions and the rise to rule of the succeeding ideal, whatever history comes to call it." Blackmur has pointed out that for expressing in fiction the "predicament of the sensitive mind" during that interregnum no education could have been better than James': ". . . it excluded him from assenting to the energies of social expansion, of technology, of the deterministic sciences, and of modern finance and business. Unconscious assent to these forces, over and above any rebellion against their moral values, caused most active minds in his day to conceal the fact of interregnum."[5]

If anything, Adams was more aware of the change than James, more aware of history, more aware of ideas as agents of time, and, characteristically, more nervously active to hunt out the new forces and test their properties. This is one reason why the *Education* appraises so carefully the later or intellectual years of its author's life while James, as a keenly equipped Small Boy who delicately recognized forces simply in places and people, could tell a valid autobiography in the assimilations of a mere twenty-seven years. Adams' Calvinistic need for certainty and order made him one of the most widely read and widely informed men of his generation, his passion for a new belief leading to Marx, Medievalism, Darwin, Im-

<hr>

[5] "Henry James," *Literary History of the United States*, ed. Spiller, Thorp, Johnson, and Canby (New York, 1959), p. 1039.

perialism, everything the tempests of the age washed in. Yet he gave them all up. Mentally, as well as socially, he was the disengaged aristocrat. In the analogy of the "Preface" to the *Education*, they were the patched and misfitting clothes, while the critical and unimpressed Adams was the manikin. In time the manikin grew into the tailor, the author who seems to find his identity not in the history of his belief but the history of the shocks to his belief.

St. Augustine also included in his autobiography the various heresies which had occupied his youth, and then refuted them with the strength of his final Christianity. In the end they were included only to be eliminated and so to isolate the superior grace and glory of the Christian faith. Adams' technique, on the other hand, is a sceptic's: he uses the false beliefs against one another, letting each overthrow the last. The dilettante art buyer, for example, watched Palgrave's confidence in the Raphael sketch give away to the Museum curator's doubt. This little anecdote is indicative of much of the rest of the book.

The value of Adams' English education as a private secretary disappears immediately upon the family's landing in New York. The City had planned no celebrations for the returning Minister. They were taken ashore from their liner by a humble revenue cutter and then had embarrassing difficulties finding hotel rooms for the night.[6] Henry observes that, "Had they been Tyrian traders of the year B.C. 1000, landing from a galley fresh from Gibraltar, they could hardly have been stranger on the shore of a world, so changed from what it had been ten years before" (p. 237). And worse than that, his generations of Puritan descent and his years of grooming in London had actually set him back in the races of the twentieth century.

Not a Polish Jew fresh from Warsaw or Cracow—not a

[6] Martin Duberman, *Charles Francis Adams, 1807-1886* (Boston, 1961), p. 334; *Education*, p. 237.

furtive Yacoob or Ysaac still reeking of the Ghetto, snarling a weird Yiddish to the officers of the customs— but had a keener instinct, an intenser energy, and a freer hand than he—American of Americans, with Heaven knew how many Puritans and Patriots behind him, and an education that had cost a civil war.   (p. 238)

Thus with American society seeking to find its way in the new industrial world, Adams arrives as a stranger who must again break his training and begin by trying to find himself. The old education is torn off in the rush for the next.

Adams finds his symbol for the United States of his return in President Grant. Grant was to be the second Washington, and four-fifths of the people, he says, had joined together for his election. He gave promise of being the reformer young journalists like Adams could support and behind whom they might work for their own advancement. He could bring the very things Adams was hunting. "Grant represented order. He was a great soldier, and the soldier always represented order" (p. 260). With his poor choices of cabinet members and the rotten scandals of his administration, Grant turned out instead to embody the forces Adams was fighting. Henry and his brother Charles followed the trail of Gould and Fisk's "Gold Conspiracy" until the scent seemed to lead right into the White House. There they met a man who was "simple-minded beyond the experience of Wall Street or State Street." He had force, but he did not know how to apply it. His only claim to intelligence was a number of sententious commonplaces like "Let us have peace!" or "The best way to treat a bad law is to execute it."

Adams' recourse with Grant is similar to the one he uses at other times against himself: he brings up another "education," social Darwinism, to knock him down: "That, two thousand years after Alexander the Great and Julius Caesar, a man like Grant should be called—and should actually and truly be—the highest product of the most advanced evolution, made evolution ludicrous" (p. 266). With Grant, Adams goes on, Darwinists might have believed America reverted to the stone age. The country that "had no use for Adams because he was eighteenth-century . . . worshipped Grant because he was archaic and should have lived in a cave and worn skins." By making the Theory of Evolution a basis for fabling, Adams both destroys its status as a Deity and slays the dragon to which he applies it. And at the same time the little man Henry Adams emerges as the leader of the movement he thought he failed to understand and which did not understand him. In this instance, Adams was on the side of progress and modernity. "For once, he was fifty years in advance of his time" (p. 267).

The chapters "Free Fight" and "Chaos" carry on the ironic exposure of social Darwinism. The one leads into the next and both end in the chapter on his teaching at Harvard, "Failure." As J. C. Levenson has observed, "Free Fight" makes a Darwinian struggle for survival out of the political arena in which Adams and his small band of reformers were taking on the might of Gould and Fisk and their various accomplices.[7] It ended in chaos because the ground on which Adams was standing had broken up beneath him. American society had momentarily ceased to care about the stupidity of its elected leaders and their suspected collusion with business. ". . . A young man fresh from the rustic simplicity of London noticed with horror that the grossest satires on the American Senator and politician never failed to excite the laughter and applause of every audience" (p. 272). He noticed this with horror because the vacant laughter was the measure of the people's fecklessness. They turned their backs and went "to work harder than ever on their railroads and foundries" (p. 273). In 1872 the public shrugged and re-elected Grant. ". . . Young men were forced to see that either some new

7 *The Mind and Art of Henry Adams* (Boston, 1957), p. 319.

standard must be created, or none could be upheld. The moral law had expired—like the Constitution" (p. 280). Adams was left "remarking what a purified charm was lent to the Capitol by the greatest possible distance, as one caught glimpses of the dome over miles of forest foliage" and pondering "the distant beauty of St. Peter's and the steps of Ara Coeli" (p. 282). One thinks of Jefferson's question whether American constitutional democracy could survive the religious and moral certainties on which it was founded.

Ready for a change from Washington, Adams spent the summer of 1870 in Europe. While in London he tried to sell his article on "The New York Gold Conspiracy" and was amazed when first *The Edinburgh Review* and then the *Quarterly* refused it. "Respectability, everywhere and always, turned its back the moment one asked to do it a favor" (p. 287). *The Westminster Review* was less afraid of the Erie Railroad and less afraid of libel suits and finally accepted the piece.

So far chaos was recognized only in the social and political world. Some weeks later Adams received a telegram summoning him to Bagni di Luca. His eldest sister had been thrown from a cab and was dying of tetanus. He arrived at her side and watched through ten days of "fiendish torture" until, while the sun blazed over the Tuscan landscape, his sister died in convulsions. This, says the author, began "the last lesson—the sum and term of education" (p. 287). Up to then, the young man had been spared the blow of the death of intimates; the common pieties of religion and poetry were no preparation. Louisa Adams Kuhn remained courageous and as soft and as full of vitality as the landscape, but this did not hold back the advance of Nature in them both. Nature generated life and death simultaneously, treated them impartially. Adams was forewarned of what was to strike him fifteen years later at the time of Marian's suicide, and there is reason to believe that the author uses Louisa's death to stand for them both.[8]

The bitter lesson of his sister's death was an opening of chaos because there was no religious or philosophic order in which it could be understood.

> The usual anodynes of social medicine became evident artifice. Stoicism was perhaps the best; religion was the most human; but the idea that any personal deity could find pleasure or profit in torturing a poor woman, by accident, with a fiendish cruelty known to man only in perverted and insane temperaments, could not be held for a moment. For pure blasphemy, it made pure atheism a comfort. God might be, as the Church said, a Substance, but He could not be a Person.   (pp. 288-289)

At this moment Adams' senses told him what his intelligence was to be another thirty years in grasping: Nature was anarchy. The young man's reflections at this time, seated in prospect of Mont Blanc a few days after Louisa's death, anticipate the lesson dated 1903 in the chapter, "The Grammar of Science," namely "Chaos was the law of nature; Order was the dream of man" (p. 451). Mont Blanc, if the reader bears in mind the pun and Shelley's related musings before it, was as well-chosen a site for this intuition as the steps of Santa Maria di Ara Coeli was for other ones. Facing the erstwhile vacationist was "a chaos of anarchic and purposeless forces" (p. 289). In the course of many days, illusions once again

---

[8] See *Education*, p. 287: "Flung suddenly in his face, with the harsh brutality of chance, the terror of the blow stayed by him thenceforth for life, *until repetition made it more than the will could struggle with;* more than he could call on himself to bear" [italics mine]. And p. 289: "He did not yet know it, and he was twenty years in finding it out; but he had need of all the beauty of the Lake below and the Alps above, to restore the finite to its place." This is one of the several instances of Adams' use of the "education" of the omitted twenty years despite their omission; it is also another interjection of the experience of the older man and author in the story of the young man.

wrapped the mountain in pure snow and splendid light; the lesson was as forgotten as previous lessons had been. Furthermore, the Franco-Prussian War suddenly erupted to throw society into a chaos which mirrored the chaos of nature and yet distracted one from seeing it.

The traveling journalist went by way of Paris to the Gaskells' retreat at Wenlock Abbey. There he installed himself as another of the "monks" and tried to work out the confusion of politics, Darwin, war, and death. Then, as if this much disorder, this much challenge to education was not enough, a letter came from Harvard offering him an Assistant Professorship of History, and he once more confronted a new education of the occupational kind. President Eliot's letter thus begins to tear Adams from his identity as journalist in the way that the brother-in-law's telegram had demolished the naïve reformer who was unprepared for the fact of death. This is worth noting because the author uses these rapidly arriving communications not as aids to education but as interruptions which break the coherence of one education by interposing another. As the railroads are a symbol of force, the telegrams, which later catch Adams everywhere from the Arctic circle to the upper Nile, are a method of introducing shocks. The *Education*, with its counter-marches and right-abouts, is in matter and manner a work of the Age of the Telegraph.

The final blow of "Chaos" is the little item of news received on returning to the United States that Senator Timothy Howe of Wisconsin had described Adams, in a refutation of an article published that July, as a "begonia." The "Gold Conspiracy" work was to be similarly damned and copied; this was his reward for "two long, dry, quarterly, thirty or forty page articles, appearing in quick succession, and pirated for audiences running well into the hundreds of thousands" (p. 292). So, after two years of journalism and a summer of war and death, the young man had the public recognition of being compared to a showy flower inclined to growing in public places. The simile better fitted a senator himself, Adams observes, while at the same time hinting that if decoration he was to be thought, then decoration he would cleverly become.

From reformer to bereaved brother to orphan of war to monk, and to begonia in one summer, the confusion of identities is a representation of the chaos the young man had discovered. This was valid experience for a student. It was, however, the very opposite of valid preparation for a teacher. This seems to me essential in realizing the significance of Adams' vision of his years at Harvard as "Failure." Adams defined a good teacher as one who prepares his students to "react with vigor and economy." This will naturally happen if education succeeds in its classic task of "running order through chaos." But Adams began as Assistant Professor of Medieval History knowing hardly a thing about the middle ages and knowing chaos, not order. Evolution was a lie. The moral order which had supported the Constitution had broken down. Nature was anarchy. Likewise, history was "in essence incoherent and immoral" and "had either to be taught as such—or falsified" (p. 301). Therefore, the job of the teacher of history, like the job of the ex-historian writing the *Education*, was the job of finding the thread of order with which to bind chaos. Unless there was coherence, it could not be taught; if it was coherent, it was false. This is the dilemma with which Adams wrestled as "Assistant Professor" and the one he bequeaths his readers when he admits he was a failure.

Critics and biographers have marveled long enough, it seems to me, over Adams' presentation of himself as a failure. The implication is that the *Education*, in being artful, is also deceiving. All the achievements which critics feel called upon to restore to him—his essays, his *History*, his introduction of seminars and advancement of graduate programs—all these successes and more are honestly mentioned in his autobiography. The only notable omissions are his two novels, which, after all, he never publicly recognized. But in acknowledging these achievements, he also dwells upon their inconsequence. He puts them in their place. The faith of society in works is like the Assistant Professor's students' faith in education—pathetic.

As a conclusion to the education of the eighteenth-century boy and the education of the nineteenth-century journalist and teacher, the chapter on Harvard anticipates the conclusion of the education of the twentieth-century man and of the *Education* as a whole. The manikin has tried out and been forced to discard a number of suits. As one lesson has contradicted another and as the author has *made* one lesson contradict another, so has no single suit proven adequate as an identity in which to live in a complex and changing world. Telegrams announcing a sister's tetanus in Italy rush in to break up the reformer's vacation in London. Grant's dullness confounds social evolution. The manners of an ambassador's private secretary are of little use to a newspaperman interviewing Congressmen from the West. But in the midst of this helter-skelter and sometimes delightful variety, the work-a-day Henry Adams is forced by his conscientiously accepted duties as teacher to stop and try to organize. Professionally, he taught his history courses in terms of the history of law, seeing the relation between his students and the Medieval Church as "dangerous." But personally he continued to organize his life in terms of his own insuppressible curiosity, wit, and good nature. That essential humanity was all he could be sure of. What it was and how it operated is best seen in the second half of the book. There, at age fifty-four, education started all over again.

IV

Of all the carefully designed puzzles of the *Education*, the clean omission of the twenty years 1872-1891 is the one that perplexes readers most. Numerous explanations can be offered. Adams did not want to go into the matter of his marriage and of Marian's suicide. The *Education* was a book for young men, as *Mont-Saint-Michel* was a book for "nieces," and matters of private life had nothing to do with "fitting young men, in universities or elsewhere, to be men of the world." Finally, Adams might have felt that the division between himself at age thirty-three and age fifty-three was so great that it was more eloquent to emphasize the contrast than to attempt to close it with explanations. In 1891 he wrote his confidante Elizabeth Cameron that he had ceased to care about his *History*. "It belongs to the *me* of 1870; a strangely different being from the *me* of 1890."[9] The second being, he said, cared more for *Esther*, the novel. There are references to some of the events of the omitted years, but declining to treat them directly has the effect of splitting the *Education* into two volumes.

This split produces a significant departure from conventional autobiography. After moving accounts of youth, in which the "hero's" prospects are broad and the possible implications of the life great, most autobiographers slip into more limited stories of their occupations and causes. Gibbon's *Memoirs of My Life and Writings* builds up to his performance as author of the *Decline and Fall*. Trollope's vivid stories of childhood dwindle into stories of his maturity as an author. The subjects of other autobiographies are so much the life in the work—when not the discovery and defense of religion—that critics often catalogue them by the author's occupation: autobiographies of generals, of businessmen, of actors, novelists, financiers, and so forth.[10] Adams, as I shall also argue of Henry James, stubbornly resists such classifications. The *Educa-*

[9] *Letters of Henry Adams (1858-1891)*, ed. Worthington Chauncey Ford (Boston and New York, 1930), p. 468.

[10] See Richard G. Lillard, *American Life in Autobiography, A Descriptive Guide* (Stanford, Calif., 1956). Mr. Lillard lists twenty-two occupational categories, alphabetically, from "Actors and Show People" to "Writers, Critics, Literary Editors, Men of Letters."

tion, by not being the autobiography of an historian, a husband, or a Washington social lion, is the education of Henry Adams. Twenty chapters of preparation lead up to twenty years of performance, and there the story stops. The result is the story of a man instead of a career.

Furthermore, Adams' omission of these twenty years goes a long way toward making the *Education* poetry rather than history. Obviously, autobiography must always describe fact, "the thing that has been," more than it describes possible fact, the "kind of thing that might be,"[11] but dismissal of so much that is mere history indicates Adams' concern with universals at the expense of particulars. During his period as husband and practicing historian, Adams was committed to one set of roles, and could not so easily portray himself as the man of his age forced into one identity after another. The generality of his experience consisted in the variety of his roles. As Henry Adams, eighteenth-century boy and twentieth-century man, he could play many roles which made him the "consciously assenting member in full partnership with the society of his age." The Adams of 1872-1891 had found himself, whereas the earlier and later Adams had to be found anew. Without writing fictions and while remaining faithful to history, he also came closer to the real truth of art, a truth more suggestive, more representative, and graver. "A———'s historic sense amounts to poetry, and his deductions and remarks always set my mind sailing into new channels," John La Farge noted during his travels with Adams in Japan.[12] He might have said the same thing of the *Education*.

The author's own explanation for the jump of twenty years is that those years had nothing to do with education. "Once more! this is a story of education, not of adventure!" (p. 314). "Education had ended in 1871 . . ." (p. 316). If "edu-

[11] Aristotle, *Poetics*, trans. Ingram Bywater (Modern Library: New York, 1954), pp. 234-235 (Ch. 9).

[12] *An Artist's Letters from Japan* (London, 1897), p. 25.

cation" here means learning rather than teaching, the seeking after order rather than delivery of it, then the explanation is entirely justifiable. Announcements like these broadcast a fresh start, a new beginning. This is a kind of second volume, and the author is introducing a new character. The boy was born in the eighteenth century; he did his work in the nineteenth. Now the calendar alone makes him a man of the twentieth century. The protagonist has shed his old clothes and prepares to prepare again. "Life had been cut in halves, and the old half had passed away, education and all, leaving no stock to graft on" (p. 317). But by 1892 the figure of the manikin was approaching the figure of the author, so that the learning Adams had eventually to become a teaching Adams, had to join with Adams the author in "running order through chaos."

Images of change and renewal crowd the opening pages. The scene is first Europe, where everything looks the same, except that "Pall Mall had forgotten him as completely as it had forgotten his elders" (p. 316). James had introduced him to Rudyard Kipling, and as Adams and Kipling crossed to America on the same liner, the latter "dashed over the passenger his exuberant fountain of gaiety and wit—as though playing a garden hose on a thirsty and faded begonia." But equally important, the ship (the *Teutonic*) itself was a symbol.

> That he should be able to eat his dinner through a week of howling winter gales was a miracle. That he should have a deck stateroom, with fresh air, and read all night, if he chose, by electric light, was matter for more wonder than life had yet supplied, in its old forms. . . . As the *Niagara* was to the *Teutonic*—as 1860 was to 1890—so the *Teutonic* and 1890 must be to the next term—and then? (pp. 318-319)

On arrival, the United States asked the same question it had asked in 1868—where was it going?

A gauge of the difference between the Adams of 1868 and 1892 is that the later one actively set himself on course to find out. Before he had had a living to make and a career to build; discovery of the United States was confined to what he learned as journalist and teacher. Now the education (read *occupation*) chosen by the retired gentleman is Education itself, that is, study of himself and his society, the purposeful effort to run order through chaos. The need for such a search is brought up by his return in 1892 from his voyage around the world. It is repeated after contemplation of the success of him and his contemporaries in their now nearly completed jobs and callings. It is repeated again by the crash of 1893 and the Chicago Exposition: "Chicago asked in 1893 for the first time whether the American people knew where they were driving. Adams answered, for one, that he did not know, but would try to find out" (p. 343).

At this point the manikin and the tailor have grown significantly more alike, and it is possible to connect several of Adams' identities which up until now have seemed widely separated. Those to keep in mind are the begonia, the historian, the eighteenth-century boy who is heir to the Adams tradition, the "stable-companion to statesmen" (James' Bonnycastle: "he was not in politics, though politics were much in him"), the amateur economist, the man of letters, the "Virgin's pilgrim," and the "Pilgrim of world's fairs." If society was to consider him a decoration, then like decoration in organic architecture, he would articulate what lay beneath. As historian he had long sought to comprehend the forces supporting society, and as an Adams he could not seriously content himself with being idle, a "social luxury" like Bay Lodge. He therefore used his retirement; his knowledge of history, art, and economics; his connections with politicians and statesmen; and his constant traveling to plunge himself deep into the study of his age. He forsook drift to find out where society was drifting, or whether it was drifting or driving.

He had Worthington Ford at the U.S. Statistical Bureau in Washington supply him with extensive tables on coal and steel production, finances, and employment. He briefly "took to study of the religious press" to determine whether "growth in human nature" was shown there (p. 352). He visited the rebellion in Cuba. He further cultivated the company of women and, as if they were all sibyls, asked them the character and destiny of mankind. The course of his journeys between 1892 and 1901 reads like an actualizing of the psychic journeys of the bardic Whitman. Spending a summer in Yellowstone Park "wander[ing] over the roof of the continent," he went on to the Pacific Northwest to "inspect the last American railway systems yet untried." From here "he set out for Mexico and the Gulf, making a sweep of the Caribbean and clearing up, in these six or eight months, at least twenty thousand miles of American land and water" (p. 350). Other trips, all of which are frankly included to represent Adams as a seeker, take him to Russia, to Beirut, to upper Norway, to Constantinople, to Egypt, Ravenna, Athens, the industrial Rhine, and, of course, to world's fairs and cathedrals. The steps of the monuments at fairs begin to invite the same questions as the steps of Ara Coeli. And even after 1901 he continued to make the regular summer passage to Paris and winter return to Washington. "Such lessons as summer taught, winter tested," he says later, still fixing himself between opposites.

Thus the *Education* becomes most manifestly a "study of twentieth-century multiplicity." Whether as knowledge or occupation, that is the definition of the word itself. The paradox is that the book is still autobiography, but autobiography has been cracked open and made a study of society on the one hand and of the self on the other. Adams is indeed writing both a *De Civitate Dei* and a *Confessions*. Understanding the one half of the broken shell which is the United States and the modern world is the complement to understanding the other half which is Henry Adams. Through the chapters "Silence" and "Indian Summer" the protagonist continues his journeys and his searchings and his persistent effort to see himself in terms of his environment while at the same time detaching himself from it. A favorite pose is that of the old man, the sixty-year-old trying to find his place among youths who ignore him by tolerating him. In this pose, needless to say, he finds a way of speaking while remaining "silent," of remaining young while appearing old.

This use of himself in one way anticipates the Yeats of the Byzantium poems and in a second way echoes Adams' admired Montaigne. Both the author of the *Education* and the essayist emphasize their retirement and aloofness from the prejudices of the mob ("State Street"). Both fill this retirement with reflection upon the nature of society and the nature of themselves. Montaigne, of course, manages to say more about himself and still say less about the details of his own life than any of his followers, and he is a precedent for Adams' reticence on personal matters. They both make their leisure one of the announced reasons for writing. The *Essays* are seeds to sow idle minds, the *Education* a way of continuing education and blocking an old man's introspection. The mind must reflect (both mirror and think) and not be one which "drowned itself in the reflection of its own thought" (p. 432). Numbers of other comparisons could be drawn: of style, of erudition, of self-mockery, and of "meditative egotism." But the essence of the matter has been stated by Max Baym in *The French Education of Henry Adams:* "Where morals are not the arbitrary imposition of societal convention on the will of the individual, they are the full measure of man assuming responsibility for the universe of his own mind in loneliness."[13]

[13] (New York, 1951), p. 113.

This, I think, is the most important connection between Adams and Montaigne. Much is said of Adams' scepticism, but as I have already shown, it was more of a defense against false beliefs and ersatz religions than an attack on Christianity or, like Montaigne's, a tactical defense of both reason and faith. It is difficult to place Adams securely in any sceptical tradition. T. S. Eliot[14] and others have called him a sceptic, implying that this is a sign of his decadence and the deterioration of his class. That Adams was a non-believer is true, but his non-belief was accompanied by a secular as well as a theological iconoclasm and by an intellectual curiosity and artistic strength that has little to do with his class. For Adams scepticism was a method, not a philosophy.

Eliot went on from his review of the *Education* in 1919 to incorporate parts of it into *Gerontion* in 1920. The line "In depraved May, dogwood and chestnut, flowering judas" uses Adams' description of the Washington spring beginning chapter eighteen (p. 268). It may also be, as has not been pointed out, that the portrait of Gerontion as "an old man . . . being read to by a boy" is meant to recall Adams the old man who learned "the charm of Washington spring" from young Sam Hoar and who surrounded himself with "nieces" and "nephews" like Bay Lodge. Eliot saw only the infirm part of Adams. He distorted and magnified Adams' own consciously ironic portrait of himself as the begonia or the remnant of the Adams family. But while Adams mocked himself, he simultaneously defined himself and drew energy from the mockery. He thus prevented himself from being a Gerontion or a Narcissus. He retained and gained knowledge of himself, and, in Hawthorne's phrase, opened up an intercourse with the world.

The tradition of Montaigne (or, for that matter, the whole

---

[14] "A Sceptical Patrician," *The Athenaeum* (May 23, 1919), I, pp. 361-362.

Western tradition) indicated that the individual was a microcosm of his society and that public order depended upon private order. Max Baym's remark about the foundation of morals for Montaigne and Adams can be revised to read "order" for "morals." "Where order is not the arbitrary imposition of societal convention on the will of the individual, it is the full measure of man assuming responsibility for the universe of his own mind in loneliness." If this tradition was to endure and remain green, men had to continue to think of themselves as a part of society and think of society as an extension of themselves. And they had to remain capable of defining and directing both. They must not, as Adams parodied himself as doing, live alone, "drifting in the deadwater of the *fin-de-siècle*," or become, like Dreiser's Carrie Meeber, "a waif amid forces."

Against this background, the remainder of *The Education of Henry Adams* is first a study of different areas of society and then an attempt to fit the studies together in a picture of its course and direction. Finally, the *Education* as a whole is this plus a picture of Henry Adams as a maker of himself, and as a maker of society rather than its victim. The chapter "The Dynamo and the Virgin" is a short essay on religion and the machine and a suggestion of the religion of the machine age. "Twilight" is an essay on twentieth-century politics as taught by John Hay and on geology as taught by Clarence King. Do the lessons of geology—or radiation, gravity, or magnetism—provide any analogies for the path of politics? "Teufelsdröckh" carries Adams on his tour of Russia, northern Europe, and the industrial areas of Germany. It is another side of the question: the power of coal in addition to the power of religion, politics, and nature. From there this latter-day Sartor Resartus rises to "The Height of Knowledge" and then dips to "The Abyss of Ignorance." As one might expect, the titles are partially ironic. In "The

Height of Knowledge" Adams watches Secretary of State
John Hay steer important treaties over the shallows of the
Senate, but the chapter opens on the sorrow of Clarence
King's death and closes with Adams astounded by men's
lack of control over the forces they presume to direct. Ignorance is, at least, without pretenses. The wise man was wiser
than the idiot because he knew "that his normal condition
was idiocy, or want of balance, and that his sanity was unstable
artifice" (p. 434).

Adams concludes "The Abyss of Ignorance" with the plan
for writing *Mont-Saint-Michel and Chartres: a Study of
Thirteenth-Century Unity* and *The Education of Henry
Adams: a Study of Twentieth-Century Multiplicity*. Within
the substance of the *Education*'s own legend, then, this is the
point (in time, 1902) at which the manikin resolved to become his own tailor. Moreover, the decision to write autobiography and the kind of autobiography chosen appear as a
milestone in the autobiographical history. The more traditional position for this decision is, of course, in the beginning
of the book, and in parting from this tradition Adams mag-
nifies the importance of his book. The *Education* is not a
response to some other experience, not a way of memorializ-
ing some other insight or achievement that has given life
significance; it is a response to that moment in life at which
an examination of life became essential. Education, that is,
the search for his own and his country's direction and purpose, led to the moment when the search itself had to be
recapitulated and analyzed. Education led to the *Education*.
Thus, definition of self by autobiography is put on a plane
with the definitions by other means usually only recorded
in autobiography. The pen, Adams says, is like a staff for
making one's way through the "thicket of ignorance," a way,
too, of drawing one's "line of force." The need is to create
such an order that will give to the pen power commensurate

with the power of the twentieth century. All this is from the end of the chapter, "The Dynamo and the Virgin."

> In such labyrinths, the staff is a force almost more necessary than the legs; the pen becomes a sort of blindman's dog, to keep him from falling into the gutters. The pen works for itself, and acts like a hand, modelling the plastic material over and over again to the form that suits it best. The form is never arbitrary, but is a sort of growth like crystallization, as any artist knows too well; for often the pencil or pen runs into side-paths and shapelessness, loses its relations, stops or is bogged. Then it has to return on its trail, and recover, if it can, its line of force.   (p. 389)

St. Augustine and Christian autobiographers knew themselves as seekers of God and made their *Confessions* or *Grace Abounding* the story of those quests. On a secular level, other autobiographers have used their books to tell the story of their quests for fame or fortune. Such concentration of interest upon one subject can be the result of either a concentration of purpose in life or the needs of unity in art or both. The product, as James wrote Adams, is apt to be a "thinning" of the life itself. Franklin's *Autobiography* is so much richer partially because it was a portrait of him at the different ages of composition. Adams perseveres in this kind of "self-teaching." From the moment-to-moment lessons of the life as lived, he goes on to the lessons of the life as written. Without the examination performed in the *Education*, he might have lacked any considered and unified definition of himself. "It is art that *makes* life," James wrote H. G. Wells, "makes interest, makes importance, for our consideration and application of these things, and I know of no substitute whatever for the force and beauty of its process."[15] Adams sought in

[15] *The Letters of Henry James*, ed. Percy Lubbock (New York, 1920), II, p. 490.

the *Education* a way of bringing order and power to his life. The book "served its only purpose," he wrote wryly, "by educating *me*."[16]

It should be said that Adams had begun thinking of writing his autobiography by 1883. In a letter to John Hay, he told of reading Anthony Trollope's and said, "I am clear that you should write autobiography. I mean to do mine." He had watched Trollope wipe out all heroism from his life and objected "to allowing mine to be murdered by any one except myself."[17] But it is revealing that he did not actually start until he had a more specific reason for writing, until the need "to fix a position for himself" and the twentieth century (p. 435) had replaced the crotchety wish to beat his biographers. By 1908, when he was sending a copy of the *Education* to Henry James, he spoke of having "taken" his life rather than having "murdered" it. "The volume is a mere shield of protection in the grave," he alleged. "I advise you to take your own life in the same way, in order to prevent biographers from taking it in theirs."[18] The suicide conceit is still present, but he also implies that he has taken possession, seized his life and put it to use. In the next paragraph of the letter to James he reaffirms the connection between the *Education* and *Chartres*, "the three concluding chapters of this being only a working out to Q.E.D. of the three concluding chapters of that." In 1883 Adams would have been just another iconoclast; twenty years later he was a tailor and a self-teacher, an artist.

V

The decision to write the *Education* is the book's climax.

---

[16] *Letters of Henry Adams (1892-1918)*, ed. Worthington Chauncey Ford (Boston and New York, 1938), p. 526.

[17] *Letters (1858-1891)*, p. 347. The next sentence is also of interest: "Every church mouse will write autobiography in another generation in order to prove that it never believed in religion."

[18] *Letters (1892-1918)*, p. 495.

It is the perspective from which to look back on the pages behind and ahead on the pages that follow. The numerous previous toilets of the manikin are a personal representation of "Twentieth-Century Multiplicity," while the theory of history which is to come is an attempt, in Adams' metaphor of navigation, "to fix" the position of that multiplicity and reckon its future course. He has studied his world and described it; now he must be historian and mariner and seek its prophecy.

As a critic of autobiography, I do not regard Adams' Dynamic Theory of History as "padding" or as a crankish notion that has dictated the author's earlier images of himself. It may chase off the stage details about his daily life, and it may be incorrect as history, as his later use of the second law of thermodynamics in *A Letter to American Teachers of History* was incorrect as science; but its real value is independent of these considerations. Its value in anticipating the course of the world in the twentieth century lies only in its occasional brilliant flashes of insight. What one finally appreciates it for is its interest as a valiant attempt to make order of life in the modern age. It is an attempt at myth. It is Adams' last and most concentrated effort at running order through chaos. This is the grand challenge of autobiography, and this has been the consistent task of the *Education*.

The heart of the problem Adams faced is announced in the chapter, "The Grammar of Science." Readings in contemporary works on science like Karl Pearson's *Grammar of Science* and the French mathematician Poincaré's *La Science et l'Hypothèse* had informed him that, "In plain words, Chaos was the law of nature; Order was the dream of man" (p. 451). This flatly contradicted not only the teaching of the Church down through the ages but also the assumption of science itself, at least, of science in the tradition of Bacon and Newton. For even while exploring the chaos of the unknown, these scientists had assumed that order lay behind it. M. Poincaré's book revealed that this was only an hypothesis.

> "[In Science] we are led," said M. Poincaré, "to act as though a simple law, when other things were equal, must be more probable than a complicated law. Half a century ago one frankly confessed it, and proclaimed that nature loves simplicity. She has since given us too often the lie. To-day this tendency is no longer avowed, and only as much of it is preserved as is indispensable so that science shall not become impossible." (p. 454)

The news from the laboratories only confirmed what he already felt as an historian and what his sister's death had hinted in 1870. But while the mathematician could go on forever finding chaos behind order and order behind chaos, this "mathematical paradise of endless displacement . . . turned the historian green with horror" (p. 455). Such a principle helped Adams to understand much that he had seen in sixty-odd years of education; it explained the perpetual failure of one education after another. It also explained the rise and fall of societies; but, in a grimly prophetic moment, Adams saw that "the staggering problem was the outlook ahead into the despotism of artificial order which nature abhorred" (p. 458).

The task was complicated, to Adams' thinking, by the fact that the world had already given birth to unchecked forces which were a kind of order of chaos. The strongest of these forces, "Vis Inertiae," were the opening up of China and the liberation of women. China "was to be united with the huge bulk of Russia in a single mass which no amount of new force could henceforward deflect." And women, shifted off the axis of "the cradle and the family," were whirling in unforeseen directions. They will become "sexless like the bees" and, like men, "marry machinery." Moving in this new line, they must, he says with thoughtful ambiguity, "leave the old energy of inertia to carry on the race" (p. 446). Against these forces there is no "Vis Nova" except the traditional power of the self-respecting man to meet the demands of his time. In the chapter "Vis Nova" Adams hears Theodore Roosevelt say that he could, if he wanted, prevent war between Russia and Japan and Britain and the Boers. "The listener cared less for the assertion of power, than for the vigor of view" (p. 464). This was the kind of erect intelligence he wanted to see. New forces of another kind are the St. Louis World's Fair, the automobile, and, for Adams, the Virgin of Chartres. In her was an attraction which, even if she had failed to hold together the powers that created her, still served to rally Adams' quest for unity. She gave him energy.

> Every man with self-respect enough to become effective, if only as a machine, has had to account to himself for himself somehow, and to invent a formula of his own for his universe, if the standard formulas failed.　　(p. 472)

Thus, as a way of comprehending his own multiplicity, relating himself to the world he lived in, and keeping alive his own "Vis Nova" and his sense of himself, he undertook his "Dynamic Theory of History."

Turning for a moment to the chapter on St. Thomas Aquinas which concludes *Mont-Saint-Michel and Chartres* gives another perspective to the theory of history in the *Education*. It is a magnificent piece of writing, and Adams wrote that he thought it was the best thing he ever did. In it he at once manages to interpret St. Thomas's theology by relating it to the architecture of a thirteenth-century cathedral, and to allegorize the elements of the gothic structure in such a way that the two together become a statement of Medieval unity. Adams succeeds in his ambition to show that art is an emanation of theology and theology a work of art, and he also marks that point when man and society were, to his thinking, most stable and best integrated.

The "Dynamic Theory of History" tries to do the same thing for the *Education*, with the difference that the author is not setting a point but drawing a line. Modern society has no unity. To attempt to bring it together around the church would be, as someone once said, for a gigantic cyclops to try to see himself in a lady's pocketbook mirror. It is not stable; it is dynamic; and Adams' theory was that the speed of change increased by squares. But for man to remain an individual and not a willow in the wind he had to keep an active rather than a passive relationship to this change and preserve his own valid image of himself and his world. Adams did not recognize man's power *over* nature and his destiny. He was too Baconian for that and too anxious to make scientific history adhere to Bacon's course for science. " 'Nature, to be commanded, must be obeyed' " (p. 484). Man could be a force *in* nature by his capacity to assimilate other forces. For Adams, man needed to understand history the way he needed to understand magnetism; not to know why, but how; not to control, but to use, like the compass, in steering his way.

The details of his theory of history do not concern the critic of Adams as an autobiographer. Questionable as it is, it has been as popular a subject of scholarship as Adams' own life.[19] In turning to history for an image of man and society, Adams was following the tradition of philosophy since Comte. He was also following the descendants of Comte who sought to define the laws of history according to which society moved and to give these laws scientific authority for the prediction of its future course. This brand of "scientific" history is now regarded as somewhat naïve and blind to the enormous importance of the irrational in man and his institutions.[20] While

[19] See R. P. Blackmur, "Henry and Brooks Adams: Parallels in Two Generations," *Southern Review* (Aug., 1939), V, pp. 308-334; William H. Jordy, *Henry Adams: Scientific Historian* (New Haven, 1952); Timothy Paul Donovan, *Henry and Brooks Adams: The Education of Two American Historians* (Norman, Oklahoma, 1961).

[20] Jordy, pp. 5-6.

Adams' early work as an historian is the object of more and more praise, this bent in his thinking is viewed as misguided, and detractors of the *Education* often assert that it was the victim of these theories. Such assertions, however, take the theories more seriously than Adams himself did. "For his dynamic theory of history he cared no more than for the kinetic theory of gas," he said in the last chapter of the *Education*. He felt "it would verify or disprove itself within thirty years" (p. 501), implying that he had used it and discarded it. The fact is that its function is more exhortative and organizational than philosophical. The real interest lies in the needs that evoked it, and its presence says more than it does itself. In the interregnum between the Christian-classical order and the order of the dynamo, as he satirically referred to it, Adams sought the meaning of his life in history and harangued his readers from his library the way a dogmatic Christian would have prophesied from the pulpit.

The theory of history, then, is an effort to complete education. It is meant to pay out the mooring line of the *Education* in the way that the chapter on Aquinas anchored *Mont-Saint-Michel*. It had to be a paying out rather than an anchoring because autobiography can never be brought to a definite end and because, more important, the very notion of a *dynamic* age excluded any conclusive synthesis. "We shall not cease from exploration," Eliot says near the end of "Little Gidding." The garb of "dynamic historian," the poser of shocking questions to the American Historical Association, was the best suit in which the author could step out of his book. His theory at once described his multiverse and thereby related him to society and also accounted for his own changing personality. His identities followed one another like social revolutions. It was a way into the past and the traditions of his culture and it was also a way into himself. Upon its firm but also moving ground Adams could at last be teacher as well as student. He could offer his students and himself convictions as well as questions. And from its security he could defend the values of thought and sensitivity, friendship, and personal responsibility which were the essential ones of his past. The mind must not drift. It must not hide in ignorance from the forces it has created and the forces which are shaping it. The closing sentence of the chapter on "A Law of Acceleration" is sublimely simple: "Thus far, since five or ten thousand years, the mind had successfully reacted, and nothing yet proved that it would fail to react—but it would need to jump" (p. 498).

Whether Adams "completed" St. Augustine's *Confessions* is a test the modern critic can spare himself the embarrassment of applying. It was success enough to recognize the necessity of trying to. Another chapter in the history of man's relationship to his world and himself needed to be written. In writing it, Adams revealed himself to be one of the first twentieth-century men and produced a prototypical twentieth-century book. His influence upon modern letters—upon autobiography and fiction, and especially upon poetry—has been enormous. And even where there is no provable direct connection, there are equally important anticipations of pose, of dilemma, of contemporary materials, of historic sense. Adams' most significant service was in demonstrating the strength and resources of personal experience. "Running order through chaos" was a social duty, but doing the job in the private world could be made to accomplish the public end. Adams' vision of himself as "a consciously assenting member in full partnership with the society of his age" enabled him to make his private multiple roles analogues of his multiverse, while his simultaneous grasp of himself as "Henry Adams," the son of Charles Francis Adams, who "stood alone," enabled him to avoid the false identities that buried many of his contemporaries.

Roy Harvey Pearce has shown how modern poets have tended to organize themselves in two ways.[21] Some have sought, with William Carlos Williams, to discover and rediscover their worlds exclusively in terms of themselves. Others, like Pound, have tried to subdue the violence of their isolation by "going to school to other poets [of the past] and learning thereby to delimit and to give precise form" to their truth. Adams begins by trying to do both. What is his stacking up of Augustine, Montaigne, Rousseau, Gibbon, and Franklin as models but a start at framing his tradition and trying to see himself within it? In the end, however, he pursues further and further the intricate mutations of his own individuality. That shifting figure discovers its own coherent form, and the *Education* might be said to have initiated a new category of autobiography. If so, James is the only successor who has matched him, and it may be that in going even deeper into his own origins James has excelled him. Together their "educations" sound a keynote for the beginning of twentieth-century literature.

[21] "The Poet as Person," *Interpretations of American Literature*, ed. Charles Feidelson, Jr., and Paul Brodtkorb, Jr. (New York, 1959), pp. 369-386. Reprinted from *Yale Review*, March 1952.

CHAPTER FOUR

The Lessons of the Boy and the Master

⁂

These fragments I have shored against my ruins
The Waste Land, l. 430

IN approaching the autobiography of Henry James from behind investigations of Benjamin Franklin and Henry Adams, the critic confronts certain disjunctions which force him to stop briefly. Franklin and Adams, though they are chronologically far apart, can be treated together. They are, after all, the two most famous American autobiographers, and this fame alone encourages comparison. Adams rendered his tributes to Franklin and asked his readers to consider him as the first of his American models of self-teaching. Yet there are still better reasons for studying them side by side. To the extent that Adams was an eighteenth-century man, he is Franklin's "contemporary," a man who carried on the traditions of John Adams and Thomas Jefferson, Franklin's actual contemporaries and confederates in the affairs of the Revolution. His "failure" is in part the failure of the patrician faith of these predecessors to remain workable and popular with Adams' actual contemporaries in the nineteenth century. Ironically, Franklin's implementation of the new forces of social and technological change was partially to blame. Yet Adams, who was nothing if not Franklinian in his faith in American destiny and his desire to stand with the future rather than the past, admired this implementation and sought himself to prepare a later age for the growing forces of its time.

[137]

In Franklin and Adams the reader is aware of such a thing as "forces." They write, from different angles, as public figures who have been involved in major events of their eras and have watched the world respond to them. The Philadelphia printer arose as an inspiring example of man's ability to direct his own life and to direct the course of the world as well. By contrast, Adams presents himself as a man who has been a lifelong witness to history without ever influencing it. *The Education of Henry Adams* is a significant companion to Franklin's *Autobiography* because it is in one way a rebuttal of it, a testimony of effectiveness answered by a tale of ineffectiveness. It is only the discerning reader who perceives the underlying purpose to define a modern order wherein the mind can resume control over its surroundings. Thus Adams, with his objective of fitting young men to be men of the world, bears relationships with Franklin, the now over-taught teacher of young Americans.

James' autobiography is not only less known. It is less known, presumably, because it is not felt to share these uses of Franklin and Adams. Yet the autobiographies of James and Adams are surely read together as profitably as those of Franklin and Adams. The "Education of Henry James" is one of the greatest of American educations, great in its subtleties, great in its accumulations, great in its individuality, and great in its importance to modern readers. In a sense it has been dealt a disservice by the readers it has had. They have frequently read it too narrowly, seeking only background for James' love of the theater and painting, information about William James or Henry Senior, and in general mining it for biography. Its intricate unity has been overlooked. It also has much more to say concerning the character and "forces" of American society than is commonly suspected. James was so powerfully an *observer*, and his individuality finally found its strength and security in that, just as Franklin's found its in becoming so cunningly the prototypical American Man. Therefore Franklin can appeal as the representative of the race, but James can speak as the unexcelled observer of the race. This is unimpaired by the fact that James also became the ideal Anglo-American, the Master of Lamb House. The real Franklin (as opposed to the popular image of him) also became an ideal cosmopolitan. James' *A Small Boy and Others* and *Notes of a Son and Brother* may not be the mythic "American life" that the *Autobiography* is so strangely taken to be, but, given the attention they demand, they have equally as much to say about life in America.

I

John La Farge, the painter and designer of stained glass, was a friend of both James and Adams. Some day this friendship should be studied closely and La Farge reviewed in terms of his influence upon these two Henrys, for as a young man La Farge persuaded the young James to give up painting and to concentrate upon his writing, and a quarter of a century later it was again La Farge who accompanied Adams first to Japan and then to the South Seas, where he persuaded Adams to do a little painting. The *Education* reports him to have frequently reproached that author: " 'Adams, you reason too much!' " One of La Farge's remarks about James, on the other hand, takes notice of an exactly opposite trait. In the period he spent with James in Newport he observed that James had "the painter's eye," and it was his opinion that "few writers possessed it." Most writers, he felt, "did not so much see a thing as think about it."[1] Adams reasoned too much, so La Farge urged him to do a little painting; James had "the painter's eye," so La Farge felt he had the most precious of gifts for writing.

The two comments are of interest, I think, because they point up a fundamental difference between James and Adams,

[1] Royal Cortissoz, *John La Farge, A Memoir and a Study* (Boston and New York, 1911), p. 117.

while at the same time holding the two men together as the close friends of a third man. This, in turn, points up something about their autobiographies. Contrast the titles: *The Education of Henry Adams,* an abstract, intellectual title, and *A Small Boy and Others* and *Notes of a Son and Brother,* concrete, visual titles, which at once place the subject in "relations." Yet all three emphasize youth or, at least, young apprehensions. In all there is a sense of a mind grappling at once with the sense of itself and the rest of the world, of its uniqueness and the "other" that is so different. It is also curious that Adams, who is so self-effacing in the book itself, should have advertised himself in the title while James, who asserts himself so strongly in the books, is so humble in his titles.

James was descriptive in naming his books and stories. It now strikes one as remarkably obtuse that a contemporary reviewer of *A Small Boy and Others* should have criticized the author for burying the subject ("The Small Boy—where is he?") and for cheating expectations by not having written the kind of memoirs "that he, perhaps better than any man of his time, [was] qualified to write."[2] In his way, however, this anonymous reviewer picked out important facts. If the Small Boy (and the youth) are there, they are present as very quiet, unobtrusive little men in the company of more boisterous "others" and in the very prominent company of the writer, the deep-voiced master. When the boy is seen (and he is), he is seen *seeing* something else ("the painter's eye") and also seeing where he is going. But why, to take up the reviewer's second point, did James spend so much space on mere memories of childhood? This was part of Adams' complaint in the cry, "Poor Henry James . . . actually still lives in that dreamy, stuffy, Newport and Cambridge, with Papa James and Charles Norton—and me!" In two books James

---

[2] "The Boyhood of Henry James," *The Nation* (July 24, 1913), XCVII, pp. 79-80.

gets no further than his late twenties. Adams covered the same years in two hundred pages, toward the end of which he had already started recalling revolutions in Italy, the Washington winter of 1860-61, and Civil War diplomacy in London. Nevertheless, what the Small Boy sees are the sure facts that are the cause and meaning of wars and revolutions. James did write the memoirs which he, better than any man of his time, was qualified to write.

James' autobiography is the story of a young man's discovery of the world and personal organization of the world in terms of his own relationship to it. Or more properly, it is a nest of stories of rediscovery: the older man re-examining the boy who was continually re-examining his own self and world. It is no more ponderous in style and trivial in content than his novels are, for they too make this method of inquiring consciousness the kind of ultra-violet light that illuminates the unsuspected nature of things. Granted, the James family had little immediate contact with the condition of the poor, the rise of industrialism, and most of the other throbbing "problems" of the century. The quaint world of Washington Square hardly noticed the poor. The Jameses were not church members. Science was William James' concern. The family lived on its inheritance, and never a hand was lifted in manufacture. Yet somehow the novels find and incorporate these subjects and so does the autobiography. The novels have been pointed out to move by sequences of event and re-examination of the event, so that suspense becomes more a question of What happened? rather than What happens next?[3] The critical issues and horrors of the day are always implicated in these hours of inquiring consciousness. So indeed does James' vast autobiographical inquiry go back over the events of a long and inquisitive youth to press on little things and find behind and around them all they really meant. *What hap-*

[3] Joseph Warren Beach, *The Method of Henry James* (New Haven, 1918), p. 51.

pened? But James' autobiography not only capitalized these methods of fiction; it also anticipated a whole new family of novels and stories. James writing autobiography, for example, is very much like Faulkner's Isaac McCaslin in "The Bear," particularly as Isaac scrutinizes the old plantation records in part four.

What Adams accomplished by thought, James accomplished by sight, the sight of the increasingly observant boy and the second sight of the author. There is no pretense of working over a subject logically, of writing, in the manner of Adams, cogent autobiographical essays on "Political Morality," "President Grant," or "Vis Inertiae." Nor could the autobiography be composed, as James said some of the novels were, around the widening possibilities of a tiny anecdote. The narrative had to be confined to the truth, to the facts of remembered experience. At times, of course, one such fact recalls others, this being the way of memory, so that the incident of Henry's picture being taken with his father, for instance, becomes surrounded with other incidents of his father's cultivation of his company. The challenge to the good reader, however, is to see for himself the significance such juxtaposed recollections may have, to analyze and compare the sometimes oddly associated parts and feel their combined effect. James' autobiography is comparatively loose and easily assembled—compared, that is, to one of his novels. The materials are naturally more diverse, and the span of years, to cite just one other problem, is much greater. But the ease is an asset. The story of youth reflects James' maturity without being, as is frequently the case with poorer autobiographies, directed and distorted by it.

Yet the great question, as Adams pointed out, was the existence of the belief that would finally give both life and book their real order and power. Taken together and read as one coherent autobiography, *A Small Boy* and *Notes* have such a belief. It was at once present with James as he started to write and discovered by him as he wrote. This reading will attempt to indicate some of what it was. The best way to begin is by noting that one of the things James realized as he wrote was that he was doing something he had always wanted to, namely telling the history of an imagination.

II

The impulse to write his autobiography came to Henry James following the death of William in August 1910. Their parents had died long before, in the 'eighties. Garth Wilkinson James had died in 1883; the sister Alice in 1892. The news of the death of Robertson James, the youngest brother, reached William and Henry in early August 1910, just as they were returning from Europe to William's summer home in New Hampshire. With the passing of William, therefore, Henry was the last survivor of his immediate family.

Henry's biographers and editors emphasize that at this hour his own strength was not great. As readers of the autobiography know, he was perpetually liable to fits of worry about his health. In 1909 he had consulted physicians regarding his heart. He was afraid of having angina pectoris, although Sir James Mackenzie, the great English heart doctor, had assured him that by judicious living he would be all right.[4] To these troubles were added the old anxieties about his art. The New York Edition had not sold nearly as well as he had hoped. The best information available indicates that during 1910 these illnesses, "partly physical but mainly nervous [had] deprived him of all power to work and caused him immeasurable suffering of mind."[5]

A letter from James in 1913 to his nephew Henry James, Jr., records the more direct circumstances leading up to the

[4] Leon Edel, *Literary Biography* (Doubleday Anchor Books: New York, 1959), pp. 41-42.
[5] *The Letters of Henry James*, ed. Percy Lubbock (New York, 1920), II, p. 151.

autobiographies. William's son had protested the novelist's slight alterations in the text of some of the letters quoted in *Notes*. At this later date, James wrote back explaining how the book happened to have a significance to him beyond the literal documentation provided by these sources. The idea had come during the dark days following William's death when James had been telling Mrs. William James stories of the "old life of the time previous, far previous, to her knowing us." She had been moved to suggest that he " '*write* these things,' " and "after a bit I found myself wondering vaguely whether I *mightn't* do something of the sort." The project impressed him as "a very special and delicate and discriminated thing to do, and only governable by proprieties and considerations all of its own, . . ." In doing it, in putting the experiment to the proof, he encountered "all sorts of discomfitures and difficulties—and disillusionments," but he held to the inspiration as it had come to him at that time.[6] That was the "spirit" and the "vision," one which the observing critic cannot fail to see as richly and splendidly elegiac.

It is elegiac not simply for being a commemoration of William and the James family. *A Small Boy and Others* and *Notes of a Son and Brother* more significantly resemble those elegies in which the poet himself enters. In *Lycidas*, for example, the death of Edward King is associated with Milton's own loss of inspiration, challenge to his religion, and loss of faith in his poetic powers. The sense that "sorrow is not dead" thus comes all the more strongly, and the poem goes beyond the apotheosis of King as the "Genius of the shore" to the poet's arising, "Tomorrow to fresh Woods, and Pastures new." The Muse that James feared had left him was not a fickle young thing who might have momentarily played him false but an old dame who might have left him forever. The effort to remember the events of early youth was thus

[6] *Letters*, II, pp. 345-346.

[144]

also an effort to regain his creative powers by reviving the hopes and freshness of youth. Not all of the boyhood of Henry James was spent in strong health and the certainty of great promise. That is abundantly clear. But the memory of other victories over moments of sickness and doubt was itself a source of renewal. He had done it before; he would do it again.

It might be added that James' course here was curiously parallel to Whitman's in writing "Out of the Cradle Endlessly Rocking."[7] At that time Whitman was only thirty-nine or forty, as opposed to James' sixty-eight, but the general fears of loss of audience and lapse of creative powers, followed by a turning to memories of childhood, are very similar. "A man, yet by these tears a little boy again," Whitman says of himself, and in the poem he is transported back to a summer when he would leave his bed and wander a Long Island beach. As the man seemed to be mocking himself in some barren period, so had the boy crossed "sterile sands" and "patches of briers and blackberries." Early in the summer he had found two shorebirds nesting, then noticed that the female had disappeared, and heard the male mourning his lost love. The bird's song of love and the ocean's song of death—the whisper of the waves "hissing" over the sand —mingled together in songs that began that moment in the boy. And even in the midst of the poem Whitman feels his own songs return to him. He tells the "Demon or bird":

> Now in a moment I know what I am for, I awake,
> And already a thousand singers, a thousand songs,
>   clearer, louder and more sorrowful than yours,
> A thousand warbling echoes have started to life within
>   me, never to die.

This poem, published in 1859, did mark a rejuvenescence for Whitman, and it is plain that James hoped for the same

[7] This resemblance was first pointed out to me by Mr. R. W. B. Lewis.

thing. For James and Whitman, reminiscence was creative and recreative, their Muses "echoes."

These elegiac origins must be kept in mind in considering what James calls the constantly repeated direction of his and his brothers' and sister's education: "Convert, convert, convert!" To announce this theme here, behind descriptions of the mourning and melancholy which preceded the autobiography's writing, is perhaps to imply that it was written only as therapy. It was therapy of a kind, but that is at last merely incidental. The autobiography itself goes on to enumerate so many conversions that one comes to realize that they must have become almost habitual with Henry James. The autobiography was one of the greatest of them. The extent of James' depression is the opposite end of the magnitude of his achievement. The phrases James used in describing to his nephew the effect of Mrs. William James' suggestion that he write of his youth are revealing: "That turn of talk was the germ, it dropped the seed." His figures were always carefully chosen, even when so common as this, and it is also notable that this same one occurs frequently in the autobiography and always in contrast to wastes and deserts. "W.J.," for instance, "flowered in every waste."[8] With the first trip to Europe alone, Henry "planted a seed that was, by my own measure, singularly to sprout and flourish—the harvest of which, I almost permit myself to believe, has even yet not all been gathered" (p. 551). "The fruit of golden youth is all and always golden" (p. 482), he noted, and what is his autobiography if not the gathering?

III

James' youth was golden (that being a reason so many dismiss it as without relevance to other American youths), but it scarcely seemed that way to him at the time. Though he

[8] *Henry James, Autobiography,* ed. Frederick W. Dupee, p. 117. Hereafter references will be given in parentheses.

was apparently a pleasant child he was not one who was in easy compatibility with his restless playfellows or smoothly adjusted to his environment. The essence of it was that the people and places and things that surrounded him were "other" and "queer," a distinctive criticism of nineteenth-century society or of the adult world generally and one that bears a good deal of thought. While it expresses the less articulate discontents of an Oliver Twist, it also anticipates the reiterated bellyaches of Holden Caulfield.

There was, for example, his grandmother Catherine Barber, "dear gentle lady of many cares and anxieties," whose taste was for the popular English women novelists, Mrs. Trollope, Mrs. Gore, Mrs. Marsh, Mrs. Hubback. These she read by the light of "a tall single candle placed, apparently not at all to her discomfort, in that age of sparer and braver habits, straight between the page and her eyes" (p. 5). His first memories of school included the "humiliation . . . that our instructors kept being instructresses." One was a "Miss Rogers (previously of the 'Chelsea Female Institute,' though at the moment of Sixth Avenue this latter)," and she reappears to James wearing gloves and "beat[ing] time with a long black ferule to some species of droning chant or chorus in which we spent most of our hours . . ." (pp. 11-12). The process of growing up was one of gradually becoming aware of the queerness of this little society. James recalls the introduction of Louis De Coppet, born in France, though of an American mother, and especially French for his "treatment of certain of our local names, Ohio and Iowa for instance." With perfect aplomb and no fear of the "circle of little staring and glaring New Yorkers supplied with the usual allowance of fists and boot-toes" he daintily gave these words the pronunciation of the original French explorers, "O-ee-oh and Ee-o-wah" (p. 21).

What did the young Louis do, James asks, but open a vista? The young James could not have put it that way, but with

the presence of Louis he was aware of New York and America
in a new light.

> The plain and happy profusions and advances and suc-
> cesses [of the young nation], as one looks back, reflect
> themselves at every turn; the quick beats of material in-
> crease and multiplication, with plenty of people to tell
> of them and throw up their caps for them; but the edify-
> ing matters to recapture would be the adventures of the
> "higher criticism" so far as there was any—and so far
> too as it might bear on the real quality and virtue of
> things; the state of manners, the terms of intercourse, the
> care for excellence, the sense of appearances, the intel-
> lectual reaction generally.   (p. 23)

Such is the story James in part tells. The family verandah,
when there was one, was a kind of raft of leisure *and excellence* in a great ugly and graceless sea. Otherwise the rural
scene around New York was "but that of our great shame, a
view of the pigs and the shanties and the loose planks and
scattered refuse and rude public ways; never even a field-
path for a gentle walk or a garden nook in afternoon shade."
This sounds like the lament of an expatriate, and it should
be said that James describes the little De Coppet as having
"given the earliest, or at least the most personal, tap to that
pointed prefigurement of the manners of 'Europe,' which,
inserted wedge-like, if not to say peg-like, into my young allegiance, was to split the tender organ into such unequal
halves. His the toy hammer that drove in the very point of
the golden nail." I do not wish, however, to argue James'
criss-crossed allegiances. In these beginning pages he poses as
ever-eager to get abroad—more eager, the evidence suggests,
than he actually was. The thing to recognize is that the idea
of Europe became a point of view on America, became a means
of seeing what was "queer," or what was provincial or grim
or deficient, in the native habitat. Without it the Small Boy

would never have become Henry James, and without it the autobiography would lack that "higher criticism" of American life—criticism rare enough, and extremely rare in American autobiography.

The fate of those ranks of friends and cousins who lived by no other standard than the flapping banner of the time is adequate testimony to the value of the better one James sought. One by one they pass by: Catherine James, "distinguished for nothing whatever so much as for an insatiable love of the dance; that passion in which I think of the 'good,' the best, New York society of the time as having capered and champagned itself away." Robert James, "the eldest of the many light irresponsibles to whom my father was uncle . . . who, almost ghost-fashion, led the cotillion on from generation to generation . . . an immemorial elegant skeleton" (p. 26). The fault of such a class was that it was too simple. Its exclusion from American life was expressed in champagne and the "German"; its respect for Europe was limited to the "Chelsea Female Institute." Meanwhile its own manners granted too much licence in some ways and exercised too much restraint in others. James watched some of his family and friends excessively "tutored and governessed, warned and armed" against healthy social contact, while others freely grew more and more dissipated. In this connection he brings up his "queer and quaint, almost incongruously droll" sense of "being surrounded by a slightly remote, yet dimly rich, outer and quite kindred circle of the tipsy" (p. 29). Every family had its dissipates, and James recounts how he once suspected an innocent and sober visitor of being one. The range of social possibilities was so limited that one either rushed into the category of the busy and made money or else sought pleasure, a search in which one spent money and time in places where people got "tipsy."

James is unique in writing a sort of "autobiography of manners." As a novelist so deeply concerned with manners he might be expected to. The question arises, though, how did he become one in a society which offered so few? How did he even awaken to them in a society so little aware of them? In fact, how did one survive as a frequenter of neither the place of business nor the place of dissipation when these were the only choices? These are some of the questions of the "higher criticism" of American life which James' reminiscences partially answer. In a stunning sentence, one that has won circulation despite the comparative neglect of the autobiographies, James says of the scene of his boyhood: "The field was strictly covered, to my young eyes, I make out, by three classes, the busy, the tipsy, and Daniel Webster" (p. 30).

I noted in sketching the tradition of autobiography in America that it developed so early because there were so few other opportunities for self-knowledge and self-expression. Men were autobiographers because they were not dramatists or poets, titled aristocrats, professional soldiers, dons, or peasants—because there was not that texture of history in which they inherited their identities. James illustrates this when he says that he, and others "who lived at near view of my father's admirable example," were thrown "upon the inward life" (p. 35). The first step in living as neither the tipsy nor the busy was in living inwardly. This does not mean that James immediately commenced juvenile diaries, though that is true in a figurative sense. Life became a kind of unwritten autobiography.[9] One examined everything as closely as if he were actually writing about it. One remembered everything as finely as if it were all written down and safely kept. The "inward life," then, was a place of employment and diversion in lieu of the shop and the tavern, a pattern of manners tufted up on the bare threads of American simplicity. James saw and saw,

[9] In this connection consider these sentences on "William James" from the article by Horace Meyer Kallen in *The Encyclopedia Britannica* (1941 edn.): "The real specific event is the individual; his character, his beliefs, his endeavor are an adventure in autobiography of which the conclusion is not established in advance. He integrates societies as he lives, and he breaks them."

stitched and stitched, until he built up inside himself the rich life which was superficially missing. The passions and the interest were present in the world about him, present from the start, but catching them required a great deal of looking. "To write well and worthily of American things one need even more than elsewhere to be a *master*."[10]

Now in regard to the subject of the inward life, of American manners, and of the profession of letters, it is revealing that the chapter in which James first expands on the state of the arts and the "political order" in the New York of his boyhood is the same one (chapter five) in which he describes his earliest memory. The two realms are brought together by the "inward life," for the inward life depended on both memory and what it could appropriate from art and the outer world. Just what else they have in common, the retained glimpse of the Place Vendôme and the company and work of Washington Irving, Margaret Fuller, or Tom Hicks, James does not bluntly announce. In these early chapters his mind moves forward and back from one topic to another with distressing ease and with little sympathy for the floundering reader, but he thereby brings things together in provocative combinations. The vision of the Place Vendôme slides in behind recollections of General Winfield Scott and James' uncle Captain Robert Temple, his images of American military bearing. Associated with them is his memory of hearing of Louis Philippe's flight to England, leaving the reader a sense of the Small Boy's perplexity: Generals, Kings, Monuments, and the news that one such stable and impressive figure should flee. This, surely, was a more complicated set of events than the American ground was accustomed to, and for a moment the narrative drops back to the subject of young New York ladies. His cousins remained forever "natural" while other girls led fancier lives and still remained "but *feebly* sophisticated." The cousins were more comprehending, different "by reason of the quan-

[10] *Letters*, I, p. 31.

tity of our inward life . . . which made an excellent, in some cases almost incomparable, *fond* for a thicker civility to mix with when growing experience should begin to take that in" (p. 34). There was, for the other children, so little to be sophisticated about or warned against. John Brown's raid, in James' seventeenth year, was "the very first reminder that reached me of our living, on our side [of the Atlantic], in a political order" (p. 34).

By the time James draws around to the subject of the arts and artists, one realizes that there is a submerged equation between the value of the work and the queerness of his early memories of it. Proust uses a similar correspondence in the opening pages of *Swann's Way*, where the adults about the young boy somehow all behave not only quaintly but childishly. For James, the artists were "landscapist Cropseys and Coles and Kensetts, and bust-producing Iveses and Powerses and Moziers" and a circle of females "glossily ringletted and monumentally breastpinned." Poe and Margaret Fuller are remembered with more respect, but for the most part the age of the memory is a sly index of criticism. As he was later to have a richer dose of Europe, so he was also to have a contact with richer artists. But all these contacts mattered in the gradual building up of his "inward life," that is of his powers of perception, his imagination, and his retention of experience.

This is an example of how James composes his old memories, or of how, possibly, they had composed themselves in his consciousness. The "inward life" was not one of conventional and predictable associations but of imaginative ones, which is one reason why it transcended its environment. The inward life was "queer," that is, detached; the environment was "queer," that is, alien to the boy; and the consciousness did "queer" things to its environment. Finally, the boyhood world is quite ancient to the author, but it emerges with such vividness just because the pictorial mind of the beholder was already so active. The accuracy of the image is proof of the intensity of the early imagination. It is also proof of the continuing power of the Master. And under the Master's gallant hand that far-off youth miraculously becomes "golden." It is indeed "the small warm dusky homogeneous New York world of the mid-century," as James calls it at the end of chapter five, but the measure of how it closes in on author and reader is the measure also of how the author had grown out of it and can now magically move the reader in and out of it with him. He learned to live in it by his ability to "convert," and he now goes back into it to show how the conversions were accomplished, making all the while another great conversion.

IV

It is impossible to take complete note of every step of the growth of the Small Boy into the Son and Brother and on to the Master. The parts of the autobiography are too intricately interwoven, and James does not write the kind of chronological history that lends itself most readily to recapitulation. Any respectful and sincere review of the development of the Jamesian imagination would be a biography and would be an impostor even in a whole volume. When Percy Lubbock made his widely quoted remark that James' autobiography showed "that it would be impossible for anyone else to write his life," he went on to explain what it was about that life and memory which made summary impossible.

> His life was no mere succession of facts, such as could be compiled and recorded by another hand; it was a densely knit cluster of emotions and memories, each one steeped in lights and colors thrown out by the rest, the whole making up a picture that no one but himself could dream of undertaking to paint.[11]

The wisest course, therefore, is to accept the "densely knit

[11] *Letters*, I, p. xiii.

cluster" for the fine work it is, and then to follow the important strands. The most important, certainly, is the one of the "inward life." Others are ways it, in turn, looked outward: in "gaping," in schools, in contact with father, brothers, and friends, in Europe, and in art. Trace them carefully, particularly in the first half of the *Small Boy*, and one can see how they harmonize and progress through the rest of the autobiography. All in all they are a unique order and a vivid image of James' belief.

Having spoken of James as a meditating small boy in a "queer" old world, I here want to go back to his figure of himself as "gaping." In the stories of his infant "instructresses" he includes an anecdote of the early walks home from school (pp. 15-17). One route went by some construction work on the Hudson River Railroad; the other went by a big brown house in the middle of spacious lawns and fields. At the construction site there was a good deal of blasting, and it was a "point of honour . . . nobly to defy the danger" and to walk near the waving of flags and the hurtling fragments of exploded rock. With a humorous dramatization of himself, James implies that he more frequently underwent the dangers of the other walk. In the "grounds" of the brown house was a "romantic view of browsing and pecking and parading creatures . . . : two or three elegant little cows of refined form and colour, two or three nibbling fawns and a larger company, above all, of peacocks and guineafowl, . . ." The whole autobiography, in effect, opens up behind this picture of the small boy gaping through the fence around this scene. As Whitman could recall the boy listening to the bird sing, so James can again "watch the small boy dawdle and gape," smelling "the cold dusty paint and iron as the rails . . . rub his contemplative nose." The image is expanded ("exploded," so to speak) to enormous importance. As opposed to the "riot" of the waving flags and whistling rock, "the only form of riot or revel ever known to me would be that of the visiting mind." The boy might there have had a "warning of all that was to be for him, and he might well have been even happier than he was."

The autobiographer obviously relished the privileges of hindsight in telling such a story. It is as surely a tale of golden youth from the memory of a silver head as any told by the aged Franklin or the aged Adams. But it satisfactorily accomplishes the function of such tales: it illustrates how the boy became the man. Beyond such generalities as that, it describes James' link between the "inward life" and the world of "others." Without the gaping, without the action of the lively eyes which stare from the frontispiece of *A Small Boy*, there would be no *sociable* inner life. I say *sociable* because this seems a crucial factor in the value of James' autobiography. Henry was not exclusively, in his brother's famous phrase, "a native of the James family" but a citizen of both the nations of his youth and the nations of his maturity, a citizen of the world. What makes his autobiography so revealing—so revealing of more than the growth of a remarkable mind—is the sociability of the intercourse between that mind and its environment. The inner life has viable meaning now, just as it did then, because it was so constantly looking outside itself. The endless observing and wondering was its very water and air, keeping it breathing and growing.

Chapter six of *A Small Boy* might whimsically be entitled "Food." It is composed, in a manner apparently quite haphazard, of memories of mere meanderings through the streets of New York: of being taken to the dentist with William, of walking through the downtown markets with his father, and of accompanying his father to the office of the *Tribune*. But from watching all the while, the mind of the young traveler is represented as having become aware of more than plain pedestrian intelligence. At the dentist's office he was allowed unlimited perusal of old copies of *Godey's Lady's Book*, and after the ordeal in the dentist's chair he and William were rewarded with ice cream. Most impressive about the walks through the market was not the dainty speciality of single servings, however, but the open profusion of fruits and vegetables tumbling from every corner. This "cornucopia" briefly recalls the "sort of southern plenty" in which food was consumed in the James household and then the warmth of the family spirit in the elder Henry. At the *Tribune* the father and son learned that one of the reporters had just published a novel. Its title was *Hot Corn*, and its subject "the career of a little girl who hawked that familiar American luxury in the streets." But though Mr. James was given a copy, young Henry heard the donor say that "the work, however engaging, was not one that should be left accessible to an innocent child." James observes the interest attendant to "the mystery of the tabooed book" (p. 45). The other reflection is left to his readers, namely that little boys were permitted peaches and ice cream, bushels of green vegetables, and *Godey's Lady's Book* but not one page of "Hot Corn"!

Such is the order of the imagination and the way it develops meanings from the impact of experience upon it. James repeatedly laments that his autobiography is not the supremely structured sort of work he could produce in fiction. It is, like his education, "no plotted thing at all" (p. 127). It is instead "a tale of assimilations small and fine" (p. 105). Thus the reader must give himself up to following along closely, being led over stretches of apparently endless digressions, for the sake of the sudden recognition scene or moment of illumination in which the path all becomes clear. It becomes clear only to the person willing to admit the Jamesian consciousness into his own. One is obliged to repeat with James the slow progress of the Small Boy. And although this now and then demands the ultimate in patience and unflagging attention, it is rewarding. It is a credible and natural progress, and little by little each short step fits into place.

The theater was significant in James's youth as a kind of ritual of gaping. One cannot learn to pray until he has learned to talk and one cannot learn to watch plays until he has learned to see. The machinery of the theater—the curtains, the stage, the acts and scenes, entrances and exits—made an honorable (if sometimes clumsy) ceremony of gaping, gave manners and form to an intense passion. Roughly a quarter of *A Small Boy* is devoted to the theater. James' memory of old plays, of old actors and actresses and the stages they walked, was thick and also surprisingly accurate.[12] This is perhaps understandable in view of his relentless effort to write plays and his invention of a dramatic method in his novels, but these experiences are not included simply for background to the writing of *Guy Domville*. That "world of queer appreciations," as he calls it, was the site of a great deal of wondering and a large mirror of the old days of boyhood. It was a further refreshment for the inner life.

The things he saw—productions of Shakespeare, sentimental dramatizations of Dickens, *Uncle Tom's Cabin*, and an unknown number of melodramas and spectacles and farces—are of little importance compared to the value he wrung out of them. He fastens onto them because they were a part of his education, like the stream of Westerns and television mysteries a boy might see today, and he treats them not as mirrors of Nature but, with the accompanying details of the lives of the performers and the Lyceums, Museums, Lecture Rooms, and Academies in which they performed, as mirrors of the place and the times. The proof that there was a relationship between the queerness of the stage and the queerness of old New York is the tale of the Wyckoff family that bursts in upon the middle of these memories. They were straight out of

---

[12] For further discussion of the range of James' theatrical reminiscences and a critique of their accuracy, see Leon Edel's introduction to *The Complete Plays of Henry James* (Philadelphia and New York, 1949), especially pp. 19-32; Edel's *Henry James: The Untried Years* (Philadelphia and New York, 1953), especially pp. 100-102; and Henry James, *The Scenic Art*, ed. Allan Wade (New Brunswick, N.J., 1948), especially pp. xi-xxv.

Dickens and the versions of Dickens seen at theaters: "cousin Henry was more or less another Mr. Dick, just as cousin Helen was in her relation to him more or less another Miss Trotwood" (p. 84). Toward both subjects James finally adopted an attitude which was beyond criticism. "We needn't be strenuous about them unless we particularly want to, and are glad to remember in season all that this would imply of the strenuous about our own *origines*" (p. 65).

He more than remembers, however, the occasion on which he first became aware of the possibility of criticism, of the intervention of intelligence between the viewer and the play. *Uncle Tom's Cabin* had then reached the height of its fame, and "instead of making even one of the cheap short cuts through the medium in which books breathe, even as fishes in water, [the subject of the book] went gaily roundabout it altogether, as if a fish, a wonderful 'leaping' fish, had simply flown through the air." Never having been in the medium of a book, it "flutter[ed] down on every stage" (p. 92). James saw it twice. The first time he was emotionally caught up. In going the second time, with his family, he recalls that "the point exactly was that we attended this spectacle just in order *not* to be beguiled." The result of the family's ironic guard was an initiation: a "glimpse of that possibility of a 'free play of mind' over a subject which was to throw him with force at a later stage of culture, when subjects had considerably multiplied, into the critical arms of Matthew Arnold." Appreciation was improved, and criticism could later be applied even to Arnold.

The end of these first reflections upon the theater comes in chapter thirteen in an account of some visits with cousins in Albany and along the Hudson. One visit included a tour of Sing-Sing Prison. Various are his remarks upon that introduction, but outstanding is his recognition, brought to mind by the enviable state of the prisoners at their ease, of the otherness of people about him. From earliest times he envied other people and would have gladly changed places with them. It was not that their lives were always so much richer, but that his seemed so much poorer. This observation has come up in the company of prisoners and wrongdoers, and the context makes emphatic his distinction between envy and jealousy. Envy engendered curiosity (or was engendered by it): it asked to know what was on the other side of the glass, the other side of the bars, the further rim of the horizon. Jealousy was akin to competing, "a business having in it [for James] a displeasing ferocity. If competing was bad snatching was therefore still worse, and jealousy was a sort of spiritual snatching" (p. 101). In knowing that what he *envied* was always unobtainable was his protection against active measures to obtain it. In it also was his constant abandonment of himself to "visions." The state of another person was as near and yet as far as the state of the prisoner behind bars. Furthermore, any direct attempt upon that state was "bad," would land him behind bars himself. Envy of the sweeter life, the supposed "richer consciousness" of other people led instead to visions of their condition, and this was a wellspring of the inner life.

The last of the memories in chapter thirteen concerns a visit with his father to a sister, Mrs. Temple, who was desperately sick. On hand also was Henry's cousin Marie James. She was a person of great interest to young Henry, first because she had been born in Paris and second because he had heard that she was "spoiled." Henry and his brothers and sister, he says, were not spoiled ("I think we even rather missed it") so that this trait was known to him only from books, thereby seeming all the more romantic. He watched her closely, and when her father told her to go to bed he watched her even more closely, feeling a little directed by that decree himself. Marie waited, and when her father told her a second time she ran across the room to appeal to her mother. The appeal, says James, "drew from my aunt the simple phrase that was from that moment so preposterously to 'count' for me. 'Come now, my dear; don't make a scene—I *insist* upon your not making a scene!' " Henry had never heard the expression before. "Life at these intensities clearly became 'scenes'; but the great thing, the immense illumination, was that we could make them or not as we chose" (p. 107).

The hours spent at the theater, the hours of "gaping," and the "visions" of other lives are thus brought together in a sense of the active connection between art and life. "It was a long time of course before I began to distinguish between those within our compass more particularly as spoiled and those producible on a different basis and which should involve detachment, involve presence of mind"; but the awareness had come that life somehow could have the quality of art. James' own mind, he explained two pages before, had been prepared for this idea, "arranged as a stage for the procession and exhibition of appearances." The Marie "scene" thus came as a climax upon the stage of his own mind as well as upon the stage of the Aunt's house. Just as surely as he prepared his readers for this moment with initially unrelated material, so he himself had somehow prepared for it. Art, such as the creation of scenes, could make life, but art also *did* make life. Life followed the mysterious and little-marked path of a rather unclear play or obscure work of fiction. By the same token, the "good life" was ideally life as art, something resembling life in a good play. Life could be created in art; scenes could be imagined or "made up." That is understood too. But in a way the art was already there, antecedent to the life, if one only had the discernment and acumen to pick it out. Furthermore, life was open to criticism: it was a succession of "scenes," and one needed to distinguish between those of Marie and those done with detachment and presence of mind. Life conceived of as art, life closely observed, scrutinized, criticized, and forced into meanings, forced to yield intelligence, was consequently an esthetic experience.

V

At the end of chapter thirteen James turns back to his more ordinary education, that is to schools. The Jameses changed schools with disconcerting rapidity, and Henry's recollections of his numerous halls and pedagogues constitute some of the more amusing portions of his autobiography. There was, for example, a school predominantly of "bookkeeping," which was very much like a "shop." Its proprietors were "Messrs. Forest and Quackenboss," one of them "the dryest of all our founts of knowledge" and the other "come down to our generation from a legendary past and with a striking resemblance of head and general air to Benjamin Franklin." At another stop in their course of schooling he and William had as writing-master Mr. Dolmidge, "a pure pen-holder of a man," and as drawing-master Mr. Coe, a man of great height and build who was always distributing very small cards with pictures to be copied, "as if some mighty bird had laid diminutive eggs."

At the time, however, few of these institutions were genial and even fewer of them were amusing. Most of them were just plain grim and dreary and of little immediate educational value. The Small Boy felt himself "inapt" at what was being taught and through his inaptitudes saw and felt a "queerness" about the whole experience. He suffered his way along, lost except for "a general lucid consciousness (lucid, that is, for my tender years); which I clutched with a sense of its value." The schools pursued their various but limited ends, and meanwhile James resorted to his imagination to learn entirely different things.

There presumably was the interest—in the intensity and plausibility and variety of the irrelevance: an irrelevance

which, for instance, made all pastors and masters, and
especially all fellow-occupants of benches and desks, all
elbowing and kicking presences within touch or view, so
many monsters and horrors, so many wonders and splen-
dours and mysteries, but never, so far as I can recollect,
realities of relation, dispensers either of knowledge or
of fate, playmates, intimates, mere coævals and co-
equals.   (p. 112)

It is noteworthy that James' complaint with his schools
and schooling was esthetic. It is more a *distaste* than an argument that he learned little or that they were intellectually arid
or—as Adams said of his—that they were historically back-
ward. Phrases like "fellow-occupants of benches and desks, all
elbowing and kicking presences" are horribly vivid in their
evocation of how he must have felt. At the "Institution
Vergnès" most of the students were "small homesick Cubans
and Mexicans," and the consequence of their homesickness
and their dark skin was "a greasy gloom." All the while, the
teachers were "constantly in a rage" and the air was full of
shrillness and "dodged" textbooks (p. 114). With the students there he was sympathetic. At other places where there
were numbers of aggressive students of arithmetic, he was
aggravated to find them "all agog . . . with the benefit of their
knowledge." Though he then had no name for it, he somehow
recognized that their omnipresent and advertised achievements, so prophetic of the kind of men they were to become,
represented "art without grace, or (what after a fashion came
to the same thing) presence without type." The description of
one boy makes perfectly clear James' visual *sense* of his environment, his appreciation of it on primarily esthetic grounds.
The boy's name was Simpson, and "he reeked . . . with strange
accomplishment—no single show of which but was accompanied in him by a smart protrusion of the lower lip, a crude

complacency of power, that almost crushed me to sadness" (pp. 128-129).

In a much earlier passage, just after the image of the Small Boy gaping at peacocks on the grounds of the brown house, James stated his opinion "that no education avails for the intelligence that doesn't stir in it some subjective passion, and that on the other hand almost anything that does so act is largely educative . . ." (p. 17). Various critics might take or have taken this as an intentional answer to *The Education of Henry Adams*.[13] It may apply to Adams' early years, but it scarcely applies to the older Adams, who had made an organic education the driving purpose of his life. In any case, it is the taproot of any fruitful education, and it must have nourished James from the start, for the principle was highly appreciated by Henry Senior.

The simple truth about James' "formal education," if that name can be given to such a formless attendance, is that it stirred many passions but never the anticipated ones. It is not exactly right to say of him, as people like to say of men of genius, that "he got little out of school." Unlike William, he always felt that he got a great deal; but he could not then see that what he got really had little to do with any particular school or with what that school was supposed to give or what William expected it to give. His passion was for gaping and imagining, and his schools supplied him with ample opportunity for this, even while not serving him as they were intended to.

It was a case of "conversion." The "inward perversity," as he here chooses to call it, "works by converting to its uses things vain and unintended, to the great discomposure of their prepared opposites, which it by the same stroke so often reduces to naught . . ." (p. 122). James compares the process to al-

---

[13] See T. S. Eliot, "A Sceptical Patrician," *The Athenæum*, (May 23, 1919), 361-362; J. C. Levenson, *The Mind and Art of Henry Adams* (Boston, 1957), p. 386; Roy Pascal, *Design and Truth in Autobiography* (London, 1960), pp. 141-142.

chemy, yet declares pointedly that the gold thus created was never the gold of "success" or material rewards. Such a thing would never have been dreamed of in the household of Henry James, Sr., to whom the son renders great thanks. The vision the father projected as most desirable was nothing other than "Virtue" itself. But in the James family, at least to Henry, Jr.'s thinking, "Virtue" was a condition of sensibility.

VI

What James longed for in his education, then, were more impressions, more "vistas," more "scenes," and more luxurious gaping. If the reader of his autobiography now and then inclines toward a sort of healthy irreverence, the extent and the objects of this longing tend to look a little silly. James gathered up every foretaste of Europe the way other boys collect turtles and tin soldiers. A bookstore had "the English smell." A favorite picture book was one of the mansions of England. European plays and paintings had a double appeal. "Nothing seemed to matter at all but that I should become personally and incredibly acquainted with Piccadilly and Richmond Park and Ham Common." Europe summed up Art and Manners, all that seemed missing or only sketchily provided for in the United States. The thing that needs to be said about these elaborate daydreams—and James the old man seems to delight in their boyish extravagance—is that they were in the finest sense so unspecific. They were not ambitions of snatching possession. They were not notions of giddy sensation. And they were not "merely" esthetic. It may be that the boy's yearnings did partake of some of these qualities, but that is immaterial. The Master (and he is the primary source of interest) presents him as wanting to be in Europe simply to look and absorb. Such a wish is in one respect the ultimate in empty aimlessness. But James' passionate preparation refutes that charge. The experience of Europe was the next course in his real education—that is, in the growth of his inner life.

One can further illustrate this unspecific nature of James' passion by comparing him with another autobiographer of youthful travel, George Moore. Suffocating in his Irish homeland, Moore dreamed of Paris as restlessly as James did of Europe. But for him Paris was a definite number of sweet abandonments. It was the life of an art student: polkas, mistresses, gaslight, and red wine. For Moore, and for members of the esthetic movement, life was an esthetic experience so long as it was an esthetic life. Specific directions like these were in effect biases. Moore, as W. B. Yeats has said, "sacrificed all that seemed to other men good breeding, honor, friendship, in pursuit of what he considered the root facts of life."[14] A preconception of "the root facts of life" was exactly what James luckily lacked. To have had one would have imposed another of the very kind of limitations upon experience which James, and the rest of his family, were seeking to lift.

Europe was a riot of impressions, a kind of long awaited vast enlargement of the excitements behind the fence of the brown mansion in New York. The chapter just before the one describing the family's arrival ends with the Small Boy asking innocent but confounding questions about paintings of Florence and of a "view in Tuscany" (p. 154). The last incident recalled of the United States is one emblematic "of the family-party smallness of the old New York," while the arrival in London commences with the young Henry an "overflow" of the hired carriage and "thrilled with the spectacle my seat beside the coachman so amply commanded" (p. 157). Europe was "a sensuous education," as Henry, Sr., had written Emerson, but even more of a one than the father had expected. When James quoted that letter in *Notes* (p. 353), he changed his father's justification of European travel from "get a better sensuous education than they [the children] are likely to get here" to "get such a sensuous education as they

---

[14] "Dramatis Personae," in *Autobiographies* (London, 1961), p. 403.

can't get here."[15] The young James is made literally breath-less from the impact of the new sensations. He disembarked suffering a recurrence of malaria contracted the summer be-fore in Staten Island, but the chills of the disease are used to reinforce the fevers of the new vistas. Similarly, when he came down with typhus in Boulogne two summers later, it was not so much the sickness that is seen to level him as the force of the accumulated sights and their significance. *A Small Boy* concludes with James fainting: "I fell into a lapse of consciousness that I shall conveniently here treat as a con-siderable gap" (p. 236). Loss of consciousness in all its defini-tions—for loss of consciousness was loss of impressions, loss of life, and therefore an eminently suitable interruption of the narrative.

The range of the memories is immense. But they are not random. Each one seems to blend the boy's passionate prepara-tion, his related experiences of art, and his tireless powers of observation. In chapter twenty-two of *Small Boy*, for instance, James tells of the family's return to England from the Con-tinent in the autumn of 1855 and of its settlement in Lon-don for the winter. This chapter, which may be said to begin with a supper of "cold roast beef and bread and cheese and ale" at a London coffee-house, is a sort of sketch of the "old" London. The city wears a sinister look. James' order of as-sociations leads him from his father's employment of a tutor to his and William's looking at ladies and gentlemen at archery in St. John's Wood, to reflections of Dickens and Thackeray and to figures in Madame Tussaud's wax museum. Her "Chamber of Horrors" leads in turn into a recital of the comings and goings of the family's governesses, a juxta-position which seems like a footnote to *The Turn of the Screw*. From here he wanders deeper into the scenery of "old" London and remarks upon the stares which he and William

[15] Edel, *Untried Years*, p. 118.

used to receive on their walks. The chapter ends with a memory from several years later when Henry and his father had again just arrived in London from the Continent.

> It was a soft June evening, with a lingering light and swarming crowds, as they then seemed to me, of figures reminding me of George Cruikshank's Artful Dodger and his Bill Sikes and his Nancy, only with the bigger brutality of life, which pressed upon the cab, the early-Victorian fourwheeler, as we jogged over the Bridge, and cropped up in more and more gas-lit patches for all our course, culminating, somewhere far to the west, in the vivid picture, framed by the cab-window, of a woman reeling backward as a man felled her to the ground with a blow in the face.   (p. 175)

The autobiography has a greater compass of observation than is generally thought. However, this passage is even more typical of James' memories for the connection it has with a previous experience of art. As is often the case, the art is that of Charles Dickens and his illustrator. The books and the pictures are demonstrated to have prepared the way for the apprehension of the "life," arranged the mental stage. Then, as if to confuse and deny any attempt to separate "art" and "life," the glimpse of the latter comes as "the vivid picture, framed by the cab-window." This technique is familiar to students of James' "scenic method." What is remarkable is not that the boy saw the action as a picture within a frame, but that the autobiographer continues to see it that way—the boy "set" in the coach, the event "set" in the window. Art is used not only as a preparation for life but as an enhancement of seeing. Without art sight is deprived of an essential resource. It bears notice that in the ensuing sentences there is no editorializing and no rendition of Henry's boyhood reaction or his conversation with his father. He finishes instead with praise of Hogarth (recourse to another artist)

[167]

and comments on the London of his present day. If one can *see* clearly enough, there is little left to say. Under a high enough pressure art supplies the morality.

James retained this image as a sort of landmark in his experience. Other images were grouped around it. It was an aspect of London, a shock to his own innocence, and a sign of the meaning of horror. In the broader perspective, it is included in the autobiography because it is not only a part of the growth of his imagination but a part of his own character. Being able to recollect it and being able to revive it in all its grimness is an assurance of the survival of his literary powers and also of his strength of being. Should he forget it or should it cease to have meaning for him, he would no longer be Henry James, no longer be himself. It defines an aspect of London, describes the state of the poor, and represents conditions at a certain moment in history, but it does all these things while also expressing a part of the picture of Henry James. This is James the observer, and his inner and outer observations, his observations through art and through life were constantly related.

The sociability and generality of these observations should give *A Small Boy and Others* and *Notes of a Son and Brother* interest for a large audience. The books are not the narrow history of the growth of a writer, but the broad and searching history of the growth of an imagination. Their readership should not be limited to students and critics of James' fiction. From this audience they have received the highest praise, but still in all they are regarded as tangential, as stepchildren or as side lights to the greater action. This attitude is accepted by no less an authority than the autobiographies' modern editor, Frederick W. Dupee, who says they belong to the period of "summing-up which began with *The American Scene* . . . and continued with the prefaces to the 'New York Edition'" (p. xi). In Dupee's equation, "the prefaces are his critical justification of his practice as a novelist; the autobiography his

revelation of the man within the novelist." The same thinking comes in a different form from students of autobiography.
Roy Pascal, for example, discusses them in his chapter on
"The Autobiography of the Poet." To him they are the life
of an artist, as if that is somehow different from the life of
a man. This is a vitiating concept, partaking of the journalistic
notion that politicians must always be given the "life of a
politician," actresses the "life of an actress," and so forth. I
grant that in the case of many empty figures of prominence
this is all their lives have to offer, but great autobiography,
like great art, transcends its subject. Inferior autobiography
may carry the subtitle of its author's profession or trade, just
as inferior novels are stories of types. But no one calls Franklin's *Autobiography* "the story of a Philadelphia printer,"
and few but Fielding have ever called *Tom Jones* "The History of a Foundling."

The fact of the matter is that the author himself was aware
of the practice of notching people's ears with their occupations, birthplace, and citizenship; and in consequence he has
taken measures against it. In some ways he has rubbed out all
the marks, and in others he has painted on his own. For one
thing, the practice was indicative of the simplicity of American
manners. In this regard it also was the cause of a standing
family joke about Henry, Sr. James explains how the brutish
Simpson boy had let it be known "that the author of *his* being
. . . was in the business of a stevedore" and this prompted
the question of what the James father "*was*." This is reported
to have amused him, and James' version of the answer is:
" 'Say I'm a philosopher, say I'm a seeker for truth, say I'm
a lover of my kind, say I'm an author of books if you like; or,
best of all, just say I'm a Student' " (p. 278). The father
was similarly without categories about his religion. To the
children their "pewless state" was as much of a discredit
as "a houseless or a cookless" one, but Henry, Sr., replied
"that we could plead nothing less than the whole privilege

of Christendom and that there was no communion, even that
of the Catholics, even that of the Jews, even that of the
Swedenborgians, from which we need find ourselves excluded" (pp. 133-134). The lack of the usual social labels
was an early encouragement of individuality. The father was
even constitutionally reluctant to see his sons assign themselves to a profession, for whether it was writing, painting,
or medicine he felt all of them "narrowing." He always
wanted more than any single one represented.

> What we were to do instead was just to *be* something,
> something unconnected with specific doing, something
> free and uncommitted, something finer in short than
> being *that*, whatever it was, might consist of. (p. 268)

Henry did not entirely agree with his father's broad universalism. There is, in these memories of the far-flung and
various outcroppings of it, a sort of detachment and amusement. His brother Garth Wilkinson (named after one of
Henry, Sr.'s, philosopher friends) was the most extreme em-
bodiment of the father's sublime sociability, and Henry recognized early that there was much to be gained by a concentration of talents. Wilky made him "tormentedly aware" that
even with many ways of taking life, "we are condemned practically to a choice . . . reduced to the use of but one, at the
best, which it is our interest to make the most of, since we may
indeed sometimes make much" (p. 163). Therefore, once
Henry knew he wanted to be a writer he went to work at it
with admirable concentration. His progress was not easy, but
his application was passionate. This is most evident in *Notes
of a Son and Brother*, for it naturally contains more of the
matter of his literary apprenticeship than the history of his
boyhood.

So if these volumes are the "life of a writer," that is because writing was such a natural fulfillment of his life. James

was first of all a man of imagination and a man who lived by his eyes. In due course, however, it became evident that such a man was also an artist, and specifically a painter of scenes and a man who wrote. Leon Edel and others have frequently commented on the way he has omitted from *Notes* many of the circumstances of the beginning of his career.[16] The customary explanations of these omissions invoke James' respect for his privacy and his effort in his older years to "re-write" the story of his youth. He was just as anxious to blot out the traces of his premature scribblings as he was to revise the style of his early novels. And he wished, this theory goes on, to idealize the history of his authorship, disencumbering it of failures and false starts. It should be added, however, that to have included in his autobiography all the details of his literary beginnings would have made the autobiography too simply the "life of a writer." As it is, free of intervening and unbalancing statistics of this sort, the volumes have a more general and universal appeal. That he may (or may not) have intended them to have this appeal is, of course, no assurance that they do, but they reward reading in the light of this higher intention. James converted his father's vocation of universalism into a vocation as artist, but the artist became, in turn, a universal.

VII

Now I have said above that James' solace in the American dearth of rich appearances was in the "inward life" and that this life was fed by books, plays, and paintings and by "gaping." The realism and sociability of the inner life was increased by the accuracy and perceptiveness of the gaping; and the gaping, on the other hand, was stimulated by art. Art was not only a subject for scrutiny but also a method. It was the picture or the play, and it was also the techniques

[16] *Untried Years,* pp. 215-216; *Literary Biography,* pp. 43-46.

by which they were made vivid and compelling. In the broader term "scene" James brought "art" and "life" together, for it took in everything from the tantrums of a spoiled cousin and the subject of a painting to the life of a nation, "The American Scene." Scenes could arise on their own, they could be "made up," or they could furtively lurk just beneath the surface, needing the force of art (method) to bring them attention and significance. This last kind was in a sense the most interesting because it presented the greatest challenge to perception and because it combined both art and life. The meaning lay in the order (either as sequence or as arrangement) that had been built up in the viewer's consciousness. In that case "life" was "art" because it seemed to have a method and because it became a subject for intelligence and, in the fond phrase of Arnold, "the free play of mind." In making life an esthetic experience, then, James was not preaching art for art's sake but devoting to life the powers of taste, thought, and disciplined sight. Life faced criticism.

This may not sound unusual until one places beside it other ways of "taking life" (to use James' phrase). There is, for example, the traditional Christian concept, illustrated in the autobiography of St. Augustine, of life as service to God, in which God alone knows its order and meaning and in which man comprehends as much as he ever may in his obedience to Him. There is, to give my second example, the concept of Benjamin Franklin in which both the heavens and the earth follow rational laws which man can understand. In the meantime, Franklin's vision of service to God was in service to his fellow man. Adams' course, seeing Christianity threatened by science and seeing science awaken forces of technology and wealth which Franklin's ideal of service was powerless to control, lay in working out the historical laws by which man and society would continue to change. While James, more aware of the religious feeling than of religion and finding the order of industry crude and spiritless, made his life have the order and passion of art. To devote to life the best of one's taste, intelligence and perception was only in the most worthy tradition; the remarkable fact was the new basis on which he did it.

The strength of James' religious application of esthetic standards to life is subtly yet inescapably revealed in the chapter in *Notes* in which he commemorates his early Newport years and his novitiate in art with John La Farge. The constant effort, he says, was to bring the "forces about us" to the "level of representation."

> Anything suggestive or significant, anything promising or interesting, anything in the least finely charming above all, immensely counted, claimed tendance and protection, almost claimed, or at any rate enjoyed, worship; as for that matter anything finely charming does, quite rightly, anywhere.   (p. 281)

Simply to point out the metaphors and the religious images here is sufficient evidence for the depth of this passion, though that alone can not convey the genuinely religious atmosphere built up around the experience. For the group of young men gathered about William Morris Hunt's studio, Minnie Temple was "the supreme case of a taste for life as life," and with her grace and moral spontaneity she was "the very muse or amateur priestess of rash speculation" (p. 283). Hunt's studio was a "temple," and though James recalls himself to have entered "by the back door"—the one of honor reserved for more promising painters like William James, Hunt, and La Farge—James also recalls that he learned more there than from the curate of Trinity Church. The "tuition 'in the higher branches' " with Rev. Leverett "failed to give me the impression that anything worth naming had opened out to me, whereas in the studio I was at the threshold of a world" (p. 285).

Notes of a Son and Brother continues the thread of memories of personal and family experience so delicately thrown in the first volume. The Son and Brother, however, is older than the Small Boy, and his studies and his observations of ways of "taking life" are that much more conscious and diligent. One might expect radical differences and changes, but about the most prominent is that *Notes* contains passages from family letters and *A Small Boy* does not. James the author, as Theodora Bosanquet said, had finally brought William "to an age for writing letters,"[17] his earliest memories having been enough for a whole book. The letters signal, in a way, the fact that James the young man had now become aware of people as separate individuals with their own multiple concerns and not just as "others" who existed only as near and far areas of his private experience. This makes them, however, that much more interesting to the young James and that much more valuable as methods and "notes" of perception. Other people become points of reference in the grand and spiritual question of how to "take life."

But the autobiography as a whole bristles with names, and almost all of them represent, like little Louis De Coppet of *A Small Boy*, a Value. James did not have the autobiographer's vice of complimenting friends, damning enemies, and stuffing the pages with stories of his famous acquaintances. Or, perhaps more correctly, he practiced this convention as a virtue, bringing people in naturally and inevitably according to the role they played in the author's own history and in the relation they hold to the themes of his book. They are all part of the "assimilations small and fine."

Such a person is "our kinsman Robert Temple the younger," the eldest brother of Minnie Temple. At a fairly young age, "soon after the death of his parents," he was sent away to "an unheard-of school in a remote corner of Scotland" and forever after he became a sign to Henry of "what

[17] *Henry James at Work* (London, 1924), p. 11.

Europe again, with the opportunity so given, was going to proceed to." Such cases were fairly common in the Jameses' circle, though still rare enough to be objects of curiosity. He became "a character," in James' opinion, "in the sense in which 'people in books' were characters, and other people, roundabout us, were somehow not"; and this, needless to say, further embellished his interest. When he first came home James had a chance to review the progress. What had happened, in the modern idiom, was that he had become the professional expatriate, the man whom Europe had civilized beyond civility. "He rose before us, tall and goodlooking and easy, as a figure of an oddly *civilized* perversity . . ." (p. 323). As time went on he was "to neglect no occasion, however frankly forbidding, for graceless adventure" and to become more derisive, more mocking. Mixed with this, on the other hand, was a sufficient amount of education and elegance to make him "successfully impertinent," particularly in his letters. For James, who seems constantly to have waited for the best in people, this "just saved him," that is until a later age when he appears to have dropped into a state of unrelieved "sardonic cynicism." One of the shocks he delivered to his family was his conversion—while in Scotland, of all places—to Catholicism; yet when back in Newport his endless banter never approached the subject of his "faith." The surprise to Henry was "that here was a creature quite amusedly and perceptively, quite attentively and, after a fashion, profitably, living without a single one of the elements of [the inward] life . . ." (p. 325). Those were the elements James "would most have missed if deprived of them" and Robert Temple had none.

Against Temple might be placed Vernon King, from the closing pages of *A Small Boy*. He had been given as strong or stronger a dose of Europe, only at the hands of a strenuous and domineering mother and sister. James describes him as "always smiling and catching his breath a little as from a mixture of eagerness and shyness." In a way, he had been fed so thoroughly on Europe and culture that he could never digest it all. The consequence was that when the Civil War broke out while he was in the United States attending Harvard Law School, he promptly and independently went off and enlisted. He had no commission, and he certainly did not have the approval of the proud mother, who was, on top of everything else, "sharply hostile to the action of the North." The "layers of educational varnish" fell clean away, and he was wounded in battle in Virginia. His mother had briefly returned to America, and while she nursed him back to health she believed he had promised not to return to the front. Whether there was such a pledge or not, he in fact did re-enlist and was killed near Richmond (pp. 219-222).

These stories of Robert Temple and Vernon King are not included as garrulous anecdotes or even as side lights to the "question of Europe." They are small blooms from the main theme of the autobiography. The great question, which becomes sharper and sharper toward the end of *Notes* is the one of how and for what, in James' plain phrase, to "take life." This subject ripens side by side with the ripening of the young Henry's powers as an artist, and the careful reader cannot escape the general conclusion that James lived his own life so richly because he was an artist and also was an artist because his life was so rich. Part of being one—a person "in whom contemplation takes so much the place of action"— lay in imagining the life of other persons, in not only observing them but observing *from* them.

It is well known that the second volume of the autobiography ends with a chapter of letters from Minnie Temple to John Chipman Gray. But this chapter is frequently isolated from the others as only a fine memorial to the heroic cousin who was the model for Millie Theale in *The Wings of the Dove*. Actually James pays other tributes to her in *Notes*, and this final chapter is the climax of them and the greatest example of the styles of life the book projects. Beginning with the story of James' own life in the schools of Geneva, the second volume progresses through sketches of the "values" represented by a score of people and their experiences: Henry, Sr., William, Wilky and Robertson James, Mrs. James, John La Farge, William Morris Hunt, Robert Temple, Harvard classmates, Boston men of letters, and fellow boarders at James' Cambridge rooming house. The progress is not even, and it is only roughly chronological. What holds them together is the fact of their interest, past and present, to James himself and to his developing interest in life and art.

One of the most important indices of the influence of these men and events on James is the imagery in which he recalls them. Certain people, for example, are "ghosts," like Robert James, who was left in *A Small Boy*, leading "the cotillion on from generation to generation . . . an immemorial elegant skeleton." His opposite number in *Notes* is Chauncey Wright, the scholar, who seems to call to Henry from the depths of his library sofa, " 'But what then are you going to do for me?' " (p. 406). He haunts the autobiographer not necessarily because he is dead or nearly forgotten but primarily because he seemed sterile and pathetic even in his life. He was "wasted and doomed, the biggest at once and the gentlest, of the great intending and unproducing (in anything like the just degree) bachelors of philosophy, bachelors of attitude and life" (p. 406). He emerges from the sofa as James is quoting letters from his father written while Henry was abroad in the 1870's, so that the contrast between Wright (and those others of his circle) and Henry himself is here at the greatest. Had he time, had he room, in his life and his book, he would do more for this "good society that was helplessly to miss a right chronicler," but the best he can do is look "wistfully after them as they go" and ask them "to turn a moment more before disappearing."

It was in this society that James met Charles Dickens in 1867. Dickens, commencing his American readings, had been invited to a dinner party at Charles Eliot Norton's. By special arrangement Henry and his friend Arthur Sedgwick dropped in after the meal and there they were introduced, just for a moment, to the guest of honor. The incident could have been dumbly anticlimactic and the preservation of it could have been mere name-dropping. Instead, the sense James carried away was of Dickens' meeting him "with a straight inscrutability, a merciless *military* eye." There was an "economy of apprehension" in it which indicated both the author's great strength and also his great fatigue, the wear of "his monstrous 'readings'" which took so much when there was so little left. This is what made the moment so full of action for James, and he says, "It was as if I had carried off my strange treasure just exactly from under the merciless military eye—placed there on guard of the secret" (p. 390). This image of Dickens is heightened by the reappearance of military imagery in a later chapter in which James equates his own early break-through as an author with the Northern victory in the Civil War, and also by the universal importance James attaches to seeing and gaping. Chauncey Wright had "strange conflictingly conscious light blue eyes"—the opposite of Dickens. And for Henry, "when one should cease to live in large measure by one's eyes (with the imagination of course all the while waiting on this) one would have taken the longest step towards not living at all" (p. 443).

VIII

James' affirmation of "living" seems to be both the vaguest and also the highest of values. In the lives of his fictional heroes and heroines (Hyacinth Robinson, Fleda Vetch, Lambert Strether, or Millie Theale) and in the lives of the "characters" of the autobiography (Henry, Sr., Mrs. James,

William, himself, and Minnie Temple) this great value, however various its manifestations, acquires a reality that is impressive to behold. None are great men of action like Franklin and not all of them can claim great friends and inside knowledge of great historical forces like Adams. What they do have in common with Franklin and Adams is an integrity, a completeness of body and soul, which imparts an immortality.

In *Notes of a Son and Brother* Minnie Temple, as I have already said, arises as the person most gifted with a taste for life. She is first celebrated fairly early in the book as an inspiring influence on Henry's and William's life in Newport after their return from Europe in 1860. At that time, while Henry was dabbling in painting and then, at the suggestion of John La Farge, turned to writing, the "originality, vivacity, audacity, generosity, of her spirit" made her a regular conversational resource and an outstanding presence in the local "scene." In the last chapter James also recalls a vacation with her and Oliver Wendell Holmes, Jr., and John Chipman Gray in the White Mountains in July 1865, though the date and names are not included in his account.[18] Of that experience James remarks that she was the heroine of their drama. He does not mean the word in the "pompous or romantic sense" but in "the technical or logical," meaning that "everything that took place around her took place as if primarily in relation to her and in her interest: that is in the interest of drawing her out and displaying her the more" (p. 509). Her letters to Gray, which were mainly of the years 1869-1870, while Henry was in Europe, back up everything that he has said of her. She was indeed "the very figure and image of a felt interest in life."

Her predicament, like that of Millie Theale, is in its surfaces so melodramatic, so soap-operatic, that it is easy for the critic to fall into appreciations barely above the common-

[18] Edel, *Untried Years*, pp. 230-231.

place. The subject of an attractive woman in her early twenties plagued with a fatal disease is a difficult one to treat with originality and fresh sympathy. What keeps James from slipping into the maudlin is the use of her letters as well as his own strong sensibility, and what keeps her letters above the merely tearful is her own indomitable personality. The reader follows her in her removals from one city to another and awaits other plans to put her in a better climate by sending her to Rome or California. The course of her tuberculosis sets on with increasingly serious lung hemorrhages, and during the hideous nights she speculates widely on the power of God and faith. She asks questions few others have the courage to ask. And through it all, surrounded by a circle of cousins little more than incomprehending and genial, she persists in believing that her happiness or unhappiness depends most upon herself. Her strength of mind and aptness of perception do not decline. In listening to Phillips Brooks, the very popular Episcopal minister, she wondered "what he really does believe or think about it all, and whether he knows the reaction that comes to me about Thursday, after the enthusiasm and confidence made by his eloquence and earnestness on Sunday. To-morrow will be Saturday, and I shall be glad when Sunday comes to wind me up again" (p. 517). Some months later she wrote that Phillips Brooks "was good for those within the pale, but not good to convince outsiders that they should come in" (p. 537).

Minnie exists not only in her own right but also in her meaning to James. Behind her sense of life is James' own. For one thing, as Leon Edel has observed, Henry may have altered her letters the way he did William's and his father's,[19] not to falsify them but to prevent them from impairing the image of her he wished to present. He was deeply proud of the last chapter of *Notes* and very compli-

---

[19] *Untried Years*, p. 313.

mented when old friends congratulated him on it.[20] She clung to consciousness just as he himself might have and just as he was doing at the time he wrote about her. Her "felt interest in life" finally emerges as an emblem of the greatness of the felt interest itself: of its tenacity, its courage, its brilliance, and ultimate honor. The power to preserve her "life" was, of course, a further work of art. It had to be done, he wrote Mrs. William James, "with tact and taste and without overstrain." The art went way beyond that, however, for it included the whole development of his autobiography around the theme of life as an enterprise in intelligence and sensibility. Without the methods of art there would have been no story of the life; without art there would have been no life to begin with.

Shortly before writing his autobiography James contributed an essay "Is There a Life After Death?" to a volume entitled *In After Days.* Published by Harpers, the book is a collection of 'turn of the century' uplift by worthies like Howells, Julia Ward Howe, and Thomas Wentworth Higginson. James' piece is still readable, not only for the unusual source of expression it gave him but also because he treated the now little-attended question with an elegance missing in his fellow essayists. It is, he says, "the most interesting question in the world," but the interest is in the value it gives to life. And as for those who do not undertake this speculation, one might ask them if they are really living. "How *can* there be a personal and a differentiated life 'after,' " he goes on, "for those for whom there has been so little of one before?" In his own case, the more he accepted his consciousness as finite and thus learned to work it the harder, the more it gave to him and the more it undermined the position on which he had started—the less finite, in other words, it became.

[20] See S. P. Rosenbaum, "Letters to the Pell-Clarkes from Their 'Old Cousin and Friend' Henry James," *American Literature* (March, 1959), XXXI, pp. 46-58; *Letters,* II, pp. 362, 402.

I do not mean to treat autobiography as a branch of eschatology or to imply that James left one in order to defy the grave. What I do come around to, however, is my earlier point that *A Small Boy and Others* and *Notes of a Son and Brother* were elegiac books *written* to defy it. To give up the inward life was in effect to die, die in the only sense death had any real meaning to James. Whereas to keep his imaginative life open was to remain alive. Recognizing himself as mortal was a challenge to the artist to make the best of himself, namely a living man, and that man is immortal.

CHAPTER FIVE

Adams, James, and Autobiography

*But my world has become one of infinite possibilities.
What a phrase—still it's a good phrase and a good view
of life, and a man shouldn't accept any other; that much
I've learned underground.*

Ralph Ellison, *Invisible Man*

FOR this study of autobiography, the value of James' and
Adams' long friendship and association is that it enables
the critic to compare closely the manners of life and expression out of which the "Lives" grew and to see them in a kind
of third dimension. The written versions of Adams' and
James' lives stand like monuments in public squares or like
country houses in landscaped parks, and the carefully preserved letters, the related fiction and biographies, and the
minor bits of gossip are like the roads and walks and hedges
which lead up to them or provide the necessary space and
perspective around them. They are not just "biographical
background" in the often maligned sense. They are fore-
ground (if only in the architectural sense), and they are the
more interesting because they are so often about autobiography or descriptive of the men themselves in a way directly
relevant to the autobiographies. This, in turn, is of further
value because of the considerable differences between the
Education and *A Small Boy and Others* and *Notes of a Son
and Brother.* First, what is common in the experience of the
two authors provides a kind of benchmark for the survey and
study; second, the differences and the different treatments of
the experience, which are initially apparent in the men's let-

ters, prepare us for locating the contrasts of the finished books. Therefore, although James' and Adams' lives and letters are by no means the central issue of this essay, they are part of its frame or its "field" and setting.

I

Both the *Education* and James' volumes were written in the decade just preceding the First World War, and, whatever name we give to this period, its complacency, its mounting quantities of armaments and uncontrolled industrial power, and (particularly among the rich) its ridiculous extravagance and pretentiousness constantly surrounded the lives of the authors. They were as vividly and solitarily aware of these conditions as were Joyce, Proust, and other younger experimenters in autobiography; and, what is more, in that decade both James and Adams felt an intensification of the homelessness and displacement which was to be so strong in the work of their followers. But where the War was a beginning for the writers of the Twentieth Century and for the American Lost Generation, it was for James and Adams the end. James died March 1, 1916; Adams March 27, 1918. Unlike their less conscious contemporaries, however, James and Adams could in their ways see what was coming, could see the moral waste land which was the anticipation of the physical one. After all, they had the honesty to face the need for order in their own lives and experience, and this reflected the need around them. The great autobiographer is never really a typical man of his time, but he can be an especially acute witness to it.

The War and its prelude thus form the frame of reference of the last chapter of James' and Adams' lives in a grim extension of the way the Boston connection and the comedy of the international scene formed earlier ones. For more immediate purposes, this is also the period between Adams' autobiography and James'. And as James' *William Wetmore Story and His Friends* and other works may in certain ways have affected the writing of the *Education*, so did the *Education* and Adams' trenchant letters stand very distantly behind *A Small Boy* and *Notes*. Adams had been talking of decadence since the 1890's and of insufficiency and impotence in the political structure since even earlier. James comprehended these matters only in a uniquely personal fashion, but what he did become freshly and more directly aware of late in his life was social change. *The American Scene* (1907), for example, illustrates his startled recognition of all that had happened in the United States in his twenty-year absence. It seems clear that had he not revisited the country in 1904-05 and again in 1910-11, having its changes so forcibly impressed upon him, his autobiography would not have rendered the memories of his youth in such a golden and far-off antiquity. The aura of youth as so long ago was his subtler or more graphic representation of the things Adams stated by reference to the growth of railroads, world fairs, or "A Law of Acceleration." But in the matter of evolution and change, Adams was a sort of prior authority, and it is interesting to see James acknowledging him and yet holding to his own perceptions, agreeing with Adams only so far as he could find Adams really justified. In a letter from Adams' house in Washington in 1905, James speaks of his host as "a philosophic father,"[1] that is, as instructor but also as a liberal and permissive old man. As he had learned to sift the sometimes strange instruction of his own philosophic father ("father's ideas"), so did he weigh carefully what might be called "Adams' ideas."

When James was in the United States in 1910-11, following William's death, he did not accept invitations from Adams for another visit to Washington. Adams' requests were

[1] Letter to Mary Cadwalader Jones, January 13, 1905. Houghton Library.

darkened by his "old cardinal" tendency. "Washington is
deadly dull, and gloomy beyond my experience, but that
suits us well enough, and I can't say that Paris, when I left
it, was any gayer,"[2] he wrote in one, and apparently James,
like Holmes, was then in no mood for such "dust and ashes."
To say such things lightly was to do violence to whatever
serious truth they held. To affect gloom was also to threaten
possibilities of gaiety and was surely an invidious extreme
of sophistication. A year later, on hearing of Adams' stroke,
James excused his not accepting the invitations by speaking
only of his own dejection and unfitness then for "the high
pitch of Washington"! He concentrated on what was strong
and admirable in Adams, and when he finally turned to the
ruins of the society they had known, it was with an innocence,
yet frankness, entirely free of Adams' cultivated acidity.

My dear Henry.

I have heard of your sad trouble and I think of you
with deep and tender participation. Mrs. Cameron has
been my main and most trusted source of knowledge,
and has in a manner given me leave to tap at your more
or less guarded door. Of this I have the more promptly
availed myself as I was already (as I intimate) hovering
much about it, very near it, and weighing the discretion
of my venturing to ask for admittance. That may have
been wrong—and yet I stand by the fondness of my
desire that some echo of my voice of inquiry and fidelity
shall somehow reach you. In these great stresses friendship reaches out to the making of an image of the friend
who has suffered assault—and I make one of you thus
according to my sense of your rich and ingenious mind
and your great resources of contemplation, speculation,
resignation—a curiosity in which serenity is yet at home.
I see you in short receive tribute of all your past, and

[2] Letter to Henry James, January 22, 1911. Houghton Library.

at the same time but keep your future waiting to render
you the same, or something very like it. Even if this
evocation doesn't strike you as hitting the remark please
believe that for me it does a great deal, and I require what I can get—so I give myself to the confidence. Upwards of three years ago I had a very grave
illness, for which I had long been spoiling and from
which I have long been incompletely emerging; I have
now light on these things, I am an authority (really
one of the rarest, I think;) and while I build myself
up again, or do my best to, I draw you, by your leave,
into the same course of treatment. May my devoted
attention thus all soothingly and not at all importu-
nately, rest on you! I spent a year ago a twelvemonth in
America—a very difficult and rather dreadful time—
without seeing you, I know; but that was because I was
unfit for adventures—condemned to hang far below the
high pitch of Washington. I saw, alas, very little (and
as regards persons very few,) that were propitious to
my state—and I departed with an overwhelmed sense
of having no nook or corner there. The whole scene
struck me indeed as unfavorable to works—and I hied
me back to *this* one, which more or less corresponds to
the idea.

But I've spent the whole past winter in London—
only lately returning thence, and even there I seemed
to find more of a frame and a *fond*. There I saw again
after something like 25 years poor Carlo Gaskell; looking very ill and very sad, altogether altered and per-
ceptibly (save the mark!) "improved"—in the sense
I mean of being gentler, softer, kinder. He was a strange
old-world apparition—and it was stranger still to me
that I had once, years ago, felt him contemporary! Lady
Cattie is terrible—she has shed, by the dull wayside, every

grace—of human garniture; and the thought that *that* (of old) had been the germ of *this* struck me as again a theme for the moralist. Then there was a young daughter—who was as absolute nought. It was a whole grim impression—including Everard Doyle; and I afterwards almost wept over it on the bosom of Gwynllian Palgrave, dear thing, a good friend of mine (the youngest of Frank's daughters) and quite the most sympathetic bit of wreckage of all that particular little circle of the other years. But I should add that Carlo G. projected himself with great concern into all newses and echoes of you. I just hear from Edith Wharton that she motors over hither from Paris a few days hence, and will spend 3 nights under my roof; which I bless because, with other reasons, I shall be able to talk of you with her. Think of us as infinitely and insistently so disposed, and believe me, my dear Henry, all faithfully yours,

Henry James[3]

The common ordeals of illness, the mounting years, and the interest in a dwindling number of old friends all gave James and Adams as strong a bond as they had ever shared. Furthermore, during these years when James was actually at work on his autobiographies he knew he had in Adams an attentive future reader. But at the same time, even in the ups and downs of his health and his anxiety about his future powers, tributes came to him from younger artists and writers which were a sure justification of his perseverance. Although both men were continually encircled by younger admirers, James' band appears to have been larger, more diverse, and more spontaneously assembled. His own slightly humorous bachelor phrase for Adams and his brilliant and

---

[3] Letter to Henry Adams, July 15, 1912. Massachusetts Historical Society.

devoted attending "nieces" was "dear old Henry Adams
and his somewhat austere seraglio."[4]

My dear Henry!

It is long, much too long, that I have been saving
you some expressions of the extreme pleasure I have
taken all these months in your magnificent rally (by all
I hear,) from your sharp illness of last year. I began
to want to rejoice with you over it from the moment of
my getting from you the so benevolent letter which
first gave me the clear image of it; but the case was,
all too sadly, that about in the measure in which you
found yourself so unerringly again, I went down, and
still more down, like the other bucket in the well—
quite out of the bottom of which dank and dusky shaft
I should have fell. I was calling up to you till a very
short time since. I have had a difficult and hampered
winter—very much so indeed—after an all but impossible autumn; but a persistent effort to emulate your
gallantry, keeping it all the while steadily and shiningly
before me, appears at last to be bearing some fruit. Take
this belated "answer" to your admirable last as a sign
of what your example is helping me to. It helps me
particularly as vividly and gratefully portrayed by dear
little Ruth Draper, who kindly came to keep me company this a.m., truly kindling a tender light in my poor
old bedimmed countenance while I gave Sargent his 3rd
sitting for the portrait he is by a fantastic turn of the
wheel of fate (*his* fate above all) doing of me. He likes
his sitter to be enlivened, and to provide therefor, and
Ruth is (in the most exquisite way,) a positively professional enlivener . . . I came up from the country
hither at the New Year (in physical case that made even

[4] Letter to Mr. and Mrs. Henry White, October 26, 1914, in Allan
Nevins, *Henry White, Thirty Years of American Diplomacy* (New York,
1930), p. 329.

that move rather a sad scramble:) and I depart again on July 1st. But it's literally but the change from the blue bed to the brown, and such exploits as your crossing of the sea and re-installing and re-adventuring makes me grovel before you even as pale compromise before flushed triumph. I feel that I shall never again quit this agitated island. I met 3 weeks (about) ago your brother Charles, whom I had, oddly enough, never before encountered—and felt that he was contributing in no small degree to its agitation. I mean that I gathered him to have delivered an address (at one of the meetings or banquets of the Historical Congress) which had had a great retentissement. But of course you know all about that—and at the George Trevelyan's Sunday afternoon, where I met him, he enlivened my sitting as much as Ruth the charming did so this morning in the studio. I published some weeks ago the most impudent volume that ever saw the light—an invitation to the world to be regaled on the interesting emotions and reflections of its serviteur from his 1st or 2nd year to about his 16th—but such as it is I should like to send it to you—now that I have an address for the purpose—if you haven't happened to see it or become possessed of it. Make me that negative sign in 3 words, and you shall instantly have it. But make me none others, I beg you—for I myself fear daily more and more the weight of postal matter—I mean of the despatch of it, not the receipt. . . . Let me add that a very charming thing happened to me here the other day—or week—the signs and tokens of which will, I feel, amuse you (in that noblest sense of the word). So I am sending them on with the earnest blessing of yours all faithfully

Henry James[5]

[5] Letter to Henry Adams, May 26, 1913. Massachusetts Historical Society. Ellipses are mine.

The "very charming thing" was none other than the present, in honor of James' seventieth birthday, of the exquisite "golden bowl" and the portrait by Sargent for which he was sitting. A copy of the accompanying "Letter," with its long column of signers, and of James' reply was enclosed. Such evidence of a loyal following was all James needed to show that the gloom around them did have, for him, its personal bright spots and that his work as artist had moreover *made* an order and illumination for certain others and himself.

Adams answered immediately. Ruth Draper had "helped" him in his recovery. Edith Wharton, whom James had asked about, was sick in Paris but "promises to get up." He himself was absorbed in his twelfth-century songs, a kind of scholarship and passion for which his brother Charles "cares nothing." He also said that he would have liked to have been one of the participants in the birthday tribute. And he had already read *A Small Boy and Others*: "On the sea [crossing to France], I had three nieces reading to me your infancy, and I left in New York all your friends racing to put down their names—and mine—on your role of American adherents. You stopped us, it seems, after I sailed, but we were all there, pretty girls and matrons and old sages."[6] Whether in the sentence beginning "You stopped us . . ." Adams meant to imply reservations in his admiration—ones based on reading *A Small Boy*—is hard to tell. If he really liked James' "most impudent volume that ever saw the light," he might be expected to have said so. If he did not, it was hardly the impudence that would have bothered him, and not even the emphasis on the "infancy." In all likelihood Adams probably appreciated the book simply as light entertainment, something read to him by obliging companions. And meanwhile he may have waited for later installments which he hoped would be more explicit about the limitations of education, the

[6] Letter to Henry James, May 29, 1913. Houghton Library.

gulf between past and present, and the disorder around him. This expectancy would make his great shock a year later on reading *Notes of a Son and Brother* all the more understandable.

And the proper word for his reaction to *Notes* is shock, not disapproval, as some people may believe. Until such time as his letter to James of March 1914 is found, the best we can go on is the response he described to Elizabeth Cameron, and this was that the book had "reduced me to a pulp." It did, apparently, because the memories were so vivid and awakening to Adams while the era of them seemed to him so wasted, so buried and irrelevant. According to the *Education*, Henry Adams had spent his life in fighting Boston, not just State Street but the Boston influence of moralism, excessive intellect, and provinciality. In this he knew he had the co-operation of James. Then in a flash James revealed a kind of tolerance for the old province and affection for the memories of it which he had forbidden himself. And the success with which James' book brought all this back to him was disquieting evidence of the lack of success of his own repressions. "—And me!" Adams cried: "Poor Henry James . . . still lives in that dreamy, stuffy Newport and Cambridge, with papa James and Charles Norton—and me!" He was still in that world and it was still in him, much more than he had cared to realize. Thus the shock and the reduction, without his defences and supporting illusions, "to a pulp"; and Adams should have seen that "education" had taken one more stride. Whatever disunities might appear to exist between that "terrible dream," as he called it, and the "quite loony" one which was 1914, he had to confess that there nevertheless were long and delicate connections right within himself. His violent reaction was proof. He had the "great resources of contemplation, speculation, resignation" which James admired him for, and he also had the old memories and sensibilities *Notes of a Son and Brother* had reinspired in him. Therefore, far from being a condemnation of the book, the melancholy it brought to Adams is really a testimony to the book's rather terrifying power.

My dear Henry,

I have your melancholy outpouring of the 7th, and I know not how better to acknowledge it than by the full recognition of its unmitigated blackness. *Of course* we are lone survivors, of course the past that was our lives is at the bottom of an abyss—if the abyss *has* any bottom; of course, too, there's no use talking unless one particularly *wants* to. But the purpose, almost, of my printed divagations was to show you that one *can*, strange to say, still want to—or at least can behave as if one did. Behold me therefore so behaving—and apparently capable of continuing to do so. I still find my consciousness interesting —under *cultivation* of the interest. Cultivate it *with* me, dear Henry—that's what I hoped to make you do—to cultivate yours for all that it has in common with mine. *Why* mine yields an interest I don't know that I can tell you, but I don't challenge or quarrel with it—I encourage it with a ghastly grin. You see I still, in presence of life (or of what you deny to be such,) have reactions —as many as possible—and the book I sent you is a proof of them. It's, I suppose, because I am that queer monster, the artist, an obstinate finality, an inexhaustible sensibility. Hence the reactions—appearances, memories, many things, go on playing upon it with consequences that I note and "enjoy" (grim word!) noting. It all takes doing—and I *do*. I believe I shall do yet again—it is still an act of life. But you perform them still yourself— and I don't know what keeps me from calling your letter a charming one! There we are, and it's a blessing that you understand—I admit indeed alone—your all-faithful

Henry James.

The author of this letter could never be overcome by his friend's historical pessimism. He did not think in the broad historical framework, and this removed him from oppressive generalizations. But what was an even more important safeguard was that, paradoxically, he had a stronger sense of the presence of the past than did Adams, the historian. Therefore it was not so wasted and neither was the future so bleak. Although the past may have been "at the bottom of an abyss," James could still reach it, because the abyss was never deeper than the depth of his own consciousness. James was really a kind of prince of antiquarians; that is, he had what mere antiquarians do not, namely, a consciousness to match the scope of his researches and so to make the researches significant. "I still find my consciousness interesting—under *cultivation* of the interest." By contrast, Adams' current research in twelfth-century music was a more normal kind of antiquarianism— something manifestly out of touch with the contemporary and pursued for that reason, as well as for the pleasure of new personal tastes. He could never have found there "the reactions—appearances, memories, many things" which James found in autobiography, because James' youth was full of vital continuities with his present. Because of their nature, it was, perhaps, the most "impudent" act of his career to expect others to share them, but they were nonetheless rich in values: the values discovered as a young man and the interest rediscovered and affirmed fifty years later. Just as an example, there could be nothing more immediately and simply pertinent to the blunt immorality of an armaments race than the recollection of the face of Simpson, the schoolboy in *A Small Boy*: "a smart protrusion of the lower lip, a crude complacency of power, that crushed me to sadness." And over all, in the whole course and order of his volumes, James had told the story of the growth of an imagination, the making of a life, the stature of a man. The very writing of the books had been a part of it, "still an act of life." It is a sign of the impressiveness of this defence of his books that in it the words "monster" and "obstinate" are made magnificent—heroic.

II

At this point it seems unnecessary to say much more about James' and Adams' relations and more important to try to reconcile the two kinds of autobiography they wrote. Some definition and justification of the two kinds has already been implied in the history of the long dialogue between the two men. Each revealingly displays his own personality and inevitably projects the basis for his interests and his style. Thus, and in their two achievements, they have also offered a possible foundation for the understanding and criticism of autobiography, if we are wise enough to discern it and use it.

We can begin by going back to Franklin's *Autobiography* and recalling an aspect of the difference between the Twyford section written in 1771 and Philadelphia section of 1788. Not only is the first part the story of a young man (Franklin from childhood to his twenties), while the last part is the story of Franklin as an adult citizen and emerging colonial figure; there are also corresponding differences in form and intent. The first part is nominally more "private"—begun as a "letter" to his son for the purpose of putting down some facts of family history and mainly concerned with the adventures of an unknown youth. Furthermore, in telling these episodes of his life, Franklin is busily concerned with the question of how his youthful self anticipated and became his adult self, the established gentleman at the writing desk. Certain acts were plainly "errata" and inconsistent with his later convictions, and yet other acts were curiously prophetic—like the child's "project" for the swimming wharf, even if misguided—and Franklin lovingly identifies these fine threads of continuity. By 1788 several things have changed. The colonial agent of 1771 has become the national hero, and the apprentice printer

[195]

of part one has grown into the more widely active and influential Franklin of part three. Indeed, the parallelism of these changes seems just right. Their consequences to the later section's form, though, are a loss of the guise of "privacy," a further objectification of the "protagonist" into an American image of the public man, and a new desire to record not just personal history but civil and national history.

These contrasts, or rather developments and evolutions, in Franklin's *Autobiography* are worth reviewing because they anticipate in embryo some of the differences between the *Education* and James' *Small Boy* and *Notes* and even possible definitions of two branches of American autobiography. They are not simply the qualities of autobiographies of childhood and autobiographies of maturity, though this is a factor. In 1771 Franklin was clearly writing for different reasons than he was in 1788, as I have explained in chapter one. And brief reflection on the *Education* will show that even Adams' earliest memories are told by a man who is fundamentally most interested in an historical problem—in the meanings of "the eighteenth century" and "the twentieth century," for example—and in the great social necessity of man's understanding his destiny. In critical terms, that is the book's tenor; the memories and the life are its vehicle. This, incidentally, is why some readers and critics assert that the *Education* is not an autobiography but an historical essay or work of philosophy.

"I am clear that you should write autobiography," Adams said in the letter to Hay in 1883, "I mean to do mine." The date of this statement bespeaks at least twenty years of conscious gradual preparation for the task, and something to recognize about the *Education* is the extreme self-consciousness of the book. Adams' reading of other autobiographies was exhaustive. He chose his models and studied them carefully, which is one reason why he was, generally, a more profound critic of the subject than James. In the course of his preparations he also arrived at definite intentions about his book. It was "to fit young men, in universities or elsewhere, to be men of the world." It was "to complete St. Augustine's *Confessions*," though this ambition had to be declared "half in jest." So important was the arrival at the book's proper purpose and design that Adams actually included the discovery of it in the book as a climax of the concerns and speculations of his later years. "From that point [of unity in the thirteenth century] he proposed to fix a position for himself, which he could label: 'The Education of Henry Adams: a Study of Twentieth Century Multiplicity.'" All of this planning and stalking of the subject was the result of and led to one of the boldest possible conceptions of autobiography, the equal, in this respect, of Rousseau's imposing "man in all the truth of nature." For at this point, not to have been supremely bold and not to have undertaken the study of society, century, and history as well as himself might have been to waste decades of inner and outer examinations. It would have been a sign of permanent circumscription within the Boston "nervous self-consciousness—irritable dislike of America, and antipathy to Boston" he had fought to break out of. Or to put it most simply, to have written the kind of autobiography James eventually wrote would have been impossible for Adams, and to have tried it would have been fatal.

In a certain finely developed and peculiarly restricted way, then, Adams writes as a public figure.

> Under the shadow of Boston State House, turning its back on the house of John Hancock, the little passage called Hancock Avenue runs, or ran, from Beacon Street, skirting the State House grounds, to Mount Vernon Street, on the summit of Beacon Hill; and there, in the third house below Mount Vernon Place, February 16, 1838, a child was born, and christened later by his uncle, the minister of the First Church after the tenets of Boston Unitarianism, as Henry Brooks Adams.

He implies that he was born a public figure, like an heir apparent. This is surely one of the most symbolically generative beginnings any book ever had, for Adams has announced his theme and committed himself to it; in fact, shown himself committed to an inheritance of which the book is the outcome. Here, as in many passages that follow, Adams has been able to invoke the inheritance for an instantaneous identification of self and the *res publica*, or for a kind of epic magnification and ennobling of the self. What Franklin could not do until his eighties when he really was a national hero, what Whitman had to do by song and celebration, fate granted Adams to do by the merest reference. State House and boy, public affairs and private person, were intricately linked. Capitals, domes, and forums would be the background of his life. Their architectural harmony would be the ideal sought in governments, institutions, societies, and history and in life and autobiography. Such grandeur, however, also had its darker shadows and such traditions their mazes and crooked corridors, like the devious way actually connecting (or separating?) the State House and "the third house below Mount Vernon Place." Therefore, what we finally admire is not the inheritance itself but the *development* of it, or all the intellectual and esthetic ripening that went into such understanding of it as underlies this passage. The use of the inheritance is only one example of Adams' self-conscious projection of his own life as an American symbol and as a figure in which to study vast modern problems. It assists him in a monumental effort to be as teacher and scholar what his ancestors had been as statesmen. Such a grandiloquent assertion, however, leaves itself open to irony; first to Adams' own mockery of himself as but "stable companion to statesmen." He is fully aware of the national preference for doers to thinkers, and even moved by it himself. His suspicion that "Thought" was "a more or less degraded Act" seemed confirmed by contemporary physiologists.[7]

[7] Henry Adams, "A Letter to American Teachers of History," *The*

And whereas Franklin's or Whitman's autobiographical edifices aspire to light and hope, Adams' rises to tragedy. The reasons for the irony and the status as public figure *manqué* are to be found, after all, in the pessimistic nature of Adams' message, in his stout resistance to the currents of his time, in his scepticism, and in his dedication to a cause more profound and more deeply conservative than politicians and mere "public figures" of the modern age seem capable of comprehending. Yet for this, too, there was family precedent, and Henry seized it. It is partly because of the inherited quarrel with State Street, he would have us believe, and because of being a descendent of men who stood alone, that he will not pander. Instead he practices "Silence," or his version of the protest that in times such as these the place for the honest, real public man is in the privacy and concentration of his study. There are greater issues needing his attention than those disputed in Congress and in the market place.

Holding in mind Adams' ambitious aims for his autobiography, one might venture to add that his constant battle with disorder and his image of the twentieth-century "multiverse" are in a way inevitable consequences of these aims. It has already been noted how the third section of Franklin's *Autobiography* lacks the neatness and unity of the first. Once he ceased methodically noting the threads connecting his past and present and began chronicling his part in greater activities further removed from his own powers and inner life, he immediately found himself in the midst of harder materials to shape and integrate. He barely made a pretence of trying to give them significant position and shape. In "Song of Myself," where Whitman is attempting much more and including mythic experiences of a still wider range, form, narrowly understood, is a value critics despair of describing. In the

---

Degradation of Democratic Dogma, ed. Brooks Adams (New York, 1919), p. 203. See also p. 243, "Thought then appears in nature as an arrested,— in other words, as a degraded,—physical action."

Education Adams is more greatly disposed to desire form and control in spite of, and because of, the chaos around him. The result is a consciously dramatized struggle between Henry Adams, the modern man who dreams of "order" and "education," and a modern world in which "chaos is the law of nature" and no education ever adequate. Autobiography at this reach of inclusiveness, a reach as great as Cotton Mather's in the *Magnalia* or T. S. Eliot's in *The Four Quartets*, seems bound to encounter a struggle of such a kind. In the *Education* the conflict is first designedly incorporated into the subject of the book and made a technique of its own internal structure, a practice in which Adams has had several notable followers, including Eliot.

The best name for Adams' kind of autobiography, I think, is epic autobiography. Another possibility might be the autobiographical anatomy, in the sense in which Northrop Frye has revived the word in *Anatomy of Criticism*, except that this term describes only certain features of the *Education* and, misconstrued, suggests some rather bizarre operations! The ways in which it resembles an anatomy—its passion for ideas, the purpose of covering ideas as unrelated as geology, biology, literature, history, sex, politics, electricity, economics, diplomacy, and industrial society, and at the same time fixing them in some new order—are also part of the way in which it resembles an ancient epic. A revealing difference is that where in the classical epic all these aspects of the culture are in their places around the imposing power of the hero, in the *Education* each threatens to break loose from the others and to overpower the hero and the culture. The hero, while not an Aeneas, is as high-born as he can be in America and also as aristocratic, in the Jeffersonian sense. And from Whitman to Hart Crane and Ezra Pound there is good precedent for the author as epic hero. As the American epic has tended to be autobiographical, so in the *Education* does autobiography become epic.

Some readers of the *Education* may want to improve this definition by calling the book an "ironic epic autobiography" or even a kind of "anti-epic." Clumsy as such phrases are, it is tempting to make a case for them. The book is not moved by the unities of its culture but by the disunities. In so far as can happen in a democracy, the hero is born to power, and yet the story is of his inability or disinclination to assume it. Neither does the author-hero eulogize himself or his society. Adams is a "failure," the society energetic without intelligence, "drifting," unconscious, or hysterical. Yet none of this detracts in the least from the scope of the book, and we must see that irony and nay-saying are not denials of the epic but a route the modern epic takes, for example, *Moby Dick*. Furthermore, Adams' humility is in some respects only the cover to his arrogance, and his tearing and shaking of his society are fundamentally the sign of his allegiance to it and his dedication to reawakening and redirecting it. The image of disorder is so clearly presented and the search for education so enfolding that the book builds and informs even as it despairs. This quality has actually surprised some belated admirers of Adams. Among these, significantly, is Lewis Mumford. In his 1957 introduction to a reissue of *The Golden Day*, Mumford wrote that in 1926 he had been "damnably irrelevant" about Adams. It had taken this great modern critic many years to recognize "the sound structure for which, willy-nilly, [Adams] had laid the foundations." If we can learn, exactly as Henry James did learn, how to see the great life and strength in Adams, keeping his posturings in their place, we will someday realize what a cultural hero he was, and is. In the *Education* he indeed did give an image of modern man in a multiverse. If we better understand this explosion of power today and are better equipped to recognize the disintegrations, we owe it in no small measure to the foresight of Henry Adams. Since the twentieth century has had to build from the ground up, where mere repair has been futile, its representative course has been a search for order rather than a following of it. To put it in a way which is relevant to all these problems, Adams was a hero not by having *been* one but by having *become* one.

III

It is quite consistent with the differences between their autobiographies that whereas Adams had begun contemplating his twenty years before writing it, James was not so inclined until very late in his life. Then, all at once, the coincidence of his brother's death, a lapse of power to write fiction, uncertainties of health, and the sense of a kind of lonely, psychic homelessness set him to it very quickly. It is true that James' *Notebooks* contain various brief excursions into personal reminiscence, such as those of 1881-82 and 1904-05, but they do not indicate further, more formal intentions in this direction. In fact, they also were commenced in moments of loneliness or sudden confusion and pursued as a means of regaining contact with his primary self. As the writing of the *Education* illustrates the "long starting and beginning late" of the epic poet, so can *A Small Boy* and *Notes* be associated with the lyricist's or elegist's response to immediate feeling.

The similarities to the first part of Franklin's *Autobiography*, though primarily superficial and somewhat accidental, are still interesting. Both concentrate entirely on the experiences of youth. At the times they were written, the authors were of approximately the same age. Both wrote in England, after having been living there for a considerable time. And both books create a tone of familiarity—Franklin's "letter" to his son and James' "family book." Finally, both authors are moved to look for their obscure connections with their origins and delighted to discover them. This is the most important similarity because the development of these relationships is a large part of this kind of autobiography's organic unity. Where there are underlying links between the child and the man, there are also links between the various ages of the child. One lesson or one newly realized feature of character leads into others, and little by little they all grow together into the ripening individual. Consequently there are not only links to be found but linkages to be made, so that the book really can reflect the sure, though sometimes awkward and irregular, unfolding of a definite organic process. About such stories as these there is also a quality that can even be called mystery. Granting that the young organism begins undefined, what will he, what might have he, become? And to the really self-conscious mind the other question is equally curious, how did he become what he did?

Where Adams was the more self-conscious as a critic and designer of autobiography, James was the more self-conscious man. Adams' self-consciousness, as he himself admits, was too apt to be only nervousness and embarrassment, while James' was a long-trained habit both of observing himself and of observing how he observed. This is of enormous importance to his autobiography. The reason James was so well equipped to write autobiography, despite lack of explicit "preparation," was precisely that all his years he had studied every action and impression that it would be about. There was only one story to tell, and that the growth of such a consciousness; there was only one way to write it, and that by this method of consciousness. The story held within it an order and structure of its own, confirmed by his very existence as the man he was and the memory he possessed, so that in a sense all he had to do was let it out. And he could not, as he said on the first page, go into his memory for the story of William without bringing out his own story too. "To recover anything like the full treasure of scattered, wasted circumstance was at the same time to live over the spent experience itself . . . and the effect of this in turn was to find discrimination among the parts of my subject again and again difficult—so inseparably and beautifully they seemed to hang together. . . ."

In the best meaning of the word, therefore, the education of Henry James is more truly an education than Adams'. It was continuous, it was his own, and it stuck. It is comparable in all these ways to the recollected "education of Nick Adams" in the early Hemingway stories and to the stories of childhood, "true" or fictionalized, of many American authors. "It seems to him," James reflected, "an education like another: feeling, as he has come to do more and more, that no education avails for the intelligence that doesn't stir in it some subjective passion, and that on the other hand almost anything that does so act is largely educative. . . ." Yet the difference in Adams' "education," if this remark does indeed point to it, is that Adams felt that his character had been shaped from birth—inherited—and that the new education more and more required the destruction of the old casting. Such a record of shocks and repeated new beginnings joined with his epic purpose of seeking the radical education of a new civilization. The passion might be doubted, but it was there as a passion finally to discover and build rather than to accumulate, perfect, and memorialize, as in James' case. James' education was therefore more rounded, interconnected, and compressed, whereas Adams' obviously could not be. James' passion could be *subjective* because it was always a question of watching the new internal growth; Adams' passion had to be *objective*, reaching further and further beyond himself and avoiding the pain and destruction going on within. But the usual, more desirable kind of education, that is, of personal growth and experience, is definitely James'.

The evidence is that the years of childhood and youthful exuberance are almost always lyrical. Elsewhere in American literature there is probably no better example than certain ecstatic pages of Wolfe's *Look Homeward, Angel*. Yet everywhere, even in epic poetry, those periods dealing with a hero's early education are always set off in a kind of enclosure of outward stillness pierced by the interior joy. Adams can recreate those hours, but we still know that they are short and unreal and that Quincy is held in rein by Boston. To James, however, they *are* what is real. James is hardly a typical singer of hours of ecstasy, but to him the calmer moments of rare insight clearly are real, for they make intelligible all the rest. Furthermore, for James the solitary Master who was recovering the story, those moments were of utmost meaning. By renewed contact with them he was able to regain a freshness missing from the present and to recreate the home and circle of "relations" around him which he had lost as the last surviving member of his family. And even where there was disappointment and frustration in that past, the triumph over it was precedent for the newest "conversion."

"A man, yet by these tears a little boy again, . . ."

The line from "Out of the Cradle Endlessly Rocking" provides a finely suggestive description of what James was doing. Although he was in London and Rye, he was writing mostly about the United States. As he told Adams, he had left the United States of his old age "with an overwhelmed sense of having no nook or corner there. The whole scene struck me indeed as unfavorable to works." And as he wrote his sister-in-law about a year later, "I could come back to America (could be carried back on a stretcher) to die—but never, never to live." Yet the further he drew away from it in time and space, the more he needed the simple, barren America of the 1840's-60's as what might be ambiguously called a place of ultimate inspiration and rest. Its simplicity and meagerness of appearances, once a liability, lived on in his imagination as a perennial stimulant. The observation and concentration of consciousness which had started long ago as a compensation now went back for new strength and recreated both childhood and the innocent America of childhood with a richness only James could display.

IV

James' autobiography, like the *Education*, is an extremely rare and inimitable kind of work. This, of course, can be said of any classic, a work which paradoxically joins and stands among many others and yet remains unique. A criticism of James' books, however, is that they are possibly too unique. Great sensibilities succeed in art by imposing on their audience in various ways so that the audience both sees freshly and also sees familiarly, but not as it has before. Thus do they change visions. This is magnificently true of Adams' effect in the *Education* and of James' in his novels. Yet in James' autobiography we may be too close to the mighty sensibility itself, where we always see freshly but where the form is so dense and its larger design so distant that we can neither identify what we see very securely nor ever be easy in how we see it. This is to elaborate what R. P. Blackmur implied when he spoke of the "excess of sensibility" in James' very late work: "excess of sensibility sterilises the significance of form."[8] Moreover, later in life James sufficiently hated and feared the popular institutions by which most men live, the theater and newspapers for example, that he developed a peculiar ignorance of how other people and society at large manifest themselves. From 1910 to 1916 Adams was much more isolated from society than James, who at the outbreak of the war even tried to throw himself in the thick of its efforts, but Adams appears nevertheless to have had the clearer view of all that was going on. The sign of these phenomena in James' autobiography, finally, is its uniqueness or its cultivation of a private vision nearly invisible to any substantial former audience.

Nevertheless, more rewarding reading of *A Small Boy and Others* and *Notes of a Son and Brother* depends upon taking it less as merely James' own story and more as one of

[8] "Henry Adams: Three Late Moments," *Kenyon Review* (Winter, 1940, II, p. 17.

a long line of different though related stories of American
initiations, all the way from Franklin's picaresque first part
of the *Autobiography* to the *Notes of a Native Son* of James
Baldwin. The prevailing approach, to James as to other men
and women, is to do the opposite. Autobiographies are entered
as anterooms to some other monument; each is read only as
this or that person's autobiography rather than in the numerous possible classifications of such books. Naturally, this also
contributes to confusion and to the proliferation of the most
disreputable memoirs; critics assert the wrong standards or just
none at all. James' books will seem less isolated and less forbidding, therefore, after they have been juxtaposed on more
occasions with other American autobiographies, with other
rediscoveries of childhood and with the other modern explorations of consciousness to which they are a kind of introduction. Ironically, their real utility to the understanding
of fictional autobiography and to his own fiction (as a kind of
gallery of portraits of the "inward life" and their reviewed
images and methods of recapture) will then be more apparent
also.

As this chapter has again tried to illustrate, James and
Adams lived on that divide in the late nineteenth century
which had to look down onto two different worlds—"unity"
and "multiplicity," as Adams forebodingly put it, or, less emotionally, "eighteenth century" and "twentieth century." For
all that the two comrades had in common, their responses to
their unsteady footing were almost entirely opposite. This,
however, enabled both men to open up independent courses
of reaction and action which, the longer we look, seem increasingly wise. They seem so because the courses were prophetic
of two of the most representative directions taken by our own
contemporaries. The one might be described as jumping from
Adams' shock and dismay over, finally, to James' deeper interior investigation and inner order. The other moves from
James' refinement and introspection toward a search for the

larger, objective order Adams pursued. It might be suggested that very late in their own lives both James and Adams tried to start afresh on the other's course, James into work with refugees and the Allied cause, Adams into his new recognitions in poetry and music. Certainly neither response today has been very viable without some sympathy for the other. How long, if ever, it will be before inner and outer worlds will bear much in common—until a political structure, for instance, will be as vast and lovely and still as curious and ornate as the consciousness of Henry James—there is no way of telling. The way is weird, or, as Adams quipped, "quite loony." Yet it is interesting, in this connection, that such a notable autobiographical—or roughly autobiographical—novel as Ralph Ellison's *Invisible Man* has gone behind both James and Adams to a picaresque structure more akin to Benjamin Franklin's. The masks and wildly varied roles of Ellison's hero show us that Franklin's *Autobiography* still has unappreciated possibilities for imitation, and it may well be that in the next fifty years Franklin's deceiving simplicity, as well as his great versatility of intelligence, will have as much to teach as James and Adams have taught in the last fifty years.

INDEX

Abelard, Pierre, 6
Adams, Brooks, 45, 74, 87
Adams, Charles Francis, 44, 46, 97, 101, 102-03, 108, 135
Adams, Charles Francis, Jr., 45, 46, 190, 191
Adams, Henry, vii, 17, 45; early relations with James, 46-58, 72-74; criticism of James' work, 57, 72, 77-81, 89, 191-93; move to Washington, 58-60; change in life after 1885, 62, 119; political sense, 64, 185, 206; self-consciousness, 48, 51, 86, 99, 197; compared to Franklin and James, 110, 137-39, 172; later relations with James, 183-95, 205, 207-08
  The Education of Henry Adams: viii, ix, 14, 46, 64, 65, 73, 79, 80, 85, 87, 88, 192; models for, 3, 7-8, 12-13, 34; problem of order in, 90-94; on boyhood, 95-101; on Civil War and shocks, 101-09, 111; chs. "Free Fight," "Chaos," "Failure," 111-18; effect of omitted twenty years, 115n, 118-21; search for 20th-century order, 121-36; "Dynamic Theory of History," 130, 132-35; influence and historical setting, 184, 201, 206, 207-08; as epic autobiography, 196-201, 202
  other works: Democracy, 62, 65-71, 117-18; Esther, 62, 65, 68, 70-72, 117-18, 119; History of the United States, 73, 91, 117, 119; A Letter to American Teachers of History, 130, 198, 198n; The Life of George Cabot Lodge, 80-81, 83-86, 122, 125; Mont-Saint-Michel and Chartres, 63, 88, 119, 127, 129, 132, 134
Adams, John, 27, 44, 137
Adams, John Quincy, 44, 95, 97

Adams, Marian Hooper (Clover), 49-51, 62n, 63, 76; remarks on James, 52, 53, 58; James' fictional use of, 55-57; suicide and effect on Adams, 62, 63, 114f, 115n, 119; Adams' fictional use of, 63, 65, 70, 71-72
Aldridge, Alfred Owen, 27n
Aristotle, 120, 120n
Arnold, Matthew, 100, 158, 172
autobiography, ix-xi, 83, 101, 134; definitions of, 4-7; modern problems in writing, 16-17, 92-94; Adams' departures from convention, 119-21, 127, 136; "thinness" of, 128f; Adams' influence on, 135, 203; in 1920's and after, 184, 200, 204, 206
  American autobiography: vii, 33-43, 137; James' uniqueness in, 149; Adams and epic, 196-201; James and elegiac, 196, 202-08

Baldwin, James, 206
Baudelaire, Charles, 100
Baym, Max, 124, 126
Becker, Carl, 25
Bell, Whitfield J., Jr., 18n, 21n
biography, 79; James' view of, 80, 83
Blackmur, Richard P., 65, 88, 110, 133n, 206
Blaine, James G., 54, 69, 70
Brooks, Phillips, 70, 180
Bunyan, John; Grace Abounding, 6; Pilgrim's Progress, 20
Burr, Anna Robeson, 4n, 45n
Butterfield, Lyman H., 44n

Cameron, Elizabeth, 86, 89, 119, 186, 192
Carlyle, Thomas, 94
Cellini, Benvenuto, 8, 41
Chanler, Mrs. Winthrop, 74, 74n